The Psychology and Philosophy of Eugene Gendlin

This book brings together a collection of essays written by scholars inspired by Eugene Gendlin's work, particularly those interested in thinking with and beyond Gendlin for the sake of a global community facing significant crises.

The contributors take inspiration from Gendlin's philosophy of the implicit, and his theoretical approach to psychology. The essays engage with Gendlin's ideas for our era, including critiques and corrections as well as extrapolations of his work. Gendlin himself worried that knowing about a problem is too often conflated with actions that might lead to change; the essays in this book point to a form of understanding that is activated, an embodied and immediate way of thinking about today's problems. Throughout the volume, the contributors creatively engage with Gendlin's work and its applicability to the complex, pressing crises of our time: the Covid-19 pandemic, environmental/climate issues, racism, sexism, economic inequality, and other factors threatening human persons and communities.

Gendlin's theoretical approach to psychology is naturally interdisciplinary, making this book an essential read for anyone interested in moving to the boundaries where psychology meets philosophy, theology, art, environmental studies, science, technology, and much more.

Eric R. Severson is a philosopher specializing in the work of Emmanuel Levinas. He has edited several other Routledge volumes, including *Race, Rage, and Resistance* (2019), *Memories and Monsters* (2017), and *The Ethical Turn* (2016). Severson is also the author or editor of seven other books. He teaches philosophy at Seattle University, USA and lives in nearby Kenmore, Washington.

Kevin C. Krycka is a professor of psychology and associate dean for Social Sciences and Graduate programs at Seattle University, USA. He has authored over 20 articles and book chapters extending Gendlin's philosophical and psychological works in the areas of psychotherapy and qualitative research. He was the inaugural chair of the Gendlin Research Center and continues as a member of its board.

Psychology and the Other

Series editor: David M. Goodman
Associate editors: Brian W. Becker, Donna M. Orange and Eric R. Severson

The *Psychology and the Other* book series highlights creative work at the intersections between psychology and the vast array of disciplines relevant to the human psyche. The interdisciplinary focus of this series brings psychology into conversation with continental philosophy, psychoanalysis, religious studies, anthropology, sociology, and social/critical theory. The cross-fertilization of theory and practice, encompassing such a range of perspectives, encourages the exploration of alternative paradigms and newly articulated vocabularies that speak to human identity, freedom, and suffering. Thus, we are encouraged to reimagine our encounters with difference, our notions of the "other," and what constitutes therapeutic modalities.

The study and practices of mental health practitioners, psychoanalysts, and scholars in the humanities will be sharpened, enhanced, and illuminated by these vibrant conversations, representing pluralistic methods of inquiry, including those typically identified as psychoanalytic, humanistic, qualitative, phenomenological, or existential.

Recent titles in the series include:

Neoliberalism, Ethics and the Social Responsibility of Psychology
Dialogues at the Edge
Edited by Heather Macdonald, Sara Carabbio-Thopsey and David M. Goodman

Anacarnation and Returning to the Lived Body with Richard Kearney
Brian Treanor and James Taylor

The Psychology and Philosophy of Eugene Gendlin
Making Sense of Contemporary Experience
Edited by Eric R. Severson and Kevin C. Krycka

For a full list of titles in the series, please visit the Routledge website at: https://www.routledge.com/Psychology-and-the-Other/book-series/PSYOTH

The Psychology and Philosophy of Eugene Gendlin

Making Sense of Contemporary Experience

Edited by
Eric R. Severson and
Kevin C. Krycka

Routledge
Taylor & Francis Group

LONDON AND NEW YORK

Designed cover image: Crystal Cove Sunset © Claire Esparros

First published 2023
by Routledge
4 Park Square, Milton Park, Abingdon, Oxon OX14 4RN

and by Routledge
605 Third Avenue, New York, NY 10158

Routledge is an imprint of the Taylor & Francis Group, an informa business

© 2023 selection and editorial matter, Eric R. Severson and
Kevin C. Krycka; individual chapters, the contributors

The right of Eric R. Severson and Kevin C. Krycka to be
identified as the authors of the editorial material, and of the
authors for their individual chapters, has been asserted in
accordance with sections 77 and 78 of the Copyright, Designs
and Patents Act 1988.

All rights reserved. No part of this book may be reprinted
or reproduced or utilised in any form or by any electronic,
mechanical, or other means, now known or hereafter invented,
including photocopying and recording, or in any information
storage or retrieval system, without permission in writing from
the publishers.

Trademark notice: Product or corporate names may be
trademarks or registered trademarks, and are used only for
identification and explanation without intent to infringe.

British Library Cataloguing-in-Publication Data
A catalogue record for this book is available from the British Library

Library of Congress Cataloging-in-Publication Data
Names: Severson, Eric R., editor. | Krycka, Kevin C.,
1959– editor.
Title: The psychology and philosophy of Eugene Gendlin :
making sense of contemporary experience / edited by
Eric R. Severson and Kevin C. Krycka.
Identifiers: LCCN 2022054335 (print) |
LCCN 2022054336 (ebook) | ISBN 9781032280042 (paperback)
| ISBN 9781032284057 (hardback) | ISBN 9781003296706 (ebook)
Subjects: LCSH: Gendlin, Eugene T., 1926–2017—Influence. |
Psychology—History—21st century. | Social psychology—History—
21st century.
Classification: LCC BF121 .P7956 2023 (print) |
LCC BF121 (ebook) | DDC 150—dc23/eng/20221114
LC record available at https://lccn.loc.gov/2022054335
LC ebook record available at https://lccn.loc.gov/2022054336

ISBN: 978-1-032-28405-7 (hbk)
ISBN: 978-1-032-28004-2 (pbk)
ISBN: 978-1-003-29670-6 (ebk)

DOI: 10.4324/9781003296706

Typeset in Times New Roman
by codeMantra

Contents

Acknowledgments

A book like this one involves a great deal of work and support from people and organizations whose names do not appear in the table of contents. We are grateful for the individual and collective support of The International Focusing Institute (TIFI) for their early and continued support, for the support of the philosophy and psychology departments at Seattle University, and for a wide array of generous people who provided support for the 2021 Symposium ("Saying What We Mean") that inspired this collection. We are grateful for the helpful editorial eyes of Kurtis Biggs, Gerson Semedo, Misha Severson, Samantha Recalde, Taylor Kelliher, and Sashivadana. Most poignantly, we acknowledge gratitude for the intellectual inspiration of this volume, Eugene T. Gendlin, surely among the most creative thinkers of our times.

Contributors

Edward S. Casey is Distinguished Professor of Philosophy at SUNY Stony Brook. He is past president of the American Philosophical Association (Eastern Division), and was the chair of the philosophy department at Stony Brook 1990–2001. He is the author of 12 books, among them *Imagining, Remembering, The Fate of Place, Getting Back into Place, The World at a Glance, The World on Edge,* and (most recently) *Turning Emotion Inside Out: Affective Life Beyond the Subject.* He was a friend and associate of Eugene Gendlin for decades, and is also the co-editor of Gendlin's *Saying What We Mean: Implicit Precision and the Responsive Order.*

Robin Chalfin is a practicing psychotherapist of 25 years, teaching, training, and writing from feminist and queer disciplines, trauma studies, and existential-psychoanalytic praxis. As adjunct faculty at Lesley University Graduate Division of Counseling & Psychology and board member at the New England Center for Existential Therapy, she is devoted to developing embodied and liberatory modes of human understanding and relatedness. Writing contributions include "Being Broken and Unbroken: Trauma, Heidegger and Befindlichkeit" in *In the Wake of Trauma* (Duquesne), "Identity-as-disclosive-space: Dasein, Discourse, and Distortion" in *Race Rage and Resistance* (Routledge), and the recent essay "The Entanglement of Being: Sexuality Inside and Outside the Binary in Studies" in *Gender and Sexuality (Taylor & Francis).*

Robert Fox is a clinical social worker with a practice of consultation and psychotherapy in Somerville, Massachusetts. He is the founder and director of the Institute for Existential-Psychoanalytic Therapy, and the founder and on the steering committee of the New England Center for Existential Therapy. He was an instructor at Lesley University for almost 40 years. His passion is teaching philosophically to therapists and other healing professionals.

Akira Ikemi, Ph.D. is a professor at the Graduate School of Psychology at Kansai University. A former student of Eugene Gendlin at the University of Chicago, he has been active in the focusing community for many years. He is one of the founders and past-presidents of the Japan Focusing Association. He has authored and co-authored over 180 books, book chapters, and academic articles in Japanese and English. He was awarded the Humanistic Psychology Award from the Japanese Association for Humanistic Psychology in 2020. A former board member and current coordinator of the International Focusing Institute, he now serves as chair of the Eugene Gendlin Center for Experiential Philosophy and Psychology.

Kevin C. Krycka is a professor of psychology and associate dean for Social Sciences and Graduate programs and Seattle University. He has authored over 20 articles and book chapters extending Gendlin's philosophical and psychological works in the areas of psychotherapy and qualitative research. He was the inaugural chair of the Gendlin Research Center and continues as a member of its board.

Shimpei Okamura, Ph.D. is a lecturer at Kobe Gakuin University, Faculty of Psychology. He has worked as a psychotherapist at schools and in psychosomatic medicine. As a certified trainer of the International Focusing Institute, he conducts workshops in various locations in Japan. He completed his doctorate with Prof. Akira Ikemi, and has recently worked on the somatology of architecture from the perspective of Gendlin's philosophy. Since 2022, he has been a board member of the Japanese Association for Humanistic Psychology.

Riley Paterson is a psychotherapist, Focusing-oriented therapist in training, and independent scholar based out of Seattle, Washington. He received a BA in military history from the University of Maryland in 2009, and an MA in existential-phenomenological psychology from Seattle University in 2019. He has previously published in *Human Arenas* and has a paper forthcoming in *Psychiatry, Philosophy & Psychology*. His overarching project is to articulate a thoroughly political approach to psychology, psychotherapy, and mental health broadly. To this end, he is currently at work on a book project tentatively titled "How to Talk about Mental Health as a Political Problem."

Ole Martin Sandberg is a philosopher specializing in environmental and political philosophy. He has done research on embodied critical thinking, biodiversity, climate change, and evolution and ethics. He teaches at the University of Iceland and does research on the concept and value of biodiversity at the Icelandic Museum of Natural History.

Robert C. Scharff is Professor of Philosophy Emeritus at the University of New Hampshire and Executive Director of ITERATA, a non-profit institute for the study of interdisciplinarity in science, industry, and higher education. He is author of *Heidegger Becoming Phenomenological: Interpreting Husserl through Dilthey, 1916–1925* (2019); *How History Matters to Philosophy: Reconsidering Philosophy's Past After Positivism* (2015); and *Comte After Positivism* (2002); and numerous papers on 19th- and 20th-century continental philosophy, philosophy of technology, positivism, and post-positivism; co-editor (with Val Dusek) of *The Philosophy of Technology: An Anthology* (2003, 2014); and former editor of *Continental Philosophy Review* (1994–2005). He is also currently finishing several papers on philosophy, science, and technology and a manuscript, *Inheriting Technoscience: Essays on Heideggerian Themes*.

Donata Schoeller is guest professor of philosophy at the University of Iceland. She is the Academic Director of the Erasmus+ Strategic Partnership in Higher Education's program Training Embodied Critical Thinking (trainingect.com). Among her recent publications are *Close Talking: Erleben zu Sprache bringen,* (Berlin: De Gruyter, 2019), *Saying What We Mean,* ed. with Ed Casey, (Chicago: Northwestern University Press, 2017), and *Thinking Thinking,* ed. with Vera Saller, (Freiburg: Alber Verlag, 2016).

Eric R. Severson is a philosopher specializing in the work of Emmanuel Levinas. He has edited several other Routledge volumes, including *Race, Rage, and Resistance* (2019), *Memories and Monsters* (2017), and *The Ethical Turn* (2016). Severson is also the author or editor of seven other books. He teaches philosophy at Seattle University, and lives in nearby Kenmore, Washington.

Hideo Tanaka, Ph.D. is an adjunct lecturer at Kansai University, Japan. He has been focusing for over 25 years. He talked to Eugene Gendlin about the philosophical background of *Experiencing and the creation of meaning* (Gendlin, 1962/1997) in a TAE workshop (2004) in New York. He completed his master's degree with Prof. Naohiko Mimura, studying Gendlin's philosophy. He completed his doctorate with Prof. Akira Ikemi, studying Gendlin's psychology. He received the incentive award from the Japanese Association for Humanistic Psychology in 2021.

Sigridur Thorgeirsdottir is professor at the Department of Philosophy at the University of Iceland. She launched along with Donata Schoeller two Gendlin-inspired projects: The Embodied Critical Thinking research project (www.ect.hi.is) and a Training Embodied Critical Thinking (www.trainingect.com), a training program for graduate students and researchers in methodologies of embodied thinking, including Thinking at the Edge and microphenomenology. Among recent publications are *Methodological Reflections on Women's Contribution and Influence in the History of Philosophy,* co-edited with R. Hagengruber (Springer 2020), and *Nietzsche as Kritiker und Denker der Transformation,* co-edited with H. Heit (de Gruyter 2016). She is presently editing a volume on embodied thinking in scholarly research and teaching along with D. Schoeller and G. Walkerden, as well a learning to become a Thinking at the Edge trainer.

Greg Walkerden is a practice researcher with disciplinary roots in philosophy, psychology, and environmental management. He designs practices for environmental managers and for felt sense centered reflective practice. He has published extensively on both environmental management and reflective practice, with a particular emphasis on climate change adaptation, professional sensibilities, and reflective practice experiments. He worked for 18 years as an environmental manager, using professional practice as a medium for action research, and has taught felt-sense-based decision-making to environmental professionals for over 25 years. He is based at Macquarie University in Sydney. His work has won a number of awards.

Introduction

Kevin C. Krycka and Eric R. Severson

This volume was inspired by a gathering of scholars, students, and practitioners held to advance the work of American philosopher and psychologist, Eugene T. Gendlin, who passed away in May 2017. "Saying What We Mean: A Symposium on the Works of Eugene Gendlin" was held virtually in 2021 where participants explored the implications of Gendlin's posthumous collection *Saying What We Mean: Implicit Precision and the Responsive Order* (2018). This extraordinary collection, edited by Edward Casey and Donata Schoeller, contributors to this volume, brought together a series of essays demonstrating Gendlin's creative and insightful ability to balance conversations across a wide range of voices in philosophy and psychology.

Gendlin had a unique capacity for thinking "at the edge" of conceptual formulations. He was able to discover, in words and concepts, the evasive connection between idea and experience. Gendlin sought to open up phenomena by exploring ideas that can only be thought in the mode of embodied practice. Gendlin's hope was that he might awaken an appetite in his readers, a yearning to understand how "the experiential side always exceeds the concepts." In this regard, Gendlin invites expansive efforts to explore embodied thinking and experiencing.

The presentations and dialogue at the symposium demonstrated the power of Gendlin's philosophical principles in action. Gene would have delighted over the breadth and complexity of thinking brought into conversation at the symposium and the crossing of these conversations with others with varying interests and backgrounds. It is not hard to imagine Gene sitting back in his well-worn chair taking in and sensing the interaction of ideas and possible solutions to some of our most tricky contemporary problems. He would encourage us to dive in and explore the contradictions inherent and urge on the budding new thinking just about to find its fresh words. He would likely have nodded his head slightly with a twinkle in his eyes signaling he was deep inside himself, resonating and sensing where he joined and pulled back. The resultant interaction of already formed ideas with others

DOI: 10.4324/9781003296706-1

that employ his "process model" carried many ideas forward, some arriving newly shaped in this volume.

The contributions contained here come from academics, scholars, and practitioners in the fields of philosophy and psychology. Such diverse backgrounds and occupations can sometimes yield too much divergence without retaining a sense of the whole project. What we've attempted here is to allow the authors wide space to explore their topic all the while attending to the whole of Gene's lifelong project of making sense of life-as-lived. For Gene, philosophy and psychology are living, not dead systems. Neither is hopelessly trapped by whatever modality of reasoning was current or favored. He certainly recognized the pull of flavor-of-the-day contemporary analysis and its tendencies to isolate and make polemic causes and effects. But he did not let these tendencies in our thinking go unexplored.

Gendlin understood that psychology and philosophy are capable of bringing so much to the world, so much newness that goes beyond solipsistic post-modern fascinations. He encouraged thinking at the edges of these disciplines, noting that to stay centered in them would likely only result in superficial alterations to an existing framework wherein contemporary issues would remain as they are. Fresh thinking is needed, Gendlin often said. Both his philosophy and psychology set a course to get the settled unsettled, to decenter issues from the confines of existing already-patterned thinking, encouraging language to speak new truths, in effect to have our concepts and solutions say what we mean.

To get there though, Gendlin worked in and encouraged others to work in the space of a pragmatist. Likely due to the influence of the American philosophers he encountered such as Dewey and McKeon, and psychologist Carl Rogers, Gendlin's kind of pragmatism, the kind that he invites us to employ, wasn't bereft of human care and meaning or saturated with uninspected broad categorical reasoning. Rather, he asked us to play with our assumptions, not abandon them or shame ourselves for having them. After all, anything existing is living and as such is of a responsive order that can be opened. He was always a teacher, helping us to find the very end of the trajectory of our amazing projects, where they broke or dissolved into others and, from that point, find again the part of it that lived and would carry forward.

As a mentor, Gene was wholly committed to finding that original thing inside of each person, and helping bring it out into public life. What mattered most to Gene was that we enjoy the thinking process as an embodied event. Conversations that revolved around something incomplete, something that need saying – often just for us, but sometimes needing to be said for others – excited his own ideas too. He allowed his students – be they from the University of Chicago days in lecture halls or strolls in the quads, or meeting him one-on-one in his small Manhattan apartment, at countless conferences and workshops, or later in his final days, living along the Hudson River – their own romantic, spiritual, or intersectional take. He encouraged us to build our own playground, if you will, of nascent wonderings, depth of feeling, crossings, and most importantly, of critical analysis.

The authors in this volume played with the central theme of the posthumus collection of his writings, *Saying What We Mean*. In their own ways, each explored a contemporary tension through the lens of implicit precision and the responsive order. The contributors reveal through their analyses that precision (of idea or thinking or solutions) is never fully finished and goes on. Each responds to their topic, often one already substantially defined by contemporary society, as if it presented us with a new order to consider. The ideas presented here emerge from fresh thinking about a topic, the kind of freshness that is embodied, disciplined, open, raw, reflective, inclusive, and horizonal. The chapters articulate a new order in relation to their topic and importantly demonstrate to the reader how a new thing (i.e. a new way of thinking about) can come from embodied precision that is open to more and can merge with other ideas and positions.

Gendlin has left for us a collection of intriguing enactments of this embodied thinking, with essays and books ranging across the spectrum of his adventurous thinking. Our hope is that anyone who picks up this volume will be enticed to go further into whatever grabs their attention. We encourage you to dwell with a chapter and, metaphorically or physically, sink down into your most favored place to enjoy what it offers, and then take up critical, embodied reflection as part of reading these contributions.

Gene would often say whether coming or going, *hello hello*. It was his way of embodying in language the sense of ongoingness found in all his works. Our sincerest hope in presenting this volume is that you will find the places here that say to you, hello hello.

Chapter 1

Starting from experience, and knowing when you do

Robert C. Scharff

In the 1997 Preface to *Experiencing and the Creation of Meaning*, Eugene Gendlin says that its philosophy "fits the times much better" today than it did in 1963 because "most philosophies and most disciplines are now on the brink of it."[1] He sees that the favorite concepts and methods of the mid-20th century have been overtaken by our experience of the world as we actually live through it. In what follows, I want to explain why I think he is right, but why I cannot express this in Gendlin's hopeful tone of voice.

What's to be done with "experience"?

Given the chance, experience always has the power to remind us that no matter how glorious our conceptualizations of it are, they always fall short of full disclosure. It is not just that there is always more to say; there is always more to say that would take off in other directions if given a voice. Moreover, once something is said, the mere saying of it changes our sense of what to say next. Experience, says Gendlin, is always experienc*ing*, that is, an unfinished process of meaning-explication. Only sometimes do we act as if we have hooked words onto a subject matter in completely satisfying way.[2]

Occasionally, a philosopher will take this fact too seriously and build a whole system around the idea that we can never say what we really mean, but for the most part philosophers tend to show too little interest in this condition.[3] "Experience" itself is rarely a dominant topic in philosophy for very long. In a sense, of course, "starting from experience" is obviously unavoidable. But the point, so goes the common wisdom, is to stop dwelling on experience "itself" and get on with the logical and practical task of clarifying its essential confusions, correcting for its natural limitations, and solving the problems it presents to us. In other words, what we initially sense, feel, and live-though must be turned over to reason; and once we recognize this, there are only two main options. Either, as rationalists believe, experience is really just a kind of unstructured putty or mush or "blooming, buzzing confusion," and the task is to create intelligibility from its disordered failure by imposing conceptual schemes on it.[4] Or, as empiricists hold, experience

DOI: 10.4324/9781003296706-2

is the "basic" source of meaning, but it is also mostly unprocessed and subjectively distorted. Hence, the task is to clarify and formalize its raw material through induction, abstraction, and reconstruction. In both cases, however, the modern consensus is that what deserves philosophy's primary attention is not experience itself, but the cognitively structured version that sets it straight.[5]

Yet actually starting philosophy with one of these approaches is a terrible idea. It makes experiencing an unnecessarily contested notion—not because of some intrinsic features of its own, but because modern philosophers have already chosen selective and competing notions that tell us what it really is.[6] Some critics object to both rationalism and empiricism on the grounds that their views neglect the non-cognitive dimensions of experience—as found, for example, in religion, ethics, aesthetics, and politics.[7] But these replies miss the main issue. The fact is, neither approach to experiencing can actually be fundamental. Both views have the relation between experiencing and its conceptualization backwards. For both come *from* experiencing before their explications tell us what one is permitted to say *about* it.[8]

I will return to this backwardness in a moment. But first, it is important to be clear about how to access the viewpoint from which both this backwardness, and the fact that it is so easily ignored, can be understood.[9] Gendlin addresses this issue in several articles. In one, he analyzes the once-popular theory that every reference to self, subjectivity, or inwardness is really a sign of narcissism. In another, he reviews the allegedly scientific literature that seems to define our lives as if they were entirely a function of socio-cultural conditions (e.g., Gendlin 1986a, 1987). Yet instead of criticizing these theories, Gendlin grants that life can sometimes feel precisely the way these theories depict it; but he then asks whether there aren't lots of experiences that would seem to be deeply mischaracterized by the ideas of hopeless self-absorption or social conformity.

What makes Gendlin's question powerful is that it calls for something more radical than opposition or critique. It amounts to a refusal, on phenomenological grounds, to follow the usual practice of privileging of conceptual schemes *over* experience. Experiencing, he says, "must stop dancing to the tune of philosophy's rules of intelligibility."[10] These rules demand (in Gendlin's phrase) a "full turnabout" from experiencing, such that the complexities and intricacies of life "are made [to seem] derivative from ... imposed ordering forms" (Gendlin 1987, 19). It is high time for this turnabout to cease dominating the philosophical conversation and for experiencing—that is, the whole process of living through life—to be restored to its rightful priority.

Gendlin sometimes calls this restoration "another Copernican revolution," that is, an undoing of the modern reversal of life and reason initiated by rationalism and empiricism and codified in Kant.[11] The point is to start over, with a refreshed awareness that all schematizations emerge selectively "from and out of" the course of experiencing. Phenomenologically speaking, experiencing is "not yet" any of those conceptually pared down experiences that we call sensible intuitions, sensations, sense perceptions, pure subjectivity, unobservable inwardness, raw feeling, or whatever. Wilhelm Dilthey has a nice way of putting this.[12] To understand experiencing "in its own terms," he argues, one must resist the temptation to go conceptually "behind it," that is, to always think of experiencing in some preconceived way. The German verb "*erleben*" means what it says. Experiencing is the living-*through* of our lives—hence, a temporal *process*. Of course, one *can* go on to divide it into episodes. Aristotle was not wrong to think of time as the measure of movement from before to after; he was only wrong to think that, having once conceived it so, he had grasped the universal truth about time "as such."

Here is the root of Gendlin's sense of kinship with phenomenology. It is always *possible* to restrict one's interests to one line of life-concern—for example, a scientific concern to develop predictive knowledge of our surroundings, or to create an algorithmic language for Information and Communications Technology (ICT). But phenomenologists do not select any one concern, let alone then work backwards from its explication to impose this on the rest of life. Rather, they try to stay "where we originally are," namely, dwelling experientially in the movement of conceptualizing, and thus remain open to the purely descriptive study of any articulation. A phenomenological philosopher, says Gendlin, "stands at the edge of thought where familiar meanings open into unseen possibilities, where words can combine in odd sentences to say what those words have never said before ... [and once] we can think at that edge, we cannot help but develop our own thinking further ... [and] open any topic in many ways ..." [13] "Thinking at this edge"—where experiencing is coming to be "said" and where experience and language have not yet been conceived as if they were two things with a problematic relation—is Gendlin's late language for what has always been his primary concern—and what marks him as a philosophical original.

How to think like Gendlin

It is clear, then, Gendlin's work presents a phenomenological challenge to traditional modern philosophy's favorite ideas about experience, thinking, conceiving, and speaking; but it also poses questions for Contemporary Continental philosophers.[14] Gendlin himself was hesitant about playing up this feature of his work, because he worried that it would encourage the sort of oppositional mood in philosophy for which he had little sympathy. The trouble with "being opposed" to a way of thinking is that it lets the pre-established assumptions of this very way of thinking set the rules of engagement, and this cuts us off from directly referring to the experiential source, both of the life-concern of *this* kind of thinking and also from our own felt sense of the reasons for resisting it.[15]

Yet there remain familiar and tempting objections to all this talk of directness that will not go away. For example, Gendlin's account of the intricacy and meaning-richness of experiencing is likely to strike many as just another attempt to conceptualize what experiencing is really like, designed to replace traditional schemes. Gendlin addresses this issue in detail in ECM, where he shows that "directly referring" to experiencing—that is, following out various processes of explication while also keeping an eye on the way felt meaningfulness continues to function in them—can be talked about in a way that is fundamentally different from developing a conceptual scheme. I can't give a full-dress ECM commentary here, so let me address the matter in another way.

Imagine a conversation between two experienced parents about how to raise children. As everybody knows, such conversations often turn squirrelly. Spanking, or no spanking? Lots of rules, or general permissiveness? The birds and bees first, or straight to The Talk? Now imagine further that you are an expectant first-time parent, listening to this exchange. The experienced parents might already be quarreling over the Right Way. For you, however, there need not yet be any right way, because there is not yet any need for "my" way. For you, the matter can still be left open to multiple descriptions—and for now, all of them are only projectively yours.

But now turn your attention away from the content of this exchange and consider the mood in which you are listening. From your perspective, the question of who is right *can* be irrelevant. All stated opinions *can* be left to appear as different expressions emerging from the experiences of child-rearing, but now disclosed to you in a situation where you may be deeply interested but with no need to make judgments or choices. For you, it can be easier to regard what the parents say, even when *they* are squared off against each other, as explicating possible aspects of a practical process, not as candidate-assertions about a topic-thing to be defined. You can still treat each parent's claims as expressively opening-up a subject in potentially illuminating ways.

Many of you will already see what I'm sneaking up on here. I want to suggest that what Gendlin calls "the struggle to stand where the phenomenologist stands" is not just a philosopher's idea. Nor is it true only for philosophers that when this stand is taken, one is "never again limited just to already existing concepts." This is the topic of one of my favorite essays, "Two Phenomenologists Do Not Disagree" (Gendlin 1983, 2018a). In it, Gendlin grants that philosophers who have defined their job as one of analyzing concepts and evaluating arguments no longer think "from" experiencing. Yet he asks whether those who call themselves phenomenologists always do better. Like him, they say they start with experience, and like him they do so with the stated intention of getting at life's disclosures without prior conceptual commitments. Yet Gendlin notes that this initial pledge cannot guarantee its sustained adoption. Some phenomenologists remain phenomenological only long enough to develop what they take to be the "essential" account of something. Some take themselves to be phenomenologists mainly because they follow Husserl, Merleau-Ponty, or Heidegger. And this has sometimes led to the paradoxical situation of two phenomenologists squaring off against each other over different descriptions of a single phenomenon, as if their descriptions were like traditional schemes that cannot both be "correct." Yet if one remains oriented like my prospective-parent listener—then encountering different articulations can lead, not to arguments over the right account, but to a conversation in which each party is open to learning how one can "come differently" from experience, even when the topic (as we often say too quickly) is "the same."

Of course, ordinary conversations come to an end, with greater or lesser degrees of clarity and agreement, when life intervenes. But Gendlin's kind of phenomenologist will want to give an account of *this very process*, and do so with the understanding that just as in ordinary life, so also in philosophy, no particular account can ever be final, even if some of them seem for a while to be especially illuminating.[16] My concern here is with the standpoint from which one gives such accounts—the standpoint Gendlin says we can "enter into" and sustain without expecting to produce definitive accounts of anything.[17]

But let me be picky here to make the point. Strictly speaking, there can never *be* an "entering into" the standpoint of experiencing, because no one ever really leaves it—even if there are perspectives that define themselves as requiring that one do so. The so-called objective standpoint, for example, is supposed to be the wholly detached perspective of an ahistorical mind; but it is nothing of the kind. The very idea of "being objective" expresses the outlook of a richly determinate, modern, Western consciousness—that is, the view of a mathematically minded, science-favoring, disembodied, individualized, secular, voluntaristic, and technique-following Self. And at least in the "developed" world, this is widely understood to be the default perspective for every well-educated person, even in the presence of experiences where it feels ill-suited. One sign of this hegemony is precisely our inclination to think of any talk of pre-objectified life as involving an "inward" turn, as if an external perspective were more normal and natural.

Of course, Gendlin knows all this—as is shown by his everywhere insisting that one "*cannot* stand outside" the experiential process, if the point is to study it as it is. And yet he obviously thinks it is helpful for us to think of this phenomenological stance *as if it were* a "going inside" and further, to expect it will be a "struggle" to do so and require us to stay "constantly reflexive" as we try. There is an important point here, and it brings us back to Dilthey.

As Gendlin explains in his MA thesis, Dilthey calls the modern claim to objectivity the expression of a life-manifestation [*Lebensäußerung*]—in this case, the manifestation of our concern to gain predictive knowledge of our material surroundings and express it in "concepts, judgments and larger thought-formations." But Dilthey reminds us that this concern and its expressions constitute only one sort of life-manifestation. Others, he notes, are "human actions and practices," and also any especially revealing "expression of lived experience," including everything from gestures to artworks and autobiographies. These other sorts of expression are mostly studied by the human rather than natural sciences, and their aim is to understand how lives are actually lived rather than how individuals and social groups behave when observed.

Dilthey's interpretation of the sciences themselves is dated. But his most important legacy is not his substantive account of the epistemic dualism of natural vs. human science. It lies in the perspective from which he tries to distinguish them—not only from each other but from other human practices. Most philosophers of science, in his day as in ours, tend to start by analyzing one kind of science—usually a natural science—and on the basis of this analysis, develop a model for studying all the others.[18] But Dilthey starts by considering all of them equally, as expressions of the life-concerns that animate their practices. To do this, he takes up what he calls "the standpoint of life" itself, from which all human activity, scientific or otherwise, is first of all disclosed as the expression of a life-driven activity. As I explain elsewhere, this is fundamentally the same outlook that the young Heidegger calls the "basic philosophical standpoint" that must replace Husserl's transcendental outlook so that phenomenology can be genuinely phenomenological.[19]

I turn to Dilthey, Husserl, and Heidegger at this point with some uneasiness. For here is the place where I feel both closest to Gendlin's "new philosophy" and also the farthest from his optimistic statements about its prospects. On the one hand, Gendlin himself is among the most conscientiously and consistently phenomenological thinkers I know. His "directly referential" analyses of the "intricacy" and "precision" of experiencing as an embodied and temporalizing process, his account of its inevitably "more than any forms" character and consequently also of the inevitably limited nature of all conceptualization, his insistence that every sort of explication be studied without playing epistemic or ontological favorites—all of this is unsurpassed.

Moreover, and perhaps equally important, Gendlin does not become a phenomenologist by denigrating objectivity.[20] He is especially clear that even if explication is *in principle* always open-ended, the degree to which this is so depends upon the experiential concern being explicated. Hence, on the one hand, it is your body, as the title of one of his books puts it, that interprets your dreams, not your self-help book on dream interpretation (Gendlin 1986b). It is the poet's lived sense of what words go at the spot where, at first, there is only an unfinished line that matters, even if "what goes" violates all the rules of poetic form (Gendlin 1992). It is the client, not the theorizing therapist, who gets hit with a wave of recognition so that words about what's bothersome start to come. In such cases, we might say, some felt-sense of things guides the explication.

Yet on the other hand and for some purposes, a line of conceptualization may need to be formalized and made more responsive to logical analysis, conceptual revision, and theoretical systemization than to any further experiencing. Here, the established routines of a group may well replace the felt sense of individuals as the ultimate guide for expression. Gendlin stresses, however, that this is not a problem. Yes, to operate under some reasoned resolve to limit one's explications to whatever a rigorously established method allows us to encounter is to "objectify." In fact, "everything" is open to objectification. This only becomes a problem when one claims that everything only "really" comes into its own *as objectified*. Ontologically speaking, then, Gendlin's "new philosophy" is an equal opportunity phenomenology. To him, for example, there cannot be any positivist or existentialist phenomenologies, because they privilege The Objective and The Subjective, respectively. But there also can be no new philosophy that fails to address the life-concerns expressed by positivists and existentialists.

But there is, I think, another "on-the-other-hand." As Gendlin acknowledges, we still live in an intellectual atmosphere that privileges established conceptual models—especially models initially created for scientific purposes that have silently spilled over into life to enframe its wider order, often in the form of pinched and reductive schemes that urge us to distrust experiencing. ECM does perhaps "fit the times" *better* now, because the weaknesses of our inherited tradition are catching up to it. But to what extent? In the space left, I want to indicate why I think there is much more standing in the way of Gendlin's new philosophy than he attends to.[21]

Impediments to Gendlin's "success"

Stated quickly, my concern is this. The modern tradition—as an inheritance, not as a set of theories—tends to silently act on experiencing the same way that "the scientific method" does for empirical researchers—only more widely and often in unseen ways. Under the influence of this tradition—again, as an inheritance not as a set of explicitly conceived rules—it is not just that words don't come because felt sense demands something fresh; it is also that they can't come because common words already possess a powerful sanction for "what one says" on such occasions. And it is this inheritance, not what we can existentially understand from Dilthey's standpoint of life, or Heidegger's basic philosophical attitude, or Gendlin's inward-turning stance that shapes our intellectual default position, both in philosophy and in life. In life, we do have episodes of life-driven meaning-creation that mostly elude the power of this inheritance. Sometimes, poetry does happen; children are lovingly raised; therapy transforms; doctors consult patients before their machines and textbooks, and technological designs get democratized. But in philosophy, if "going inside" is tolerated at all, it is still usually in the merely supplemental form that Thomas Nagel describes in *The View from Nowhere*. The primary task, Nagel says, has always been to "understand the operation of our minds [and the condition of the world] *from a point of view that is not just our* own." Hence, first-person reports are important in philosophy mainly because they remind us that our rational quest for "unqualified results" is always flawed and human. This reminder should make us humble, but never "reduce our ambitions." Eternal and non-local truth remains the goal, even if we cannot reach it.[22]

But the problem for speaking from experience is not just the urge to settle for tradition-bound third-personism itself. Critics of this outlook often make the equally third-person assumption that the problem can be avoided simply by making another choice. One says, for example, that the allegedly objective viewpoint must be "recontextualized."[23] But *re*-contextualization suggests a move made by a context-free mind, already hovering over a con-textless outlook and now deciding what to add. At first, it may seem as if one has thereby "unmasked" every objective claim by revealing its historically conditioned nature. But all this really accomplishes is to present the ideas of objectivity and contextualization as juxtaposed before our minds and ready, as Gendlin puts it, "to obscure each other, as if [concepts] *ought to* work purely alone, and situations ... *ought to* consist of finished givens [we can] ... simply observe and represent."[24]

It is not just analytic philosophers that have this problem; phenomenologists inherit a version of the same difficulty. Throughout his life, Husserl held that no philosophy is genuine philosophy if it makes foundationalist use of natural or historical knowledge in characterizing its standpoint.[25] No mathematician, he argues, would consult historians about the truth of mathematical theories. What, then, could a historian possibly say that would make philosophers uncertain about their idea of a true philosophy?[26] As he wrote to Georg Misch in 1930, I want to "make it plain that at times, the 'ahistorical Husserl' *had to have* distanced himself from history ... pre-cisely in order to advance far enough in method to pose [objective] scientific questions in regard to it."[27]

One way to unravel this issue is to notice that two additional Cartesian aspects of our modern inheritance are causing trouble here. Pretty much everyone now knows that Descartes' *Meditations* led to a tradition that tends to excessively privilege the view from nowhere. What is less recognized is how it also set the modern tradition's standard for how to handle what appears from this standpoint. What Descartes' disengaged thinker does is bring ideas fully before itself, test them for their clarity and distinctness, and then "affirm" the ones that pass the test.[28] In other words, the judgments of a thinking subject—that is, its resolute choices—are considered just contextless as the thinker itself. The result has been that even today, long after Cartesian *thinking* has been shamed for ignoring its historicity, the idea of a totally "free" *willing* is alive and well—perhaps most destructively in the supposition that we can get rid of Cartesianism by just choosing to do so. Being somewhat right is now acceptable, but being a little bit free still sounds contradictory.[29]

The biggest remaining problem with our Cartesian legacy, then, lies in the fact that, both philosophically and culturally, the stance from which the view from nowhere should be critically confronted is still widely conceived as an outlook from which one can make utterly ahistorical "choices." This is one reason why I cannot share Gendlin's confidence that "*post*-modern debates" have put philosophy "on the brink" of his project. Post-modern opposition to Cartesianism is still largely a Cartesian move, and its opponents remain just as resolutely distanced from experiencing. Today, natural scientists tend to see the old image of an Absolute Conception of the World as having been overtaken by events, especially in quantum physics. But *philosophers* of science continue to study this change externally, by analyzing what scientists say, with no movement toward the sort of inward stance from which the felt-need for the changes in what is said might be understood.[30]

This, argues Heidegger, is what Husserl never understood. He philosophizes as what he takes to be a science-minded consciousness, but he never sees that this way of thinking is itself only one (now increasingly dated) existential possibility. So he *trains* himself to enact this possibility as if it could have no philosophical alternative and then *chooses* its vision of a total methodological self-possession as the proper model for all philosophy. Yet, in fact, the very idea of achieving "freedom from all standpoints" is itself "something historical," not a context-free choice.[31] It is a variant of the old dream of *not* being historical and of somehow thinking like the gods. To Heidegger, for a philosophy to stay phenomenological, it must learn to speak creatively *from* experiencing *in spite of* the influence of social convention and tradition over all our efforts to speak. Phenomenological analysis thus necessarily involves a constant struggle to "win" the phenomenological attitude, with no hope of finding/choosing the method that makes this possible.

Gendlin himself mostly avoids this problem; but his discussion of the ways in which our modern inheritance can obstruct his project are often cursory. In this regard, my own view is more like the young Heidegger's. He, too, comes from the experiential place opened up by Dilthey and praised by

Gendlin in his MA thesis; but Heidegger felt it necessary to explain in detail precisely how the roadblocks to thinking "from" this place interfered with his attempts to do so.[32] In the end, I'm just not sure it is phenomenological enough to report that "most philosophy and most disciplines are on the brink" of ECM's new philosophy. Inward turns and "speaking from life" are still mostly viewed as the poor relatives of observing and thinking from the outside—even when one's own felt sense of how things are stirs restively against this setup. There must be, says Heidegger, both a positive and a critical side to the question of "who" philosophizes, and the critical side needs to be taken up explicitly if there is to be widespread clarity about what kind of thinker can actually become a second-Copernican revolutionary.

What Heidegger means by this comes out clearly in his analysis of Husserl.[33] What he finds most problematic about Husserl is not his theoretical prejudice, nor his excessive promotion of supposedly "scientific" values, nor even his call for a philosophically "foundational science" (*Urwissenschaft*) that leaves the very idea of "science" (*Wissenschaft*) hopelessly ambiguous. Behind all these tradition-dependent symptoms lies a restrictive "basic philosophical tendency," namely, the assumption that even in phenomenology, "reflection" on experience is structured like a Cartesian act of "meditation"—that is, a kind of reflection (*Reflexion*) where one imagines choosing to be utterly self-possessed and ahistorical.[34] But this idea of reflection, argues Heidegger, is "already a disguised theory"— one that "thematizes" experience into the acts of a consciousness that is free to define and legitimate its own activity.[35] With reflection so defined, Husserl's hostility toward history, his distrust of unprocessed experiencing, and his verdict that Dilthey's account of lived experience is ultimately mere psychology—all these unphenomenological features of his thought are understandable.

To Heidegger, Dilthey's writings display a much more radical "basic attitude [*Einstellung*]"—one that knows all about objects but also remains open to everything that is not experienced as an object. Dilthey describes this attitude as "a new and distinctive consciousness of existence [*Daseinsbewüßtsein*]" (Heidegger 2005, 66-67) that "is inseparable from the act in which it occurs" and that "intensifies the field of inner awareness" and "illuminates and highlights its content" (e.g., Dilthey 1989, 49–51; Dilthey 2002, 46–50, 53–54, 155–156). He calls this consciousness an enhanced self-awareness (*Selbstbesinnung*) of the course of our experiences that deserves to be "the true foundation of philosophy" (Dilthey 1984, 278; cf., 254). The young Heidegger, using virtually the same language, identifies this self-awareness in his early lecture courses as the proper replacement for Husserlian reflection.[36]

Here, I think, Heidegger is clearing the way for what Gendlin actually does, more or less without further ado, and not just in relation to the Being question. For Gendlin, it is just obvious that "bringing something to thought" need not mean "placing a topic under thought, as its basis." No topic, he says, "is only its categories."

> Anything can rethink itself as a "happening." In [Heidegger's] terms, the kinds of "transitions" I study are different ways of "letting be," of "happening." Of course there is no final list of ways. Each opens more ways inside itself, and in the others. But even a few *let us learn, be, and say, much* [more].[37]

This undoubtedly states the ideal, in relation to both phenomenologists and phenomena. It is probably safe to say that some conception of this possibility incentivizes every post-Husserlian to attempt, in Heidegger's words, to recapture our "basic experience of the lifeworld" by "sinking back down into environmental life," such that we can remain in touch with "specific experiences" but with an enhanced self-awareness that "goes along with their articulation" instead of reflectively resolving to treat all experiences as, say, instances of Aristotle or Kant's categories (Heidegger 2013, 119–124, 191–192, 271).

But that, I think, is just what this is. An ideal. To this day, many phenomenologists are not very phenomenological in their stance, even if the topics about which they try to be phenomenological are extensively described. Think, for example, of Husserl's account of time-consciousness. He may have properly identified the centrality of temporality for human existence, but from what reflective position and with what results? No one could actually live out the "structure" of time-consciousness as Husserl portrays it. Of course, time-consciousness can be interpreted this way, if one is trying to theoretically reconstruct how it must work; but for Heidegger, there is a prior question, namely, *precisely how* must temporality already figure in the living-through of life, such that Husserl's reconstructions don't seem like a mere construction?[38]

So, to sum up, I agree that many philosophers are now closer to Gendlin's project than they know. But what will it take for them to be more than just "on the brink"? I think we need just as many Gendlin-like accounts of the powerful ways in which a phenomenological perspective is routinely blocked, as we do accounts of the new possibilities that thinking from this perspective opens up. For in a deep sense, Gendlin's new starting point for philosophy is precisely the outlook that the main currents of the Western intellectual tradition have been diligently trying to surpass.

Notes

1   Gendlin 1997b [hereafter, ECM], xi. ECM actually appeared in 1962, not 1963.
2   His early descriptions of this term, usually with reference to therapeutic practice, explain that it designates

(1) "a process of *feeling* (2) occurring in the *immediate* present. (3) Clients can *refer directly* to experiencing. (4) In forming conceptualizations, clients are *guided* by experiencing. First rough conceptualizations can be checked against direct reference to experiencing. (5) Experiencing has *implicit meanings*. (6) These are preconceptual. Experiencing is a concrete *organismic* process, felt in awareness.

(Gendlin 1961, 239)

This sense of experiencing is already present in Gendlin's unpublished Counseling Center Discussion Papers in 1950s, and it is this sense that appears in its full-blown ontological sense in his philosophical writings.

3 "Today non-logical transitions are emphasized, but only as a glorying in *disorder*" (Gendlin 1989, 408). Or occasionally, like Derrida, they make conceptual incompleteness the primary concern and conclude that the inadequacy of all conceptualization is itself philosophy's topic, rather than experience. I return to this briefly below.

4 It is worth noting that this famous phrase from William James is not linked to any consideration of the relation of reason to experience. The full sentence in which the phrase appears is, "The baby, assailed by eyes, ears, nose, skin, and entrails at once, feels it all as one great blooming, buzzing confusion; and to the very end of life, our location of all things in one space is due to the fact that the original extents or bignesses of all the sensations which came to our notice at once, coalesced together into one and the same space" (James 1981, 462). James is focusing here on what is now often called lived space, existential spatiality, or "thereness," and he is arguing that it is neither a "form of intuition" in Kant's sense, nor an addition of reason, but part of the structure of the living through of life from the very beginning. Indeed, he goes on to propose a developmental account of how young children become better at things that emphasizes the emergence of skills and understanding out of their relationships with nature and people in this "one space" and does *not* attribute all of this to the growing importance of rationality.

5 Gendlin (1997b, 140–148). I cite one main place for illustrative purposes, but his image of rationalist and empiricist ways of blocking the opening to the study of experiencing is ubiquitous in Gendlin's writings.

6 Gendlin (1997a) [hereafter LBP], 31. For a thorough review of the idea from the 16th to the 20th century in the developed West, see Jay (2005). Near the end of this illuminating book, Jay suggests that "The experience of reading [William Blake's *Songs of Experience*, after which this book is named] is thus one in which the self-conscious reader feels the *fallen quality of his own state*, knowing that he has to struggle to make sense out of the challenges presented to him by the poet/artist, and *may never in fact find a satisfactory resolution*" (403). One purpose of this paper is to find a way to express agreement with this idea, without accepting the mood revealed in its italicized phrases.

7 And indeed, in our world, reality is mostly what calculative cognition says it is, praxis is mostly the skillful use of engineering techniques, education is essentially STEM training with a few frills added if the community can afford them, and ideas about life's goals are largely politicized legitimations of what is desired by those who thrive in such a world.

8 Think of the matter this way. If it were always true that experiencing needs conceptual help in the way both rationalists and empiricists claim, then the question of which view is right could never be resolved and deciding between them would simply be a matter of either compromise or declared preference, and either decision would be arbitrary since by definition there could be no

perspective from which "experiencing" could be understood in its own, not yet processed condition.

9 Of course, treated merely as the source of self-defining philosophical systems, rationalism and empiricism are less problematic; but they still operate in a logically circular way. "Experience" is still what it is stipulated to be; "reason," also; and the two stipulations define the parameters of system that operates by agreement not to appeal outside of its conceptual boundaries. That there is such an outside can be recognized only by a philosophical reflection that is neither outside nor externally comparative of multiple systems, but understands that every urge to develop a system is grounded in the explication process of experiencing.

10 ECM, 146 n2. Of course, this does not make him an opponent of philosophical analysis or argumentation. The point is that when established conceptual schemes are used to judge the nature of experiencing, they get things backwards. Hence, the need for a "reversal."

11 Again, here is a "reversal of the usual philosophical order" (ECM, xiii–xvii). See also, Gendlin 1973, 2004.

12 ... as Gendlin already knew by the time he wrote his MA thesis on him. See Gendlin 1950. The question raised in this early essay is how "to *found* a scientific method which includes the comprehension of the given significance of human data," instead of moving directly instead to a method that suppresses this comprehension in favor of the physical-scientific model of experimental observation, even for the human sciences (iv–v. my emphasis).

13 Gendlin 2012, 6. In this place, Gendlin is explaining how this sort of thinking facilitates the understanding of the writings of a philosopher. For a description of how this thinking works in general, see Gendlin 2018b, 282–293.

14 Gendlin did not particularly like my way of associating his views with other philosophers; nevertheless, he was not shy about acknowledging his historical context. While everything Gendlin wrote—from the early studies of Rogerian therapy to the TAE work he did with Mary Hendricks—reflects a distinctly underived and original philosophical treatment of experiencing, he made it clear that in developing it, he drew upon the work of Dilthey. Gendlin's MA topic is Dilthey's concepts of *Erlebnis* and *Verstehen* (Gendlin 1950). He also acknowledged his strong affinity with post-Husserlian phenomenology—most recently, in Gendlin 2004, although Gendlin (1983) is still my favorite; cultivated a limited kinship to Heidegger (Gendlin 1967); and much else—e.g., Richard McKeon's "semantic schematism" (Gendlin 1989, 405) and most surprisingly perhaps, Aristotle (Gendlin 2012, also Gendlin 1995).

15 Dilthey knew, says Gendlin, that "in principle, anything human is understandable," not because we apply the right concepts to it but because, as human ourselves, our own references to it can be "direct" and in no need of mediating rules (Gendlin 1989, 405–406).

16 In *A Process Model*, Gendlin presents a systematic account of what such a *detailed* phenomenological philosophy would cover, and how it can start in such a way that explication can be inclusive of the whole of Being, without ontological prejudice in favor of human entities (Gendlin 2019).

17 The spatial metaphor is used extensively in Gendlin's writings. No account of the experiential process, he says, can be given while "standing outside" of it. Experiencing and conceptualizing are only directly disclosed "in the very process of examining" it. As I am arguing, such language is a duck-rabbit—both necessary in a world that privileges external accounts and for that very reason, less phenomenological than one might wish.

18 I pass over an often-misunderstood point here, namely that Dilthey does not claim that philosophy and the human sciences should both take the same standpoint; nor does he think that "understanding life in its own terms" means the same thing for both. For example, when human scientists say that their perspective is "more intimately" related to experiencing that the perspective of the natural sciences, they are making a *comparative* judgment, based on the recognition that "observing" and "explaining" are deliberately more selective and distanced from individual differences than human scientific "interpretations." But philosophers would be playing favorites if they took this position. For them, every human practice is equally grounded in the living-through of life, even if their ways of "intensifying" the interests that drive them vary in selectivity. For further discussion, see Scharff (2019, 71, 101–104, 108–109 ns.25–28).

19 The most revealing thing about Dilthey's characterization of this standpoint, says Heidegger, is that although it seeks to study the methods that various practices develop "from out of life itself," this study itself has no fixed methodology. The proof of its phenomenological success will always lie in its results, which cannot be guaranteed in advance by adopting a special procedure, by dividing life up into regions, and certainly not by founding a school of properly trained transcendental minds.

20 Cf., Dilthey (2002): "One cannot make room for the human sciences by sacrific[ing] the legitimate independence of the particular sciences, the fruitful power of their empirical methods, and the certainty of their foundation to a subjective and sentimental mood which seeks nostalgically to recall by means of [pseudo-] science a [kind of] psychic satisfaction that has been lost forever." (49–50).

21 "Curiosity about how [my] project might be possible," he says, "is an appetite I would like to rouse in my reader" (ECM, xi). Would that curiosity were all we needed!

22 Nagel (1987, 25–27) and Nagel (1997, 6–7, 10–11 and Ch. 1). Given this widely shared attitude, is it any wonder that one of the most popular philosophy books on ethics and public policy from the 20th century is Rawls' *A Theory of Justice* (Rawls 1997, 102–168), whose major premise is that how we should live is a question to be asked only after we take an "original position" that bars us from considering our own circumstances or desires?

23 I am thinking here especially of the work of Richard Rorty and the later Hilary Putnam. For a recent analysis that comes much closer to the position I take here, see Beaney (2020, 594–614) and Beaney (2019, 725–758, esp. 753, 757–758).

24 Levin (1997, 6). It is no surprise that objectivity's critics, faced with this "ought" in an inherited atmosphere where objectivity is privileged, either double down or have second thoughts about fostering "relativism" or even nihilism. And then objectivism reclaims its ground, new critiques emerge, relativism is evoked, objectivism returns, and so on. If any reader hears the echo of Thomas Kuhn's career in this description, so be it.

25 David Carr notes that in later life, Husserl does make "history" as a topic and "tended to take up themes closer to the topic of history." But this is not the point at stake here. What Husserl objected to most in "historicism"—namely, its depiction of all thinking, even the sort of philosophical thinking that prides itself on taking a methodologically secured distancing from the historical life, remains "historically determinate"—remains in his writings beginning to end. For him, all references to the historical determinateness of thinking *reduces* thinking to its historical conditions; but this confuses the sort of external and causal accounts of today's antecedent conditions that many historians and human scientists do indeed offer (on analogy with the way natural scientists

conceived "material conditions") with the sort of hermeneutical accounts of the experience of "being historical" developed by later phenomenologists like Heidegger and Gadamer. Hence, it seems off the point for Carr to conclude that Husserl's later interest in history as a subject matter and the new "rhetorical style" he takes toward it shows that "Husserl's path finally rejoins that of the historicism of German philosophy in the late 19th and early 20th centuries" (Carr 2014, 241).

26 The full text reads: "Certainly the mathematician ... will not turn to historical science to be taught about the truth of mathematical theories. It will not occur to him to relate the historical development of mathematical representations with the question of truth. How, then, is it to be the historian's task to decide as to the truth of given philosophical systems and, above all, as to the very possibility of *a philosophical science that is valid in itself*? And what would he have to add that could make the philosopher uncertain with regard to his idea, i.e., that of a true philosophy?" (Husserl 1981, 187, trans. slightly altered).

27 Letter to Misch, cited in Sandmeyer (2009, 169, trans. slightly altered).

28 Descartes (1985, 125). For Descartes himself, we know, the only thing that can appear to such a mind is an idea, or representation of something, but even if one assumes that at least some of our encounters are more direct, how a Cartesian is supposed to deal with appearances remains the same. I am focused on the pattern of entertaining ideas, testing them, and then affirming/judging them, for it is this pattern that one can still see prominently on display in the latest textbooks on epistemology.

29 "It is above all in virtue of the will that I understand myself to bear in some way the image and likeness of God".

30 Of course, I acknowledge a debt to Hilary Putnam for this phrasing, if not quite with the same intention as his. It is in reference to Richard Rorty that he says, wearily, that behind all those noisy rejections of various facets of Cartesianism, "the attempt to say that *from a God's-Eye View there is no God's-Eye View* is still there, under all that wrapping" (Putnam 1990, 25, author's emphasis). For Putnam's critique of Bernard Williams's defense of science as seeking the Absolute Conception of the World, see Putnam (1990, 170–174).

31 Heidegger (1999, 64). Indeed, Husserl's own production of repeatedly revised accounts of how to implement his principle of all principles already suggests that the very ideal of a distance-taking, science-minded philosophical posture is hopelessly unphenomenological; and in tracing Husserl's "insufficiency" back to "what goes on" in his phenomenology "before it becomes what [he claims] it is," says Heidegger, I am showing "hermeneutically" that the very extension of his objectivism to the whole of philosophy is something much more serious than mere neglect.

32 My reference to "roadblocks" is deliberate. It is this idea that Heidegger utilizes at the beginning of *Being and Time* to explain how three "basic prejudices" in our inheritance of the metaphysical tradition "pre-answers" are efforts to raise the being-question again with a firm Don't Bother (*Being and Time*, trans. John Macquarrie and Edward Robinson (Heidegger 1962, §1). The idea that they constitute a "roadblock" comes from conversations with Reiner Schürmann.

33 Here and in the previous paragraph, I am drawing on Scharff (2019, 87–109). As I explain there, Heidegger's initial analysis of Husserl's phenomenology relies heavily on Husserl's so-called *Logos* article, "Philosophy as Rigorous Science" (Husserl 1981), which has led some defenders of Husserl to object that this ignores all the later modifications he made to this early and somewhat programmatic essay. My argument there, however, is that on the problem of Husserl's ultimately unphenomenological self-interpretation, nothing really changes.

34 This, says Heidegger, allows us to imagine ourselves engaging in an entirely detached kind of "seeing to which the seen stands opposed, over against and... outside the seeing" (Heidegger 2000, 111–112; cf., Heidegger 1999, 64).

35 Heidegger (2000, 93–94). As I explain elsewhere, Heidegger's critique is not aimed, just generally, at Husserl's reflective efforts to gain access to experiencing, but at the fact that these efforts take the form of a "thematization" that is traditionally Cartesian (Scharff 2019, 141–142 n.11).

36 For Heidegger, Husserl seems to depict a kind of "bringing-everything-to-a-reflective-standstill [*Stehenblieben*] …. instead of a more phenomenological *going along with* [*Mitgehen*], whereby I am carried away by the stream of life" in an enhanced but nevertheless "immediate participation in experiencing." In contrast, "Husserl's 'phenomenological reduction' thereby appears to be twisted into its opposite. There, I am precisely *not* participating, take no position, practice ἐποχή. One can only characterize the phenomenological reduction in such a [negative] way if when one looks at all experiences from the outset as completely *intentional*, and in addition, as thing-apprehending experiences [e.g., perceptions]—[But] if one starts out from understanding itself, one comes straightaway to the demand to "participate" in personal life-experience with the greatest vitality and interiority" (Heidegger 2010, 91–92, author's emphasis omitted).

37 Gendlin (1989, 409), my emphasis. Hence, Gendlin can, e.g., just start right in by just saying "An organism is an environmental interaction that continuously regenerates itself. It does not follow from the past, but it does take account of it," then call for a new "process model" that captures this "taking account," say a few words about an old model's unphenomenological way of splitting this interaction into perception over here in the body and things over there—and then get on with it. He certainly deserves praise for this, but it will not help most philosophers because *operating with an old model is not the main problem standing in the way of understanding him.* The cumulative effect of 2500 years of philosophizing virtually guarantees that "taking account of regeneration"—however naturally this happens for other organisms—has long since been translated into a kind of objectivist, static/dynamic language that makes it seem unnatural even to try. After the old model just described, there have been 100s of other more appealing versions, all of which "thematize" away experiencing in favor of some especially desirable form of contact selected by a "reflective" consciousness.

38 I am reminded of those developmental linguists who insist that little kids *must* be learning "grammar," or else they wouldn't be able to say the things they do. In this insistence, they are trying to give inappropriate ontological power to their "must" by reading back into children the grammatical theories they fashioned in the first place from the outside, in an effort to try to reconstruct what they could only "observe" as "linguistic behavior"

References

Beaney, Michael. 2019. Developments and Debates in the Historiography of Philosophy. In *The Cambridge History of Philosophy, 1945–2015*, eds. Kelly Becker and Iain D. Thomson. Cambridge: Cambridge University Press.

Beaney, Michael. 2020. Two Dogmas of Analytic Historiography. *British Journal of the History of Philosophy* 28(3): 594–614

Carr, David. 2014. Husserl and Classical German Philosophy on History. In *Husserl und die klassische deutsche Philosophie/Husserl and Classical German Philosophy*, eds. Faustino Fabbianelli and Sebastian Luft. Dordrecht: Springer, pp. 229–241.

Descartes, René. 1984. *The Philosophical Writings of Descartes*, vol. 2, eds. John Cottingham, et al. Cambridge: Cambridge University Press, 1984.

Descartes, René. 1985. *The Philosophical Writings of Descartes*, vol. 1, eds. John Cottingham et al. Cambridge: Cambridge University Press.

Dilthey, Wilhelm. 1989. *Selected Writings*, Vol. I, Introduction to the Human Sciences, eds. Rudolf A. Makkreel and Frithjof Rodi. Princeton, NJ: Princeton University Press.

Dilthey, Wilhelm. 2002. *Selected Writings*, Vol. III, The Formation of the Historical World in the Human Sciences, eds. Rudolf A. Makkreel and Frithjof Rodi. Princeton, NJ: Princeton University Press.

Gendlin, Eugene T. [Gene]. 1950. *Wilhelm Dilthey and the Problem of Comprehending Human Significance in The Science of Man*. [Unpublished Master's Thesis]. University of Chicago (Dept. of Philosophy).

Gendlin, Eugene T. 1961. Experiencing: A Variable in the Process of Therapeutic Change. *American Journal of Psychotherapy* 15(2): 233–245.

Gendlin, Eugene T. 1967. Analysis [of Heidegger's *What is a Thing?*]. In Martin Heidegger, *What is a Thing?* trans. W.B. Barton, Jr. and Vera Deutsch. South Bend, IN: Gateway, pp. 247–296.

Gendlin, Eugene T. 1973. Experiential Phenomenology. In *Phenomenology and the Social Sciences*, Vol. 1, ed. Maurice Natanson. Evanston, IL: Northwestern University Press, pp. 281–319.

Gendlin, Eugene T. 1983. Two Phenomenologists Do Not Disagree. In *Phenomenology: Dialogues and Bridges*, eds. Ronald Bruzina and Bruce Wilshire. Albany, NY: SUNY, pp. 321–335. Reprinted in Gendlin 2018a, 5–21.

Gendlin, Eugene T. 1986a. Process Ethics and the Political Question. In *The Moral Sense in the Communal Significance of Life: Investigations in Phenomenological Praxeology. Psychiatric Therapeutics, Medical Ethics and Social Praxis within the Life- and Communal World*, ed. Anna-Teresa Tymieniecka [Analecta Husserliana 20]. Dordrecht: Reidel, pp. 265–275.

Gendlin, Eugene T. 1986b. *Let Your Body Interpret Your Dreams*. Wilmette, IL: Chiron Publications.

Gendlin, Eugene T. 1987. A Philosophical Critique of the Concept of Narcissism: The Significance of the Awareness Movement. In *Pathologies of the Modern Self. Postmodern Studies on Narcissism, Schizophrenia, and Depression,* ed. David Michael Levin. New York: New York University Press, pp. 251–304.

Gendlin, Eugene T. 1989. Phenomenology as Non-Logical Steps. In *Analecta Husserliana, Vol. XXVI. American Phenomenology. Origins and Developments*, eds. Eugene F. Kaelin and Calvin O. Schrag. Dordrecht: Kluwer, pp. 404–410.

Gendlin, Eugene T. 1992. Thinking Beyond Patterns: Body, Language, and Situations. In *The Presence of Feeling in Thought*, eds. Bernard den Ouden and Marcia Moen. New York: Peter Lang, pp. 25–151.

Gendlin, Eugene T. 1995. Ultimacy and Aristotle: In Essence Activity. In *Being Human in the Ultimate: Studies in the Thought of John M. Anderson*, eds. N. Georgopoulos and Michael Heim. Amsterdam/Atlanta: Rodopi, pp. 135–166.

Gendlin, Eugene T. 1997a. How Philosophy Cannot Appeal to Experience, and How It Can. In *Language Beyond Postmodernism: Saying and Thinking in Gendlin's Philosophy*, ed. David Michael [Kleinberg-] Levin. Evanston, IL: Northwestern University Press.

Gendlin, Eugene T. 1997b [1962]. *Experiencing and the Creation of Meaning: A Philosophical and Psychological Approach to the Subjective*, 2nd edition [ECM]. Evanston, IL: Northwestern University Press.

Gendlin, Eugene T. 2004. The New Phenomenology of Carrying Forward. *Continental Philosophy Review* 37(1): 127–151.

Gendlin, Eugene T. 2012. *Line by Line Commentary on Aristotle's 'De Anima,'* Vols. I and II. Spring Valley, NY: The Focusing Institute.

Gendlin, Eugene T. 2018a. *Saying What We Mean: Implicit Precision and the Responsive Order. Selected Works by Eugene T. Gendlin*. Evanston, IL: Northwestern University Press.

Gendlin, Eugene T. 2018b. Introduction to *Thinking at the Edge*. In Gendlin 2018a, pp. 282–293.

Gendlin, Eugene T. 2019. *A Process Model*. Evanston, IL: Northwestern University Press.

Heidegger, Martin. 1962. *Being and Time*, trans. John Macquarrie and Edward Robinson. London: SCM Press/New York: Harper and Row.

Heidegger, Martin. 1999. *Ontology: The Hermeneutics of Facticity*, trans. John van Buren. Bloomington: Indiana University Press.

Heidegger, Martin. 2000. *Towards the Definition of Philosophy*, trans. Ted Sadler. New York: Continuum.

Heidegger, Martin. 2005. *Introduction to Phenomenological Research*, trans. Daniel O. Dahlstrom. Bloomington: Indiana University Press.

Heidegger, Martin. 2010. *Phenomenology of Intuition and Expression*, trans. Tracy Colony. New York: Continuum.

Heidegger, Martin. 2013. *Basic Problems of Phenomenology: Winter Semester 1919/1920*, trans. Scott M. Campbell. New York: Continuum.

Husserl, Edmund. 1981. Philosophy as Rigorous Science, trans. Quentin Lauer. In *Husserl: Shorter Works*, eds. Peter McCormick and Frederick A. Elliston. Notre Dame, IN: Notre Dame University Press, pp. 166–197.

James, William. 1981. *The Principles of Psychology, Vol. 1*. Cambridge, MA: Harvard University Press.

Jay, Martin. 2005. *Songs of Experience: Modern American and European Variations on a Universal Theme*. Berkeley: University of California Press.

Levin, David Michael, ed. 1997. *Language Beyond Postmodernism: Saying and Thinking in Gendlin's Philosophy*. Evanston, IL: Northwestern University Press.

Nagel, Thomas. 1987. *The View from Nowhere*. Oxford: Oxford University Press.

Nagel, Thomas. 1997. *The Last Word*. Oxford: Oxford University Press.

Putnam, Hilary. 1990. *Realism with a Human Face*. Cambridge, MA: Harvard University Press.

Rawls, John. 1997. *A Theory of Justice*, rev. ed. Cambridge, MA: Harvard University Press.

Sandmeyer, Bob. 2009. *Husserl's Constitutive Phenomenology: Its Problem and Promise*. New York: Routledge.

Scharff, Robert C. 2019. *Heidegger Becoming Phenomenological: Interpreting Husserl Through Dilthey, 1916–1925*. New York: Rowman and Littlefield International.

Chapter 2

Where is emotion?
Gendlin's radical answer

Edward S. Casey

It is too readily assumed that emotion is located in the human subject: in their brain, mind, heart, or person. Such a view reflects the early modernist view that all thoughts, feelings, and memories are ensconced in the individual subject, as with the Cartesian schema whereby "animal spirits" connect mind and body – from within the subject. But what if certain aspects of human experience such as emotions cannot be so contained? What if emotions are located beyond the strict confines of human subjectivity? How can we disengage emotion – which is to say, liberate it from the confinement to which it has been subject since the early modern period? If so, where will this leave us?

In phenomenological fact, we experience non-privatized emotions quite frequently – as when we enter a room of people who are celebrating together. Right away we pick up the celebratory emotion. It pervades the space we have come into; we sense it as situated among the celebrants, *out there* – not in here, not in me exclusively. I not only take note of the shared emotion; I enter into it; I participate in it, and it enters into me.

Eugene Gendlin's model of environment #2 helps us to understand the phenomenon of emotional contagion – which is very difficult to explain on the modernist model of emotion as exclusively subjective. In this brief contribution, I shall explore how Gendlin's environmental model illuminates such contagion and points toward a radically novel sense of emotion.

I Environment and emotion

A first clue comes from the following statement of Gendlin's: "The environment is directly involved when we act. But the environment should not be considered *external*. It is not in the here-there space of perception."[1] Not content with the single term "environment," Gendlin distinguishes "environment #1," in which body and environment are separate entities, from "environment #2," in which the body *implies* the environment. The latter sense of environment is said to "occur-into" bodily processes.[2] Note that by "body" Gendlin refers to the entire sensing-feeling organism, rather

DOI: 10.4324/9781003296706-3

than to what Merleau-Ponty designates as the "objective body." We are here talking about what Merleau-Ponty would call the "lived body," and it is this body that is continuous with environment #2: at one with it. It follows that "bodily process is body-environment interaction" (p. 122): the interaction is the primary reality, not the distinction or the difference between body and world. It follows that "because an organism is environmental, therefore it happens directly into the environment" (p. 169). To *happen-into* is to ingress into the surrounding world, so intimately that I can no longer distinguish *it* from *me*. This world is continuous with my bodily being. It follows that "We *are* environmental interaction in the universe" (p. 176; my italics). It also follows that "people ... are not inside their skins, but *are* their living-in the world and their living-with others" (p. 214; my italics).

II Two axioms at stake in environment #2

Two basic phenomenological axioms can be derived from Gendlin's idea of environment # 2:

> Axiom # 1: "We *are* [our] interactions with the environment – other people, the world, the universe – and we can sense ourselves to be just such an interaction." (p. 304; his italics). If so, then certain emotional states bear out this situation more expressively and insistently than any other experiences. There is already a presentiment of this in Kant's discussion of the sublime as encompassing us; and there are still more cogent cases to be found in what Scheler calls the "affective transmission" that occurs in certain crowd phenomena such as those to which I have already alluded. There are others that can be labeled as the generic "sociality of affect" that permeates our lives far more extensively than we may realize – and certainly far more so than early modernist accounts of emotion allow, much less explain.
>
> Axiom #2: Still more radically, Gendlin is proposing that we *are* our environment and not only our interactions with it. This radical ontological thesis goes beyond any relational model, no matter how plausible such a model may seem to be. In this spirit, we shall have to go beyond the externalist models of emotion proposed by Kant and Scheler to a *fusionist* schema whereby emotions are what meld us to and in our surroundings – not just taking us there but proposing that we *are there* in unique ways. This signifies a radical *pervasion* of the life-world by emotion, not just coloring it but deeply qualifying it, indeed *being* it.

Such pervasion as this is unique; it does not, and cannot, occur by thinking or remembering or by any other discrete human activity. Most important, it could not happen at all unless there were continuity between our living bodies and the environments with which they are fused on the Gendlinian model. This fusion, first fully established phenomenologically by Gendlin, is essential to the claim that emotion is something we find ourselves *in* and *part of* – and that is itself equally in and part *of us*. Emotion is situated in two ways: at once in us and out of us. It is everywhere in the life-world we animate and inhabit.

III How this is possible

Here we must ask: what is it about emotion that enables such interfusion to happen? One thing is very clear: with emotion, we are on the far side of affect or feeling regarded as something merely private and subjective: something we sense and hold within us (and sometimes eject beyond us: as in emotional outbursts). Emotion is less an entity – something directly nameable and designatable as such – than it is an *event*. Indeed, it is an event that emerges when body and environment converge in certain ways.

Body plays a major role here, just as Gendlin emphasizes; it is not just the intermediary between emotion and environment but the very *agent of enactment for* their bonding. This is not merely a matter of my own personal body as modernism would insist. More importantly, it is a body that is at once the agent and the subject of environmental impingement: thus a *dimension* of my being-in-the-world that cannot be reduced to being an attribute of my own discrete body, much less of my mind or brain. For it is a feature of my body considered as continuous with the environing world: at one with it, thanks to the radical merging that occurs in environment #2.

IV A new location for emotion

What is admirable about Gendlin's position is that in order to evade modernism's privatistic view of emotion, he does not go to the opposite extreme of literally externalizing emotion – as do Kant (the sublime as inherent in a breathtaking scene before us) or Scheler (emotion as experienced in the affective transmission of crowds) or Heidegger (for whom *Befindlichkeit, state of mind,* takes us away from Dasein regarded as an isolated entity). Instead of externalizing emotion, Gendlin locates it in the intimate interface between my bodily self and an environment that is not merely impinging upon me but *convergent with my experiential self,* thus at one with it.

Gendlin thereby refuses to endorse either of two dichotomies that have been central in the modern Western understanding of emotion: inner/outer and self/other. Thanks to his model of radical environmental inherence, he avoids having to choose between either side of these binaries – two of the central binaries that, according to Derrida, have been altogether indispensable in Western philosophy from the beginning, stridently so in early modern thought.

Where is emotion? If it is not in the emotionally moved subject, it is also not in the surrounding world. It is neither internal nor external. It is immanent in our ongoing experience even if this experience is not merely *mine*. Nor is it *ours* (as with the crowd-induced emotions singled out by Scheler). It is *in-between*, in the very midst of whatever we are experiencing at any given moment. This is to relocate emotion radically – a move so bold that not even Gendlin himself specifically states it or endorses it. But it follows forthwith from his model of environment #2, whose fecundity here manifests itself in a way that is unique in Western philosophy.[3]

Notes

1 Eugene Gendlin, *Saying What We Mean: Implicit Precision and the Responsive Order: Selected Works*, ed. Edward S. Casey & Donata M. Schoeller (Evanston: Northwestern University Press, 2018), p. 119. His italics. Further reference in my text will be to page numbers in this book.
2 I here leave aside environment #3, which is defined as "the environment that has been arranged by the body body-en#2 process" (Gendlin, *A Process Model* [Evanston: Northwestern University Press, 2018], p. 5). This is an environment that is the result of the body/environment interaction itself: e.g., a bird's nest, a spider's web. Such an environment is more of a deposit than a process.
3 This essay draws from my view of emotion as explored in *Turning Emotion Inside Out: Affective Life Beyond the Subject* (Evanston: Northwestern University Press, 2022). My own conception of emotional life differs in the end from that of Gendlin insofar I argue for the location of emotion *beyond* the subject in certain crucial cases.

Chapter 3

Is responsibility implicit?

Eric R. Severson

To read Eugene Gendlin's philosophy is to find oneself immediately *working on* the problems that vex. Readers today who take up his work find themselves turned toward the problems of our time, oriented in a mode of understanding that is both active and activated. The problems that arise before us – sexism, racism, environmental disaster, or some other cause of contemporary suffering – are not autonomous facts that we discover as though we are independent and disengaged investigators. We discover our own entanglement along the way and how implicit thinking about such problems has already determined the way they are understood. This essay wonders about the emergence of a particular phenomenon in the analysis of the encounter with suffering: responsibility.

Gendlin participates in a hermeneutic philosophical tradition. Among other contributions, he directs precise and expansive attention to the incredibly complex milieu in which thinking, speaking, and acting take place. This tradition, when it is at its best, operates with profound humility and openness to novelty and surprise. Using a tangible example from my spouse's work in obstetric care and my own work with the ethical philosophy of Emmanuel Levinas, this essay plays at the boundary between phenomenology and ethics. In so doing, I move toward a central question about the work of Gendlin: does phenomenology deal only in understanding? Does the pursuit of more precise, embodied, activated understanding, perhaps, reveal something already at work before thinking has begun? I will make my case for a responsibility-laden approach to phenomenology in three parts, through analyses of causation, language, and touch. Ultimately, I argue in all three cases for a Gendlin-inspired *implication* in the implicit, obligation in the oppressive order, and responsibility in the "responsive order."

Causation and carrying-forward

In recognition of a diverse audience for this volume, I have decided to fasten my deliberations to a practical example. At the same time, I have attempted to shift quotations and technical terminology into my footnotes and avoid

DOI: 10.4324/9781003296706-4

falling into common philosophical jargon in my prose. In what follows, I explore the implications of Gendlin's responsive order in light of the urgent problem of maternal mortality and obstetric safety. I highlight this situation to underscore that what we learn in an analysis of what Gendlin calls the "responsive order" arrives as both information and obligation; the latter, I believe, is more primary than the former.

In a labor and delivery room, as nurses and doctors and midwives and anesthesiologists gather around the body of a person giving birth, the importance of precision is abundant. The instruments and tools of assessment are fine-tuned. The practitioners are trained, experienced, and nuanced in their understandings of the human body and the nearly infinite things that can go right or wrong in the harrowing moments of delivering a new human from the body of the birth giver. Labs are carefully analyzed, blood pressure monitored, and heartrates tracked of both the patient and the fetus. Nurses watch for slight changes in color, breathing, posture, and positioning – any of which could indicate transition into dangerous territory for either the one giving or receiving birth. And yet, despite spending more money on the science of these harrowing moments than any country in history, and despite the earnest attention to precise science and medicine, people in the United States are dying of childbearing-related causes at an increasing and alarming rate. While maternal mortality rates drop precipitously around the world, thanks to global medical and cultural advances, the reverse is true in the U.S. America is the only industrialized country in which maternal mortality is on the rise (Martin & Montagne, 2017).

This is only one piece of an incredibly complex problem. Though high rates of maternal mortality put *all* pregnant people at increased risk in the United States, racial inequality makes the problem heartbreakingly worse. Black and Indigenous women in the United States have rates of maternal mortality a staggering three to five times higher than white women.[1] My spouse – her name is Misha – *is* a labor nurse, and I watch as she carries the burden of this dire situation with her everywhere. Something is happening in the labor and delivery room which world-class ultrasound machines and world-renowned surgeons cannot seem to stop or even slow down. I was reading Gendlin's *Process Model*, sitting next to Misha as she worked through the latest literature in obstetrical safety, and I was struck by the importance of this alignment.

The medical system in the United States is largely built on the interpretation of causation that Gendlin attacks relentlessly in his work. He claims that in the West (in particular), we are trained to "attribute causality to separate individuals" and work tirelessly to find individual explanations for any given event that takes place (Gendlin, 2018/1981, p. 31). When something goes wrong in a medical procedure, it is imperative to find the causal source. Who drew the wrong medicine? Who missed a key indicator? Who failed to intervene when it was needed? This pressure to establish singular causal origins is driven by a range of factors, from deep philosophical resonances that we can trace back from Aristotle to the modern need for litigation. Obstetrics represent one of the most litigated arenas in American medicine; when a pregnant person dies there is a mad scramble to find the singular cause, the person who committed malpractice, the individual at fault. Gendlin encourages a phenomenological model that assumes "original interaffecting" (Gendlin, 2018/1981, p. 31). The urgency to assign blame paves over the implicit, obscuring the delicate ways that events come to pass. This is particularly true in the effort to attribute a singular cause to a complex phenomenon. He teaches a process he calls "focusing," which attends to the often-ignored, precise, and implicit processes at work in any event.

For Gendlin, the individualistic thinking that dominates Western society inclines us to see events not just simplistically but incorrectly. For him, the complexity of causation is better framed as a nuanced philosophy of time he sometimes calls *carrying-forward*. My appreciation for Gendlin's work grows every time I apply such thinking to the confounding problems of our day, from medicine to politics to economics to systemic racism. We are not billiard balls exchanging energy in collisions that could be scripted by causal laws – this was, in fact, what Pierre-Simon Laplace thought, and Gendlin enjoys pointing out how wrong he was (Gendlin, 2018/1981). For Laplace, a clever demon who knew the precise arrangement of the world a century before I was born would be able to perfectly predict every event, thought, and emotion of my life (Hoefer, 2016). Some events unfold precisely in this manner: radioactive carbon decays at a predictable rate; each spring the earth reaches a vernal equinox at precisely a moment that could have been predicted by astronomers thousands of years ago. This predictive power is compelling and useful; it forms the backbone of modern science.

Gendlin insists, obstinately, that this way of thinking about causes and effects is both harmful and incorrect when it comes to the ways human beings find themselves in the world. Gendlin's nuanced understanding may not be relevant for understanding how *some* events take place. We don't need much careful analysis to determine whether it was the bat that caused the baseball to move, the flame that caused the food to burn. But, the ease with which physics and individuated causation can explain *some* events creates a kind of intoxication; under the influence of causal determinism, modern thinkers in all disciplines have found themselves desperate to explain all events similarly. Drawing deeply on his work with the ideas of Heidegger, Gendlin resists the cultural addiction to the intoxicant of simplistic causation. A similar critique arises from another close reader of Heidegger, Hans-Georg Gadamer. For Gadamer, the tendency of the modern world to be enthralled with science borders on *scientism* and undermines our ability to understand any phenomenon well. Gendlin and Gadamer both expect implicit complexity in events and urge us to join them at the murky edge of understanding where phenomena actually come together; one will rarely understand everything that happens in the carrying-forward at work in an event, but this does not release us from the responsibility to try.

My first point is to demonstrate that the medical community – and I think the psychological one as well – has largely misunderstood causation, and that this philosophical error is neither trivial nor merely academic; it is deadly. Since the same impoverished philosophy of causation informs modern politics, economics, and technology, we should expect them to produce and exacerbate this same alienation. Our tools and habits are patterned after the one-directional logic of causation; this configuration of how things come to pass in the world keeps putting people in danger.

I will not take time, in this chapter, to fully explain Heidegger's work on causation, which is summarized in his essay concerning technology (Heidegger, 2018/1954). However, it is helpful to remember that Heidegger detects an impoverishment of causation in modern times and gestures back to the complexity of causation in the work of Aristotle. The truth about how something comes to pass, about what is happening in any given event, is not for Heidegger a journey toward singularity but toward nuance and multiplicity. Modern thinking, and modern technology in particular, forgets the way the grain of a wood or texture of flour participates causally in the making of the bowl and the bread. One understands both bowl and bread poorly by focusing on the carpenter and baker as the singular causal origin for that which they make. For our purposes here, it is helpful to see Gendlin as a particular kind of Heideggerian. Gendlin sees that our bodies relate to our minds in remarkably complex ways, and that simplistic causation actually guides us into erroneous and unhealthy ways of inhabiting the lived situation in which we find ourselves thrown.

Medicine provides a perfect example of the tension between these two competing phenomenologies of an event. When a labor and delivery process leads to an emergency surgery, or to the death of the patient or the infant, a singular cause sometimes appears to present itself. In hindsight, some previously undetected comorbidity is often identified, and health care providers can point their finger at this as the "cause" of death. In extraordinarily rare cases when a particular physician or nurse can be tied by individuated causation to a death, these persons can be disciplined and their employment terminated. But, far more often, the tragedy is blamed on hypertension, a rare or unpredictable complication, lack of prenatal care, or the choices made by the birth-giving person. But the statistics undermine this simplistic hermeneutic approach. Women are dying in the United States that are saved elsewhere. The causes ascribed to their deaths are being circumvented by people who are doing the same work, elsewhere, in different ways. Remember, *all* women in the United States are at higher risk than their counterparts with similar medical resources elsewhere in the world.[2] Even when we control for variables such as poverty and prenatal care, Black and Indigenous women die at a rate comparable to regions of our world *without modern hospitals*.[3] To assess the phenomenon of maternal mortality through the lens of individualistic, separated causation is not working. In fact, this method is leading us to spend time, energy, and resources on interventions that are not improving the situation for women, especially birth givers of Color. I believe Gendlin can help.

Before continuing to use this particular example alongside Gendlin's work, I want to point out that this is not *really* a lesson for people working in maternal health. The example I am working on here has to do with complex systems; I wish to point to a Gendlin-inspired modality of phenomenological analysis that allows us all to attend to the implicit as it manifests in our bodies, our work, our families, our relation to the planet, and to the complex relational systems that human beings inhabit. Ultimately, I am building toward the claim that the implicit carries more than just accurate information about how events unfold. My hunch is that when it comes to intersubjective encounters the implicit *implicates*, that it not only teaches but *obligates* the one who learns from it.

The body itself is a complex organism, not best understood as a machine. The concept of a machine, of modern technology and computing, is built on the simplistic philosophy of causation that Heidegger critiqued. Bodily systems, including the brain, relate to one another in complex, implicit, and murky ways. STEM fields, in general, aspire to the simplicity of mathematical certainty. Psychologists, not just obstetricians, feel the pressure to exert the same epistemic approach to their fields. Simple causes mean simple fixes.[4] I detect a massive slippage between this reductive, simplistic approach to understanding and the lived world of our communal bodies. We are slapping bandages on systemic problems in medicine, psychology, politics, education, policing, and then repeatedly reaping the whirlwind as these models of assessment lead us back to death, misunderstanding, inequality, and racism. If responsibility is all about finding the singular cause of an event, and not an invitation into the murky complexity of suffering, then we'll never turn the corner on racism, sexism, homophobia, transphobia, and the range of problems – like maternal mortality – that spring from the deeper soil of the implicit. Racism and sexism cannot be starved at the register of the explicit. There is nothing linear about these complex problems, and yet we attempt to fix them with the logic of the economy – with the logic and language of the systems that are already distorted and flawed. Similarly, we will not see progress in reversing the abysmal problems with maternal mortality in the United States by tinkering with the singular "cause" that seems to appear in the explicit. We are surely wise enough, as a species, to understand that simple causation is inadequate for confronting complex and systemic problems. It is one of the unique and lasting contributions of

Gendlin that he saw this problem at this very scope. He developed a way of knowing, feeling, assessing, thinking, caring, attending, and *focusing* that coaches us into a modest uncertainty for the sake of nuanced and humble understanding.

Language fails twice

There is no simple solution to maternal mortality, or racism in health care, or racism *anywhere,* because these are powerfully framed by a broken model of causation. We know that in maternal care the mentality, control, understanding, volition, and overall psychological state of a pregnant person plays a significant role in outcomes. So, eliminating misunderstanding is a crucial component of improving safety. In this second section of my chapter, I focus on the different ways that communication fails, that *words* fail. I want to show that words fail in many ways. We are accustomed to seeing the ways that breakdowns in synchronic communication lead to problems, to suffering, but I think sometimes the failure of words turns in another direction. Drawing from the philosophy of language we find in Gadamer, and also Emmanuel Levinas, I want to establish the possibility that the failure of words can also open to something far more important than synchronized understanding.

Since poor communication correlates with high rates of unnecessary surgery and other bad outcomes, there are movements in the fields of obstetrics to improve communication and understanding (Weiseth et al., 2022). One initiative involves a whiteboard in each labor room, on which names, medicines, diagnoses, plans, etc. are outlined and referenced by all caregivers. Patients are often given a watered-down, redacted version of their own health assessments. Physicians often confer about their bodies outside of the rooms. This can be intensely alienating, objectifying, and humiliating. So instead of whispering in the hallway about a patient's situation, the conversation happens at the bedside, with efforts to include the patient in the deliberations (Spigel et al., 2022). Some physicians are annoyed at the extra work this creates, being asked to translate their jargon into terms and explanations that lead toward understanding. Others see the deep value in these practices, and the increased psychological and physical safety this provides for everyone involved. These tools are bound to make a difference and prevent the breakdowns in communication that lead to anxiety and fear. Gadamer argues, powerfully, that language is the medium of hermeneutic experience.[5] Nowhere is the art of understanding more exigent than in a conversation about bodies that hovers on the cusp of a mortal danger *produced* by misunderstanding.

Another point needs to be made here about the forces at work when words fall apart in the context of both medical and psychological care. Language is not issued in a vacuum. Physicians who refuse to use the whiteboard tool for better labor room education are themselves under tremendous pressure, swamped by debt to medical schools that train and prepare them to be providers who generate profit. The insurance system squeezes their care into impossible boxes; at some hospitals, the standard obstetric appointment is a mere *ten* minutes. Additional barriers of racism, sexism, ableism, and poverty ensure that the encounter with a provider is a constant crucible in which language is set up to fail in the most dangerous of ways.

Anxiety, of course, is not merely a mental phenomenon but an experience of the whole body, and for a pregnant person anxiety impacts at least *two bodies*. Language inhabits this murky, embodied, and social space between us all. And, when caregivers fail to attend to these dynamics of language, parents often find themselves distanced from their own care, from their own bodies. They become alienated by work being done increasingly *on* them, rather than *with* them. When patients attempt to advocate for themselves, their questions and concerns are often met with dismissive indifference. Some physicians take over as *efficient* cause of the delivery; the body of the birth giver (as formal and material cause) fades into the background. In plain terms, patients become objects of medical intervention, surgical or otherwise. They are alienated from the very labor of their bodies, from the events that transpire; the people around them reinforce and exacerbate that alienation. This alienation is at least partly the product of the failure of language.

I have painted this picture with broad strokes to demonstrate how language contributes to this escalating crisis of maternal mortality. The simple failure to tend to the patient's understanding, the psychosomatic event of thinking, nullifies the extraordinary tools and expertise that should be keeping pregnant Americans safe. Perhaps it is obvious, then, why Black and Indigenous birth givers are at an even higher risk of bad outcomes. We live in a society in which the delicate work of language has been infested with systemic racism, assumptions about people and words and bodies that repeatedly tilt away from women and persons of Color.

The problems that lead to danger in our treatment of people – in medicine, psychology, society, and politics – are far too complex to be understood by either a mathematical approach to language or a simplistic understanding of cause and effect. We must talk, then, about how words and gestures and symbols fail and lead to the alienation from our bodies and relationships. However, I think that the fact that words fail to achieve perfect synchrony of understanding is not always a bad thing. Gendlin is here to help with that too. He points out, in his essay "Words Can Say How They Work," that words are not principally correlational (Gendlin, 1993). They work toward correlation, toward understanding, but the implicity of language reveals a deeper work afoot when we use words. Gendlin invites an attentive look at how language *entrains* one person with another. He would surely appreciate recent studies that suggest that more than 90% of communication happens at a nonverbal level (Pease & Pease, 2004).

If I am charged with keeping pregnant persons safe, I must embrace responsibility for the world which presses them toward death. Implied in the situatedness of that hospital bed is a range of possible implicit comorbidities: patients may have been silenced and ignored, before and during labor and delivery. They may have been forced to speak in alienating, sexualized, or objectivized terms about their bodies and reproduction. They may have been conditioned to believe and behave as if their fate is sealed by men, or by systems, or by economic and political powers. Somehow all of this is pressed into the electrically charged atmosphere in which birth givers are asked, "How are you feeling?" That question falls on ears, on bodies, laden with more than can fall to understanding. Here, we find that responsibility is not about culpability, not merely about fault or blame. Drawing on the philosophy of Emmanuel Levinas, I use the word responsibility to refer to a condition of the human person prior to these.

The failure of words to *precisely* convey much of anything is a failure that can lead us to the meaning of language and to a far richer understanding about our shared, embodied, and linguistic existence than mathematical certainty ever could.[6] This is not to imply that synchronic understanding is unimportant; the clear conveyance of meaning is immensely important. By the word "synchrony," I mean the convergence of understanding, the convergence of ideas. We synchronize our understanding when you understand aspects of the words that I use, when I ask for an apple and you hand me the correct fruit. If you ask for a hammer and get a hamster, good soup and get good soap, the failure of language is potentially catastrophic (hopefully it is just amusing!). It is important that words (or signs of some sort) provide us with one and not the other. Still, the fact that "soap" and "soup" are differentiated with clarity in those English words does *not* mean that in this example we have found the paradigm for language. This is another way to state the problem I've been working on – as framed by Gendlin. Language-as-synchrony is not to be abandoned, but when it comes to speaking, it happens alongside a more primordial event already underway.

A word is best understood as an entrée, a summons, or an invitation, to the responsive order. As Gadamer writes, "every word, as the event of a moment, carries with it the unsaid to which it is related by responding and summoning" (Gadamer, 1960/1989, p. 458). Gadamer points out that within a word, therefore, multiple layers are offered, and some of the more important ones lay far below the meaning presented on the surface. Because words inhabit the space of responsiveness and summoning, their meanings cannot and should not be fixed; Gadamer contends that within a word there is an "infinity of meaning to be explicated and laid out" (Gadamer, 1960/1989, p. 458). Language is best understood as that which, under close analysis, can fail upward, toward a truth that hides in the explicit. The truth is not the exposure of some kernel hidden beneath many layers of partial meaning; the implicit is often that which evades the machinery of understanding and knowledge. The slippage in meaning, between what is spoken and what is understood, is an invitation to relation, to responsibility that was there before the words were spoken, let alone fell apart.

For this reason, in obstetrics, it is apparent that merely having hypertension explained to a patient – in non-technical language or in their native tongue if English is not familiar – does not necessarily mitigate the elevation of danger in labor and delivery. Arriving at understanding, converging on a common idea – hammer, soup, and high blood pressure – is the *context* (or, perhaps, *pretext*) for language, but not its main event. Birth-giving people are safer, in labor and delivery, when they are genuinely heard, when they feel like their bodies and pain matter to the people giving them care (Phipps et al., 2012). Having a handy glossary for doctor-speak does not deliver this outcome. Part of what has been eliminated in hospital rooms, and perhaps on psychotherapy couches too, is the possibility of surprise. In his work on language, James Risser (2019) points to a search for meaning that opens toward surprise, toward the unpredictable and unscripted arrival of meaning in the midst of "dynamics of language that cannot be reduced to logical calculations." The safe and successful delivery of a baby relies on *communication*, words, language, and the embodied event of speaking that happens surrounding a birth-giving person (ACOG, 2011). This is not the only requirement, of course, but it is a demonstrable difference between the act of birth giving in places where pregnant persons have similar health-care tools to the United States and yet die so much less often. Patients, and psychotherapy clients, can often tell when the possibility of *surprise* has been siphoned away from the linguistic encounter. We are deeply accustomed to performing language at this register, at the gas station, the grocery store, the dentist, and the bank. Perhaps neither birth giver nor medical provider notices that this transactional, impoverished dialect is being invoked at this bedside. If the other person cannot surprise me, perhaps I cannot hear the other at all.

In this second portion of my chapter, I am arguing that the failure of words is dangerous, inevitable, and potentially salvific. Language can fail *toward* the other person in their suffering, or *away* from them. Language can fail toward indifference or toward care, toward danger or toward life. This pivot is not arbitrary; we who hear words, particularly words of suffering, are not first of all given a meaning-puzzle to solve. We are handed words of suffering, and even in their breakdown we find that responsibility for this suffering remains as a primordial condition, the implicit "saying" reverberating in the words of the "said" (Levinas, 1974/1998). To turn away from the invitation to take responsibility for the failure of language is to turn away from the other person in indifference, and in so doing to threaten the humanity of everyone involved. Gendlin's points about language and causation, about the implicit, can provide a gentle guide to a richer understanding of our bodies, our words, and our world. But I hear in Gendlin a sterner message. The consequences of failing to attend to the implicit are not just misunderstanding, roads not taken, surprising futures foregone. A failure to attend to the unconcealing of the implicit is the unnamed *cause of death* for many human beings. The summons to attend to the implicit, to what is carried in the face and voice and words and suffering of the other person, is an ethical charge.

This transformation in thinking offered by Gendlin, and then by Levinas, is not some cataclysmic change in medical practices or psychological systems – though sometimes I think those might be called for. Rather, I am suggesting a mode of training and thinking about language in all fields that embraces responsibility for the implicit, to what Levinas called the *saying* that reverberates and inhabits the *said*. The primary work of language happens not in synchronous understanding, but in the shared, embodied, linguistic, and implicit world. Every word is an invitation to responsibility for this world that imperils the other person. The words of the other summon me to seek some humble semblance of understanding, but more importantly, they invite me to surprise, to the irruption of new possibilities. Language invites me to embrace responsibility not just for the pieces of that world I understand, but for the murky origins of that suffering. *For the racialized other, racism is a comorbidity.* For almost every woman, sexism is a comorbidity. For the disabled person, ableism is a comorbidity. One does not have to comprehend how these forces threaten the vulnerable other or have these realities established by empirical proof; they arrive not as facts about the other, but as possible dangers to which the caregiver must attune. To see them at work is to, as Gendlin put it, *thicken* one's felt understanding of the phenomenal world (Gendlin, 1996, p. 65).

Only in the posture of radical responsibility for the murky implicit is there hope to stand in the way of the racism and sexism that repeatedly claim the lives of birth-giving people in the United States. This doesn't mean that a bunch of doctors and nurses need to read Gendlin, or Heidegger, or Levinas. I have read Heidegger with enough students to know that this might not lead to the results I am seeking. Rather, what I am arguing is for a responsibility that transcends understanding, that is not contingent upon understanding, and that is *prior* to the project of interpretation.

Implication and touch

I tend to think that a great deal of the problems with maternal safety in the United States has to do with what happens to women everywhere in my country. They face implicit, embedded, complex discrimination at the grocery store too, or the dentist, but mostly it leads not to death. There are ample studies that show that the problem of sexism in reproductive medicine is similar to gender inequality throughout the American health-care system (Villines, 2021). This sometimes-implicit problem becomes explicit in maternity rooms because in this case the consequence of failing to attend to the implicit is often *deadly*. Confused, concerned practitioners wonder why women are faring so poorly in *this* situation, as though the implicit configuration of gender relations is worse in hospitals than it is everywhere else. In labor and delivery, people who give birth walk precariously close to a cliff. Here, the winds of patriarchy and misogyny can do their deadly work with the soft force of a breeze. "I don't know what went wrong!" we hear, over and over again. In this third section of my paper, I want to talk about the role of touch, of skin, and argue that the responsive order of the tactile world includes a responsibility that precedes understanding.

I have been attempting to avoid philosophical jargon, at least the kind that might distract from what I believe to be an incredible practical connection between philosophy and the way people experience the world across all disciplines. I have the honor of teaching nursing students – we have a lot of them at Seattle University – and as sophisticated and complex as Gendlin, Gadamer, Levinas, etc., may be, this message is not elitist, and abides in all human experience. My goal when I teach philosophy to undergraduate students, nurses-in-training included, is to open this mode of thinking and living and being to all work and walks of life. Since I've taken up an example from nursing, I'll continue it, but this isn't really about the medical field in any exclusive way. Walking into a patient's room, nursing students receive responsibility for the implicit. The choice to embrace this responsibility is life-or-death; it is not trivial; it is not a matter of moving from *good* to *better* practices. In the implicit – the history of a patient – resides a summons to respond, a responsibility for the other, carried forward in the modes of listening, in the tenderness of care, in noticing details, in detecting the presence of the unsaid in every saying.

The purpose of such vigilance is not first of all better *understanding*. In fact, Gadamer points out that whether it is a text, or history, comprehension "does not consist in a technical virtuosity of 'understanding' everything that is written" (Gadamer, 1960/1989, p. 483). Genuine experience of the world is, for Gadamer, "an encounter with something that asserts itself as truth" (Gadamer, 1960/1989, p. 483). The phenomenon asserts itself with both the truth and the means for its reception. Walking into a hospital room, a nurse may find complex medical terms on the whiteboard, a "birth plan" written and re-written for nine months already in the trash bin, and a chaos of words arising from the patient, family, or support persons. The nurse encounters a deluge of information, history, and emotion. Amid this chaos, the work of hermeneutics is predicated upon an urgency; to fail hermeneutically, here, is to fail ethically. In my role as a philosopher who teaches dozens of nursing students each year, I seek to prepare them for the project of interpretation. Gendlin sometimes compares attentiveness to *touching* the world with our awareness. He spends less time talking about the event of contact between bodies. My own analysis of touch is meant not to apply specifically to the physical touch of another person, but more generally to the encounter with the other that *asserts itself* to my senses.

Misha told me the story of an incredibly delicate and precarious moment that I believe provides some insight into the implication – as in obligation – of the implicit when it comes to the tactile, sensory encounter with the other person. Heidegger wrote, "That which is to become a phenomenon, can be hidden. And just, therefore, because the phenomena are immediately and mostly *not* given, phenomenology is needed."[7] As with each of my three meditations in this chapter, I offer them as an example of the responsibility that I detect in the implicit; my point is not to turn those who read my words into labor and delivery nurses. Rather, my hope is that we might better see, in all our labors, a liberating and enabling responsibility that arises as pri-mordial in what Gendlin calls the "responsive order."

During a cervical check, a nurse, midwife, or physician can often feel the head, or other body parts of the baby, through the window of the cer-vix. A rare but dangerous problem in labor involves the compression of the umbilical cord between the head of the baby and the narrow opening of the cervix. This occurs just once in 500 pregnancies; many other dangers are far more frequent (Lore, 2017). The medical term is "umbilical cord pro-lapse," and though it is uncommon it is a potentially fatal development in the labor. As the birth-giver pushes toward delivery, the cord is pinched shut and no resources can reach the baby. When it becomes apparent that this is happening, an emergency caesarean section is indicated. Whether or not the situation is fatal, or results in a healthy delivery, depends on a range of other factors. The most decisive difference involves detection, and therefore the vigilance of health-care providers. When the problem manifests on the scientific instruments, such as the fetal heartrate monitors, it can sometimes be too late.[8]

The tactile difference between the tissue of a baby and the tissue of the umbilical cord is incredibly subtle. So, most of the time when the fingers of the doctor or the nurse make contact with the cord it is likely to go unde-tected. Oftentimes, when assessing the body of the laboring person, *two sci-entists* do not agree on what is taking place. The medical professionals have different things going on with their bodies, their minds, differing pressures on their felt sense of the moment when they make contact with the fetus – or was that the cord? A prolapsed umbilical cord is rare, so the assumption is generally that it is the baby and not the cord. No doctor, nurse, or midwife, can make the detection of the prolapsed cord their primary intention. This is just one of many hundreds of possible problems to which caregivers must attend while assisting or assessing a laboring person.

Yet to miss the precise differences is to fail the other, to miss a chance to intervene and prevent a dangerous development. Twice in her two-decade career as a labor nurse, Misha has felt the pulsing of an umbilical cord during cervical checks. She says the key to detecting this subtle event is hard to describe, but it involves a momentary pause during which the subtle and tactile differences take shape in her mind. This is an awkward moment to pause, and what is detected is often not measurable or even describable. Misha allows the difference between the two phenomena to reveal itself; *the truth asserts itself, but with the quiet force of a fluttering pulse.* The provider who catches this problem before it shows up in a precipitous drop in fetal heartrate dramatically improves the chances of a safe delivery. Still, Misha finds this skill incredibly difficult to teach. Gendlin calls this calming down – which doesn't actually take more time but is a matter of focusing – a "thickening" understanding of an event (Gendlin, 1996, p. 65).

A simplistic understanding of causation and language, as I dealt with in my first two sections, led to a *thinning* of experience, a paring away of what might seem like peripheral components of a phenomenon. Thickening takes *practice*; it must be learned in less complicated situations in order for it to carry into situations as nuanced as this. This is a delicate capacity of touch, the training of an index finger to detect the difference between a baby's head and a prolapsed cord. Such focusing takes practice, takes time, and takes an ongoing attentiveness to a responsibility for the almost-born person. To an outside observer, this detection seems like some kind of magic, a sorcery not available to normal mortals. Because this is a thickening experience, attending to the possibility of a prolapsed cord does not take away from the vigilant openness to the appearance of more common risks. The danger is unmistakable after the cord becomes trapped, creating rapid heartrate decelerations and making an immediate caesarean surgery necessary. To catch a cord prolapse *before* it becomes detectable by monitoring is rare, and greatly increases the chance of a safe outcome. It is only possible when nurses and physicians practice a focusing and mindfulness that the entire system of American health care makes incredibly difficult.

The laboring body, as a site for phenomenology, is no science experiment, even as science is heavily involved. The encounter between the practitioner and the body of the other is *charged* with ethical significance. You can *get away* with missing subtlety; the lawyers and insurance companies will never know about what happens between the labor nurse and the implicit responsibility that reverberates in the responsive order. The difference between these two interpretations is not given, not offered in force, and not apparent at a glance. Misha tells me that the only way she catches this potential emergency is by breathing, calming, and feeling what does not immediately present itself as explicit. What she detects, in the delicacy of touch, is a heartbeat, an attestation of truth, a message from another person mediated by the tube of life which is not quite mother nor baby. The tactile difference between a heartbeat felt in the cord and the body of a baby is perceptible, but only to the hand that touches and feels with patience, with vigilance for the appearance of what is not apparent. The moment is carried by responsibility, for the other, for this other whose face has yet to appear to the world of light.

Before this sounds like some kind of Gendlin-esque lesson for obstetrical professionals, I return to the larger lesson from Gendlin (and Gadamer) concerning the humble posture of the phenomenologist. To best attend to the phenomenon of a prolapsed umbilical cord, one must be open to the surprise of the most delicate sort. Gendlin advocates thickening in the awareness of one's own body, and a vigilance for the nearly indetectable in the hiddenness of any event. Following Levinas, I am adding to this a strident exigency: the presence of the precarious body of the other in the responsive order undermines any indifference that I might have to the interpretive process. Whether I'm trying to understand racism, sexism, homophobia, ableism, transphobia, economic inequality, or some other form of oppression today, these phenomena deliver *responsibility for the precarious other* along with the datum that confirms their existence. The responsibility for the other – pregnant or not! – is not a curse, or a burden, but a gift. It opens me to the thickening of my own feeling, toward increasingly genuine engagement of the other that is constitutive of human personhood. To attend to the other is to use my skin – itself given the capacity to feel by and through a maternal other – to receive a message that hides in the concreteness of any word, any touch, even the umbilical cord. This phenomenon is fleeting and yet, in its subtle appearance, there is an opening toward life which must not be missed. With the fluttering pulse of an umbilical cord, there is the appearance of two phenomena. To the phenomenological nurse practicing calmness, thickening, and vigilance, there is data that could lead to life and safety. But with that phenomenon, this introduction of subtle/precise/implicit data, one discovers an event prior to the learning, more primary than the reception. This anarchic happening upon which rest hermeneutics, interpretation, phenomenology, and science, is the precondition of responsibility.

Conclusion

In conclusion, I want to gesture toward a few thoughts on this extension of Gendlin's work – and the work of Levinas – as it relates to psychotherapy. For starters, I'm advocating that psychologists practice the hermeneutical vigilance that operates with the incredible humility I find in Gendlin, Gadamer, and Levinas. *Saying What We Mean*, the very last writing we have from Gendlin, is a master class in humility. No theory is adequate; no method is to be trusted without reservation. However you are shaped as a psychologist, Gendlin advocates that you hold loosely to your tools. He demonstrates this by holding loosely to his own tools, his own vernacular, and his own model. I have gone beyond Gendlin, in some regards, particularly inasmuch as I have pointed to *responsibility* in the responsive order. My effort, however, is to honor his work by loosening some of the knots that might keep it from carrying-forward.

If I am right, then what happens in the psychotherapeutic encounter is a hermeneutical event established in the before-time of the encounter. The responsibility for the client, in therapy, arises as a condition for the encounter. The invitation to understand, given in infinitely unique ways by the client, arrives not as puzzles for understanding – not principally, not initially – but as mysteries resting on a prior responsibility for the vulnerable other.[9] The one who sits before the therapist arrives already laden with the layers of history and culture and wounds and language and emotion carried in some explicit manifestation of causation, in the apparent meaning in words, in that which is explicit to the tactile and sensible encounter. To the external observer, the therapist who is "ethical" is only responsible to do good interpretation with what is *given*, with what is presented as explicit. "You're not giving me anything to work with!" I once heard an exasperated therapist declare. After reading Gendlin, I profoundly disagree. The implicit *is* given. Heidegger was right, though; even the most important of phenomena tend to hide.[10] The excavation of perception, so important to Gendlin, leads not toward some archaeological eureka of understanding, but toward better modes of ambiguity, listening, waiting, attending.

For psychologists, this is also a pursuit of understanding that might be strange and foreign to the client. After all, people subjected for a lifetime to racism and sexism often do not *understand* the way these forces are at work. The psychotherapist inhabits this unknowing, never possessing knowledge but facilitating the encounter been the client and their estrangement. In medicine, there are always possible, undetected comorbidities. In therapy, as in hospitals, racism is a comorbidity of the encounter, a complex component of the implicit in the room. For this comorbidity, whether or not it is explicit, I am responsible, and no less so because I do not understand or detect its work. Sexism is a comorbidity, as is trauma and depression and abuse. These are not just data, offered to me as implicit beneath that which arrives explicitly in the other person. For the comorbidities of the other I am *responsible*. To care for a pregnant person is to find oneself situated as a buffer, a wind-brace, taking responsibility for the implicit that threatens to nudge her further into danger at every precarious moment. Likewise, to care for a client in therapy is to listen for the pulsation of danger even – perhaps especially – when the client does not know it is happening. The shape of this danger for any given client is never really understood, and is different, surprising, and new, for every person. Nevertheless, if we would help, we must listen and wait and embrace the responsibility that we find implicit in the psychotherapeutic encounter.

As a philosopher, these are the ways the ideas of Gendlin, Gadamer, and Levinas leave me thinking about psychotherapy. Use your tools, be they models of Gendlin, Freud, Jung, Lacan, Rogers, Erikson, Frankl, or any other tool-maker, but use them gently and humbly. I find great wisdom in all these voices, and many others. More important than these tools, however, is the injunction to hold them loosely. Slow down, to whatever degree you can, and tenderly wait for the pulsation of the other to take the lead. This is not a suspension of science, but a manner of becoming a better phenomenologist, a person whose hands are shaped and prepared for the suffering of the other.

It is in the midst of this responsive order that something pierces the game of understanding, the pursuit of meaning, the gathering of fragments, and the tracing of linguistic expression. To say that the project of hermeneutics is *pierced* is not to indicate its failure but its escalation. Standing on Gendlin's shoulders, I am attempting a phenomenological method adequate for maternal mortality, cultural sexism, sublimated trauma, systemic racism, invasive colonialism, entrenched economic inequality, and much more. I think any such method rests first on a responsibility prior to understanding.

Notes

1 For every 100,000 American pregnant persons, seventeen will die of pregnancy-related causes this year. However, that statistic spikes to forty-three women if we only consider pregnant Black persons (Petersen et al., 2019).
2 "An indicator of a society's health, the maternal mortality ratio (MMR; maternal deaths per 100,000 live births) decreased globally by about 38% between 2000 and 2017, yet, it continues to climb in the United States. Ranked worst in the developed world, the United States reports almost 700 pregnancy-related deaths annually" (Heck et al., 2021).
3 The MMR rate among Black birth-givers in the United States is an abysmal 40.8 (Petersen et al., 2019).
4 The DSM is a noble attempt to create a medical-style compendium of possible psychological categories, effects, and strict (Eurocentric) symptom pools that can guide targeted treatment protocols.
5 Gadamer titles a whole section of *Truth and Method*: "language is the medium of hermeneutic experience" (Gadamer, 1960/1989, pp. 384–404).
6 The meaning of our feelings in any situation "is never quite equal to any cognitive units. There is always more to go" (Gendlin 1978/1979, p. 52). We are left perpetually approximating our language to an implicit experience that is never fully pinned down or anticipated. This process he calls "content mutation" is a hallmark of successful psychotherapy and, I would argue, clinical communication as well.
7 Gendlin opens the first essay of *Saying What We Mean* with this quotation (Heidegger, 1927/1962, p. 60).
8 Worldwide, about 9.1% of babies with a prolapsed cord do not survive delivery (Murphy & MacKenzie, 1995).

9   "... in a past more profound than all that I can reassemble by memory, by historiography, all that I can dominate by the a priori – in a time before the beginning" (Levinas, 1974/1998, p. 88).
10 Philosopher Maurice Merleau-Ponty (2012/1945, p. 5) suggested that we think of this search for understanding through perception as "a process similar to that of an archaeologist. For the structure of the perceived world is buried under the sedimentations of later knowledge."

References

American College of Obstetricians and Gynecologists (ACOG). (2011) *Quality patient care in labor and delivery: A call to action.* https://www.acog.org/practice-management/patient-safety-and-quality/clinical-information/quality-patient-care-in-labor-and-delivery-a-call-to-action

Gadamer, H. (1989) *Truth and method* (J. Weinsheimer & D. G. Marshall, Trans.). Continuum. (Original work published 1960).

Gendlin, E. T. (1978/1979) *Befindlichkeit*: Heidegger and the philosophy of psychology. *Review of Existential Psychology and Psychiatry 16*(1–3), 43–71.

Gendlin, E.T. (1993) Words can say how they work. In R.P. Crease (Ed.), *Proceedings, Heidegger conference* (pp. 29–35). Stony Brook University.

Gendlin, E. T. (1996) *Focusing-oriented psychotherapy: A manual of the experiential method.* Guilford.

Gendlin, E. T. (2018) *A process model.* Northwestern University Press. (Original work published 1981).

Heck, J. L., Jones, E. J., Bohn, D., McCage, S., Parker, J. G., Parker, M., Pierce, S. L., Campbell, J. (2021) Maternal mortality among American Indian/Alaska native women: A scoping review. *Journal of Women's Health 30*(2), 220–229. https://www.liebertpub.com/doi/10.1089/jwh.2020.8890

Heidegger, M. (1962) *Being and time* (J. Macquarrie & E. Robinson, Trans.). Harper & Row. (Original work published 1927).

Heidegger, M. (2018) Die Frage nach der Technik. In A. Ziemann (Ed.) *Grundlagentexte der Medienkultur* (pp. 55–60). Springer VS. https://doi.org/10.1007/978-3-658-15787-6_7 (Original work published 1954).

Hoefer, C. (2016) Causal determinism. In E. N. Zalta (Ed.), *The Stanford encyclopedia of philosophy* (Spring 2016 Edition). https://plato.stanford.edu/archives/spr2016/entries/determinism-causal/

Levinas, E. (1998) *Otherwise than being or beyond essence* (A. Lingis, Trans.). Duquesne University. (Original work published 1974).

Lore, M. (2017) Umbilical cord prolapse and other cord emergencies. *Global Library of Women's Medicine.* https://www.glowm.com/section-view/item/136#.YuA0hnYpDIU

Martin, N., & Montagne, R. (2017) U.S. has the worst rate of maternal deaths in the developed world. *NPR.* https://www.npr.org/2017/05/12/527806002/focuson-infants-during-childbirth-leaves-u-s-moms-in-danger

Merleau-Ponty, M. (2012) *The phenomenology or perception* (D. A. Landes, Trans.). Routledge. (Original work published 1945).

Murphy, D. J., & MacKenzie, I. Z. (1995). The mortality and morbidity associated with umbilical cord prolapse. *BJOG 102*(10), 826–830.

Pease, A., & Pease B. (2004) *The definitive book of body language.* Bantam Books.

Petersen, E. E., Davis, N. L., Goodman, D., Cox, S., Syverson, C., Seed, K., Shapiro-Mendoza, C., Callaghan, W. M., Barfield, W. (2019) Racial/ethnic disparities in pregnancy-related deaths: United States, 2007–2016. *Morbidity and Mortality Weekly Report 2019*(68), 762–765. http://dx.doi.org/10.15585/mmwr.mm6835a3

Phipps, M. G., Lindquist, D. G., McConaughey, E., O'Brien, J. A., Raker, C. A., Paglia, M. J. (2012) Outcomes from a labor and delivery team training program with simulation component. *American Journal of Obstetrics & Gynecology 2012*(1), 1–9.

Risser, J. (2019) When words fail: On the power of language in human experience. *Journal of Applied Hermeneutics 2019*(6), 1–11.

Spigel, L., Plough, A., Paterson, V., West, R., Jurczak, A., Henrich, N., Gullo, S., Corrigan, B., Patterson, P., Short, T., Early, L. Bridges, M., Pesek, E., Pizzitola, M., Davis, D., Kirby, K., Borduz, C., Shah, N., Weiseth, A. (2022) Implementation strategies within a complex environment: A qualitative study of a shared decision-making intervention during childbirth. *Birth 2022*(00), 1–15. https://onlinelibrary.wiley.com/doi/10.1111/birt.12611

Villines, Z. (2021). What to know about gender bias in healthcare. *Medical News Today.* https://www.medicalnewstoday.com/articles/gender-bias-in-healthcare

Weiseth, A., Plough, A., Aggarwal, R., Galvin, G. Rucker, A., Henrich, N., Miller, K., Subramanian, L., Hawrusik, R., Berry, W., Gullo, S., Spigel, L., Dever, K., Loveless, D., Graham, K., Paek, B., & Shah, N. T. (2022) Improving communication and teamwork during labor: A feasibility, acceptability, and safety study. *Birth 2022*(00), 1–11. https://doi.org/10.1111/birt.12630

Chapter 4

The experiencing model

Saying what we mean in the context of focusing and psychotherapy

Akira Ikemi, Shimpei Okamura and Hideo Tanaka

Introduction

This chapter endeavors to address the intriguing question of what is happening in the relationship during Focusing in particular, and during psychotherapy sessions in general. In contrast to his philosophical writings, Eugene Gendlin has written very little about theory in his writings on Focusing. For example, he has written nothing about theory in the book *Focusing* (Gendlin, 1981/2007). In his book *Let Your Body Interpret Your Dreams* (Gendlin, 1986), a philosophical elaboration of his theory of dream interpretation is presented in the appendix, but not in the text itself. He wrote:

> If you don't like theory, don't let it get in the way of the experiential steps the book describes. They are not based on theory. You don't need the theory for them. That is why it is an appendix, here.
>
> Theory does *not ground* what I described in the book. I love theory, but it does not ground life. Many people think everything is "based on" theory. If that were so, what would theory be based on?
>
> (Gendlin, 1986, p. 141)

It seems that Gendlin prioritized method over theory. He critiqued Medard Boss' Daseinsanalysis as "theoretical" and Rollo May's Existential Analysis as not making clear "just *how* one moves from avoiding to meeting [existential challenges]" (Gendlin, 1973, p. 320). His emphasis on method helped Focusing to win world-wide recognition, as the book *Focusing* was translated into twenty languages, and it is practiced in many countries and regions of the world. A six-step method which he called *Focusing Short Form* outlined in this book showed how attending to the *felt sense* of a situation could unfold into a *felt shift*, an experiential change imbued with new understandings of the situation.

Perhaps, the advantage of prioritizing method over theory is that it enables an opening for new theoretical elaborations about Focusing to emerge,

DOI: 10.4324/9781003296706-5

while its downside is that many Focusing practitioners remain uncertain about the theoretical basis of what they are practicing. Thus, a consistent view of just what is happening in the relationship during Focusing is yet to be formulated, even among those who practice Focusing. Some Focusing practitioners seem to endorse a paradigm where "unconscious material" comes into consciousness during Focusing, while some others assert that "the body knows" without really addressing what is meant by "body" or how such a body can know. Moreover, these paradigms do not squarely address the issue of the nature of the relationship through which such processes occur.

In this chapter, we wish to present the *Experiencing Model,* which is a theoretical model to disclose what is happening in the relationship during Focusing. Since the model addresses fundamental issues such as "how one has experience" or "how is saying," the model is applicable to a wide range of human endeavors, including psychotherapy. In order to ensure that theoretical concepts point to experience, excerpts from a recorded Focusing session are presented. Theoretical assertions are explicated from the recorded session and are woven into a coherent whole, which the authors name the Experiencing Model. This session and some theoretical assertions that comprise an earlier formulation of the Experiencing Model were originally published in Japanese (Ikemi, 2022) by the first author. Theoretical considerations and assertions are augmented in this chapter with input from co-authors. As we shall discuss, the model moves beyond the views of Carl Rogers and carries forward what is often left in the shadows in the psychotherapeutic writings of Eugene Gendlin, to present a view of saying what WE mean, in the context of psychotherapy.

Excerpts from a focusing session

About the session

The session presented here was conducted as part of an online workshop on Focusing. Both the therapist (the first author), and the workshop client, the focuser, had more than thirty years of experience in Focusing. The session started in the form of the Focusing Short Form (Gendlin, 1981/2007) but followed the flow of experiencing as the session evolved. The duration of the session was sixty-six minutes. The session was recorded on Zoom and presented to the focuser for her confirmation and consent for publication. Permission was also obtained for the release of part of her email to the therapist which she wrote four days after the session describing the impact of this session.

In the following, records from the session are presented in narrative style, rather than in transcript style. The focuser's statements and utterances are written within quotation marks, while the therapist's statements appear within parenthesis. The reflection response by the therapist is marked as RF. On some occasions, the exact contents of the reflection responses are shown following the notation RF=. Pauses are noted with the notation of s for seconds and m for minutes. Thus, the notation [1m 25s] would signify that there was a pause of one minute and twenty-five seconds. Brackets { } are used to explain a situation or to suggest a translation for a word that was originally in Japanese.

The session

The session began with Clearing a Space, but the focuser said that she wants to take up a "big issue" about her mother. She tends to avoid thinking about her mother. She had not visited her in decades. It seemed to her as if she were "avoiding" her mother. She said, "I don't know why this happens, but there is a premonition that I will be overwhelmed" when she thinks about her mother. For this reason, she has not taken up this issue in her Focusing for decades. She sensed some guilt about her relationship to her mother pertaining to the time that her father had passed away. Her father had developed cancer and the physician initially said he could only live for another month, although her father actually lived on for two years after the diagnosis. Her mother became emotional and out of control in sorrow upon hearing that her husband was seriously ill, and the focuser's sisters had asked the focuser to come visit the hometown hospital where her father was hospitalized, as the focuser was a medical professional. Upon discussing with the physician in charge, the focuser decided to withhold telling her mother the diagnosis of cancer and gave her mother an alternate explanation about the nature of the illness.

"My mother believed that explanation, and was relieved to know that her husband did not have cancer ... and I kept thinking ... I have to tell her the truth, but my sisters told me that it was not time for that now ... I kept thinking 'But I have to tell her the truth', I have to, I have to, but before I could do so, father passed away ... when I think of that ... I feel sorry ... and I kept postponing ... and no one wanted to touch upon this ... and after this, for many years I did keep in touch with my mother, avoiding that subject, but deep down inside there is guilt ... it's been several decades."

(And how do you feel, when you think about this whole thing now?) "[5s] well ... what I really feel as I talk about it is, around here (chest and throat area) there is something like friction (like something stuck?) ... So, I can't speak smoothly." (How can we call that felt sense?) "What is it? ... well, it's something like, seems like it can come out but it can't come out ... a different thing just came up ... I am also hurt {wounded[1]}." (Be aware that you feel hurt.) [10s] (And how are you hurt?) "... well my hurt is, not like being scratched but like being cut" (RF) "I've never been cut with a sword, but it's like being chopped with a knife." (What could this sense be? Who is cutting you? And what are you being chopped with?) [60s] "Well, uhm ... what did you say, who is cutting me? with what?" (Well whatever, but you're being chopped here.) "Maybe I'm thinking with my head, but since I want to erase all this from my memory ... I'm cutting myself up? No, that's not it." (RF) "Yes, I'm wishing that this never happened...." (What happens to your hurt when you say that?) ... [15s] "The pressure gets weaker ... but it's still there ... It's not Focusing but something gets in the way of my thoughts. Like will the wound ever heal, or there's no life that's not wounded, but those are just some phony wise remarks" (and what is the wound telling you? Your head tells you there is no life without wounds, but the wound itself, what is it saying?)

"This ... I'm not sure what I'm doing now ... There are two wounds in the same place. Same direction. One is like a scratch wound the other is cut." (Be aware that there are two ... What could it mean, that there are two?) "Will you say that again, please" [2m]. {The focuser seemed to be thinking of something, so the therapist did not respond.} "There are two, they have different qualities ... this is ... oh, I'm sensing that it's really true ... and when I try to ask myself, what is the meaning of this ... then I get interrupted ..." (There are two wounds, and you don't know why there are two ... You can make it into a *nazokake* {riddel} if you want: what happens when the two wounds are crossed with your mother?) "When the two wounds ... uhm ... [1m] wait ... [20s] No, I feel like giving up. It's not working." (Then let us take a break.)

At this point, it was thirty-eight minutes into the session. The session resumed after a break of a couple of minutes. However, soon after the session resumed, the focuser said "[20s] ... I'm really not understanding this ... [20s] ... yes ...[30s] ...uhm [35s] ... I don't know, sorry." The session entered a second break for a few minutes and resumed at forty-five minutes since the beginning of the session.

"It's funny isn't it ... it's not that I was abused ... as the youngest of three sisters, my mother took good care of me, she loved me, and when I was little, she made dresses for me and took me out shopping to department stores and after I started working she used to come to help me when I was away for work ... that's when my father was healthy ... but after my father died, after a while ... troubles surfaced in my family ... I got divorced ... I was up to here with all those things ... and I didn't have the energy to listen to my mother and I remember I slammed down the phone once ... and that was it, you know."

(Can I say what came to me?) Yes. (Well, you slammed down the phone and well, she believed your alternate explanation and you really felt you needed to apologize, but you couldn't. Something got in the way. That's what I'm hearing you say.)

"Somehow, I can't talk serious[2] with her. (RF) {The focuser laughs} Yes, yes, and then, that's why, uhm, about my family, just before I got divorced, she called me almost every day, and she was crying and saying how worried she was about me. But I was up to here with all the work and taking care of the kids and I thought, well if you're so worried about me, then just don't call me. I was really in a mess, and she used to cry and if I could talk properly about divorce with her, maybe she didn't need to call me, but in my relationship with my mother, I never really talked to her honestly about how difficult it was with me and I would crack jokes and evade the seriousness, like that, you know, I couldn't talk to her seriously [honestly, genuinely]. (RF) Yes that's right, I can't talk to her seriously."

(I feel like I know what the other wound is about.) "Huh! What is it?" {She leans forward.} (Well, there's one wound about your father, and there's another one about the divorce.) "Ah! ... ah ... hum ... yes ... yes ... uhm ... that feels right ... uhm ... uhm ... I see". (And it's not your style to talk genuinely with her.) "Well, I'm not good at that. I can't imagine some people holding a family meeting. (RF) Yeah. [12s] If I could only say I'm sorry I didn't tell you about father's diagnoses ... I kept thinking like that ... but really, I don't know now ... [10s] it's strange to say, I don't have to apologize [10s]. Rather than that, the un-natural way I, I excessively avoid her, and thinking that I must properly, properly work on telling her the ... (The way you think you must properly tell her is not the easy and authentic nature of the relationship with your mother.) Yes, long time ago, when my children were little ..."{she recalls the time her mother came up to help her with her children when she was busy with work.} (So, the relationship with your mother was much more free and easy.) "Yes, it was easy. {omission} My two sisters and my mother go out to a hot spring spa once a year. Last year I didn't join them but went to the same spa one day later. But they invite me every year, and now I'm thinking, maybe I can join them." (RF) "They go every year and my eldest sister says 'I know you won't be coming, but if you can come along ...' And I would say 'I'm busy now' and decline. But now, since this session began, I'm feeling like I could go." (Be aware that now you have a thought that you can go with them.) "Yes [20s] yeah [omission]."

"Ah, [10s] I'm not quite sure about this yet, but *it was me*, who was setting up a rigid stance ... I realized that in this session ... *it was me*, who couldn't be natural {genuine} with her ... and when I think so, I now see that my mother is not such a powerful monster." (RF) "Yes, and I've been swelling up the wound in me. And it's now clear to me that it was *my thought* that said if I see her, then the wound in me would enlarge and fill up and conquer my heart[3]." (RF = You were thinking that if you are with your mother, the wound will become livid and you would lose your balance, but come to think of it, your mother is not a monster.) "Well, it wasn't like I was avoiding her ... yes, well, she was so warm, I just thought." (RF = Now, you are remembering your mother's warmth.) "Yes … yes… that's right … {tears}. Yes, she was always warm." [65s] "I'm glad I took this up today. I've been avoiding this … well, she was really warm" (RF = You are moved by your mother's warmth.) "…{Tears} … yes [60s] I think our time is up … I am satisfied to stop here {she laughs out}."

Excerpts of her email four days later

Since I've always had some guilt feelings about not going back to the home where I grew up, when people ask me: "Don't you ever go back to your mother's home?" I had said for many years that "I just don't get along with my over-protective mother." But as I repeated this, I may have created the image of an over-protective mother. But in the Focusing session, I realized that I felt she was over-protective and gloomy only once during the divorce process, and she had always been so warm. I've created this image of an over-protective monster and that blocked me from seeing reality as it is. It was really like the *frozen whole*[4] started to melt. Yesterday, by such a strange coincidence, my eldest sister emailed me, and I would always get depressed thinking of how to reply and procrastinate, but this time, I had no such depressive moods and I promised right away that when the corona pandemic ends, I will go with them to the hot spring spa. Not only my experience but also the whole situation started moving. Thank you so much!

The experiencing model

It is possible to discuss in some detail the technicalities of the therapist responses seen in this excerpt. However, the aim of this paper is an attempt to construct a theoretical model. For this purpose, this paper will emphasize theoretical dimensions and will refer to the technical aspects of the therapist responses only in relation to such theoretical elaborations. In the following, the Experiencing Model will be elaborated by way of five assertions articulated from this session.

Experiencing and "the unconscious"

The early part of this session before the two breaks centered upon how the focuser experienced her relationship with her mother. This was certainly not an easy task, as evident in her statement before the second break. "[20s] I'm really not understanding this …[20s] … yes … [30s] …uhm [35s] …I don't know, sorry." It seemed as if the process has halted. This halted process may appear to be *resistance* as described in classical psychoanalysis. However, just before the break, the focuser says "[10s] It's not Focusing but something interrupts [gets in the way of my thoughts]. Like will the wound ever heal, or there's no life that's not wounded...but those are just some phony wise remarks." These remarks resemble what is referred to as *mechanisms of defense*. However, the crucial difference between her experience and what is called defense mechanisms is that the focuser could distinguish these thoughts as something that "interrupts [gets in the way]" as opposed to the direct experience (direct referent) that she was trying to sense into. She therefore continued her attempt to directly sense into how the situation was felt for her.

Can the direct referent she was probing be called the *unconscious*? According to Gendlin's critique of the *repression paradigm* (1964, p. 104) or from his description of the pre-conceptual (Gendlin, 1973, p. 223), it cannot be said that the focuser was trying to probe her unconscious. Rather, any human experience is pre-conceptual, as experience is not made of words and concepts. Experience is the source from which words and concepts arise. For example, let us take up a favorite piece of music. If someone were to ask us, "what is that piece like?", how might we answer? The moment we say "It's a bright piece" we know that the word "bright" is insufficient, and much is lost when the experience of that music piece is substituted with this word. The struggle to find the right words to express the experience of the music piece does not testify to the fact that our conceptualization of the music piece is repressed in the unconscious. The difference between Gendlin, who saw experience as pre-conceptual, and Carl Rogers, who saw that "experiences not accurately symbolized in consciousness" are "denied to awareness" (Rogers, 1951, p. 510), has been highlighted in a previous article (Ikemi, 2005).

If we stand on the assumption that human experience is not yet in words, the effect of psychotherapy is not "making the unconscious conscious," but "carefully finding how to say experience, which is not yet in words." Such saying, or explication, happens in a relationship and generates meaning, echoing the title of Gendlin's first book *Experiencing and the Creation of Meaning* (1997a). In this session, the focuser was not trying to make conscious the unconscious but to say and find meaning in her experience of the "premonition that I will be overwhelmed." Consequently, as will be discussed later, novel meaning was carried forward, and that was retroactively applied to her experience, transforming her understanding of past events.

The direct referent is an "implying"

In focusing and FOT (Focusing-Oriented Psychotherapy), the direct referent is not viewed as representations of past events that may have *caused* the experience. For example, it would be unwise to ask a person who is experiencing hunger, "what (past events) has caused your hunger?" Rather, one would ask, "what do you want to eat?" The experience of hunger, like other experiences, points to a process of *further living* (Gendlin, 1973). The hunger knows implicitly what the body wants to eat, and that is not just anything. Likewise, the "premonition that I will be overwhelmed" is viewed as *pointing to a mode of relating* to her mother, which the focuser's experience (or "body") is implying. The therapist, therefore, makes no attempt to investigate past experiences which may have caused this experience.

Re-experiencing

Re-experiencing and Interaction

One aspect of what revitalized the halted process after the second break was the therapist's response: "Can I say what came to me?" This response is an instance of a type of response that Carl Rogers called *Testing Understandings (TUN)* (1989, p. 128) that is widely considered to be characteristic of his way of responding after he developed Client-Centered Therapy (Lietaer & Gundrum, 2018). In other words, in this response, the therapist tested to see if how the therapist was experiencing the focuser's experience could adequately say the focuser's own experience. Ikemi (2017) speculated that TUN is essentially Rogers' Re-experiencing[5] (*Nacherleben*) of the client's experiencing. The word 追体験, a translation of *Nacherleben*, is used widely in Japanese and to some extent in Chinese and Korean, but there is no accurate translation of that term in English.

The following example may clarify what this term means:

> When my dog, a golden retriever, was still around, she used to sit on my right side and she would lean on my leg, putting her left paw on my right foot, and sometimes she would look up to me and sometimes she would begin to drool on my jeans.

As the author relates this experience, the reader may Re-experience the author's experience. In other words, the reader may not only have a visual imagery of the dog, but also the sensation of warmth as the dog leans on the leg, the sensation of the dog's paw on the feet, or the warmth of the dog's drool on the jeans. Re-experiencing is richer than the explicit words that are spoken. Since there is no accurate translation of *Nacherleben* in English, only Ikemi (2017, 2019a) has written on the subject within the framework of Person-Centered Therapy or Focusing. Re-experiencing seems to have been translated as "empathy" in some philosophical literature, but this has been criticized, since in Re-experiencing, there is no self-projection of putting oneself in somebody else's shoes (Makkreel, 1975, p. 252).

On TUN, Rogers (1989) wrote, "I am trying to determine whether my understanding of the client's inner world is correct ..." (pp. 127–128). It must be noted here that Rogers kept "my understanding" and the "client's inner world" separate. This subject-object cleavage is evident from the first of the six conditions in Rogers' famous article on the core conditions (Rogers, 1957), where he stated that "two persons are in psychological contact." In other words, two persons were seen as separate entities that were in contact. In contrast, Gendlin (1997b, p. 41) says about *Nacherleben* that "these [the author and the reader's experiencing] cross, so that each become implicit in the other."[6] In other words, Gendlin does not view your experience and my experience as separate entities, but as our "inter-subjective experience." As Cooper and Ikemi (2012) wrote, articulating how persons are "originally entangled" is a formidable challenge for the Person-Centered Approach. Re-experiencing may hold the key to carry forward this challenge.

After the therapist expressed his Re-experiencing in what followed from: "Can I say what came to me?", the focuser's process seemed to have come alive and she mentions about the issue of divorce. Upon listening to her speak, the therapist felt as if he knew "what the other wound is about" and shared his Re-experiencing with her as: "Well, there's one wound about your father, and there's another one about the divorce." The focuser experienced a felt shift there, which is expressed in the following words. "Ah! ... ah ... hum ... yes ... yes ...uhm ... that feels right ... uhm ... uhm ... I see." In this moment, the therapist and focuser had *crossed* in that one of them had explicated what was implicit in the other's experience. In psychotherapy, it is often said that the *interaction* changes both the client and therapist. It may be possible to assert that one aspect of what is called interaction is the mutual Re-experiencing between the client and the therapist.

Re-experiencing oneself: The experiential effects of the reflection response

Looking back over his career, Carl Rogers wrote that the term "reflection" to designate a certain type of therapist response (also referred to as "saying back") made him "cringe" (Rogers, 1980, p. 138). Puzzling over the effects of the reflection response, he wrote that he had arrived at a *double-insight* (Rogers, 1989, p. 127–128). One of the insights comes from the perspective of the therapist. The other comes from the perspective of the client.

Rogers clarified that he had no intention of reflecting feelings. "I am *not* trying to reflect feelings" he wrote, with "not" in italics. Rather, he was try-ing to check if his understanding of the client's experience fit with the client's understanding. He says that such a manner of responding provided a "sound motivation" for responding (Rogers, 1989, p. 128). Rogers was afraid that the reflection response would be misunderstood to be a technique. Similarly, Gendlin (1990, p. 206) critiqued that the reflection response as a technique could get in the way of the personal nature of the therapeutic relationship.

He wrote: "'I can stay here because I have my reflecting method, I have my ping-pong paddle, so you cannot get me. You say something, you get it back.' There is a sense that we are armed, you see." Both Rogers and Gendlin saw the reflection response, not as a technique but as an encounter of two persons. As Ikemi (2017) has argued, Roger's TUN amounts to Rogers expressing his Re-experiencing of the client's experience.

The other side of Rogers' double insight is the experiential effect of the reflection response on the client's experience. The therapist's TUN response serves as a mirror where clients can see themselves reflected. "The feelings and personal meanings seem sharper when seen through the eyes of another, when they are reflected (Rogers, 1989, p.128)." Thus, from the client's perspective, the therapist's Re-experiencing or TUN serve as a reflection (RF) which can then be used by the client to Re-experience their own experiences.

Hence, Rogers' double insight shows how the expression of therapists' Re-experiencing serves at once, as TUN from therapists' perspective, and as reflection (RF) from clients' perspective. Let us pick up some instances from the session above which show how RF enhances the focuser's own Re-experiencing.

- "... well my hurt is, not like being scratched but like being cut. (RF) I've never been cut with a sword, but it's like being chopped with a knife." After RF is provided by the therapist, the experience of being "cut" becomes more detailed. It seems that with RF, the focuser Re-experienced her experience of "cut" and came up with a more finely sensed experience, "being chopped with a knife."
- "... I'm cutting myself up? No, that's not it. (RF) Yes, I'm wishing that this never happened." Again, "cutting myself up" becomes more refined and transforms into "wishing this never happened" after the RF. Such a change in content is referred to as *content mutation* (Gendlin, 1964, pp. 144–148; Gendlin, 1996, pp. 13–15). The moment the words "cutting myself up" leave her lips, the focuser notices that that isn't right. She says "No, that's not it" and Re-experiences her own experience to come up with an expression that better says her experience. It seems that "Re-experiencing one's own experience" is necessary for such content-mutation.
- "... yes, well, she was so warm, I just thought. (RF = Now, you are remembering your mother's warmth.) Yes ... yes... that's right ... {tears}. Yes, she was always warm [65 s]." After the RF, the focuser is experiencing her mother's warmth more vividly. Evidently, she was Re-experiencing her mother's warmth during the long silence.

As discussed above, one of the functions of RF (TUN/RF response) seems to be its facilitation of the client's own Re-experiencing. With regards to the focuser's statement above where she was Re-experiencing her mother's warmth, it may be noted that in the Experiencing Model, fully Re-experiencing in the here and now seems to be more therapeutic than simply "recalling" or "remembering" past events.

Saying

Saying is one of the keywords of Gendlin's philosophy, as evidenced in the title of his posthumous book *Saying What We Mean* (Casey & Schoeller, 2018). Although much can be discussed about saying in Gendlin's philosophy, for the purposes of this paper, discussions will be limited to saying as seen in one of the roots of Gendlin's philosophy, the hermeneutics of Wilhelm Dilthey.

"Perhaps the most radical impact of my philosophy today stems from Wilhelm Dilthey" (Gendlin, 1997b, p. 41). This is a rare passage where Gendlin discloses one of the roots of where his thinking comes from. He goes on to discuss how the hermeneutic circle of experiencing-expression-understanding is one, and that each is an instance of the other two. The circle keeps turning and moves the experiencing process forward, so that saying is a "further" experiencing, further expression and a further understanding. To substitute "novel," another keyword in Gendlin's philosophy, for "further," it can be said that saying initiates a novel experiencing, expression and understanding. When the focuser says that she is "hurt [wounded]," she is experiencing the hurt and hurt is her expression and hurt is how she understands herself. But in her Re-experiencing of that word, aided by the therapist RF/TUN response, the expression is found to be inadequate. A more refined expression emerges, "being chopped with a knife." Now, she is experiencing "being chopped with a knife" and that is her expression and that is how she understands herself. The circle keeps turning swiftly, as the listener responds. "I'm cutting myself up?" she says. That is her novel experiencing-expression-understanding which is instantly found to be inadequate in her experiencing as she says "No, that's not it." As the listener reflects this, the circle turns again. Now, her experiencing-expression-understanding progresses to "Yes, I'm wishing that this never happened." In its optimal form, saying is viewed in this way in the Experiencing Model, where saying keeps the circle turning to generating novel experiencing-expression-understandings.

Dilthey (2002, p. 250; 1927, p. 230) writes of experiencing or lived experience (*Erleben, Erlebnis*) that they "include what is not distinct and needs to be explicated *(aufklären)*." He also says about how such explication is possible but at the same time inexhaustible.

The completion of lived experience in the direction of the psychic nexus is grounded in a lawful progression that always goes beyond the

apprehended content of the lived experience. This progression is conditioned by the state of affairs, and every step in it involves a satisfaction
repeatedly instigated by the dissatisfaction stemming from the inexhaustibility [*Unerschöpflichkeit*] of the lived experience.

(Dilthey, 2002, p. 51; 1927, p. 29)

The focuser's lived experience includes "what is not distinct," as seen in the
case material presented above. The focuser uses expressions such as "hurt,"
"being chopped with a knife," "I'm cutting myself up?" in a "lawful progression" that can "go beyond" or change the "content of the lived experience."
Such explications are accompanied by a sense of satisfaction as much as
a sense of dissatisfaction arising from the "inexhaustibility" of experience
which propels the progression.

Now let us turn to Gendlin, to highlight how much more elaborate his formulation is. It sheds some light on what Dilthey referred to as "inexhaustible." Gendlin refers to such novel experiencing-expression-understanding in
his early work, *Experiencing and the Creation of Meaning* (Gendlin, 1997a),
as "comprehension." He writes: "To invent a metaphor to express a prior
felt meaning is comprehension" (p. 117). For example, the expression "being
chopped with a knife" is a metaphor to express a felt meaning that existed
prior to the expression. Thus, we can say that the act of saying through
which the focuser says of her experience as "being chopped with a knife" is
comprehension.

Moreover, Gendlin fine tunes his articulation of "comprehension" to
elaborate some intriguing characteristics. "Often we do feel that it [=what
we finally symbolized] has changed. We say, 'I didn't really see this about it
until I tried to express it.' It changes because it interacts with the felt meanings of already meaningful symbols ... By the time we say exactly what we
meant, it isn't quite the same; it is richer, more explicit, more fully known"
(Gendlin, 1997a, pp. 119–120).

In this session, the focuser's expression "being chopped with a knife" says
the prior felt meaning that got symbolized with that expression. But as soon
as she said these words, the felt meaning had changed. She says "since I want
to erase all this from my memory ... I'm cutting myself up? No, that's not
it." Here, she says, "I'm cutting myself up" and then immediately abandons
that expression with "no, that's not it." It can be noted here that the metaphor "I'm cutting myself up" serves both as symbolization to express the felt
meaning, while also serving as an "arbiter" to determine whether the same
expression has or has not been successful to symbolize the felt meaning.
Gendlin writes:

All through this process the felt meaning to be symbolized functions
both as selector and as arbiter. We concentrate on (directly refer to) this

felt meaning and words come to us (explication). The felt meaning also enables us to feel whether these words succeeded or failed to symbolize it (arbiter).

(Gendlin, 1997a, p. 119)

In one important sense, then, the resulting symbolization *does* symbolize the *original* felt meaning. In another sense it specifies it, adds to it, goes beyond it, or reaches only part of it – in short, *changes* it.

(Gendlin, 1997a, p. 120)

As seen in the discussion above, it is not simply the case that the felt meaning which pre-existed the expression got "represented" in the expression, for example of "being-chopped with a knife." The expression changes the felt meaning of what we meant to say. One aspect of the "inexhaustibility" of experience is that the experience keeps changing as it is expressed.

Yet another important aspect of saying is that they are not one-way streets in the interaction from self to other. Her expression "being chopped with a knife," for example, is relayed not only to the listener but also feeds back upon the focuser herself, with the help of the listener's reflection response. Thus, it can be said that comprehension functions on two dimensions: the dimension of felt meaning and symbols; and the dimension of self and other. "We use symbols not only to tell others what we mean; we tell ourselves (Gendlin, 1997a, p. 120)." This view of saying as occurring in the dimension of self and other sheds light on how the client and therapist *co-explicate* (Cooper & Ikemi, 2012) in the therapy session. It echoes George Herbert Mead (1934, p. 75) who wrote: "we affect ourselves as we affect others and mediate the social situation through this understanding of what we are saying."

Furthermore, Ikemi (2019b) adds to the discussion above on saying as a two-way interaction of experience and verbal symbols, through his term *the gives of words*. When the focuser said, "being chopped," the verbal symbol "chop" yields a rich meaning context, which implies no hesitation, sharpness, cutting with speed and power, cruelty and so forth. Ikemi (2019b) refers to these meaning contexts which accompany verbal symbols, as the *gives of words*. When the focuser said, "being chopped with a knife," perhaps the *gives of words* could not adequately say the felt meaning of her experience, thus the expression was changed to "cutting myself" and that too was found to be inadequate to carry forward the meaning of her experience. Another facet of saying can thus be seen as a multi-directional interaction of experience and the meaning context that the word *gives* us. The *gives of words* is another way of elaborating on what Gendlin simply refers to as "already meaningful symbols" in the passage cited above.

The carried forward was

In the interaction characterized by mutual Re-experiencing, the focuser was able to say her experience of her mother. Such sayings amounted to an impactful felt shift, wherein which she re-discovered the warmth of her mother.

Ikemi (2016, pp. 93–95; 2017; 2019a) coined the term *carried forward was* to point to the characteristic changes that occur when something is newly discovered in awareness. This term highlights what Gendlin explicated in similar contexts, often using italics, such as in the following sentence: "rephrasing a point *carries* the point *forward* so that we discover more of what it *was*" (Gendlin, 1997b, p. 23). The term sheds light on the characteristic temporality that is experienced when novelty comes into awareness. The experiencing process moves forward, and then we discover what is *was*. George Herbert Mead also took note of such characteristics of time. He wrote, "... for that past must be set over against the present within which the emergent appears, and the past, which must then be looked at from the standpoint of the emergent becomes a different past" (Mead, G.H. 1932/1980, p. 2).

As the focuser's experiencing carried forward, she discovered that her mother *was* warm indeed. The felt shift, the carrying forward, the *emergent* that happened here transformed the over-protective and gloomy person that her mother was into a warm mother which she really *was*. Such a realization is retroactively applied as the past is overwritten.

Surely, there is a direction of how past events shape how we experience. However, there is the other direction of how a person's reflection upon past experiences and explication arising from such reflexive awareness moves the understanding forward to overwrite how the past "really" was.

Discussion

As discussed above, the Experiential Model addresses human experience, articulating with hermeneutics, interpersonal interactions, linguistic theory and its view of temporality. This model addresses a "formidable challenge" (Cooper & Ikemi, 2012) to carry forward psychotherapy theories, particularly Carl Rogers' Person-Centered Approach, via its views of what is happening in interpersonal interactions. Furthermore, it sheds light on what is frequently left in the shadows of Eugene Gendlin's FOT, as discussed below.

More than simply stating that the client and therapist are in interaction, the Experiencing Model asserts that the felt meaning as experienced by the therapist is *already crossed* with a situated, living process that is the client. In his previous work, Ikemi (2014) presented a term *responsive combodying* pointing to how the client and therapist as embodied are not separate bodies but are an interacting body of both. Just as a school of sardines that instantly responds with each other, the bodies are already crossed as a *being-with* and as a *beings-in* situations. This perspective overcomes the view of the client and therapist as separate and independent entities as espoused by Carl Rogers (for example, 1957). The practical dimension of this perspective is shown in the case presented above.

In his analysis of Heidegger's *Befindlichkeit* which is included in the book *Saying What We Mean* (Casey, E. and Schoeller, D. (Eds.) 2018, pp. 194–224), Eugene Gendlin carefully considers the German term to articulate the nuance of "how-are-you-ness" or of "finding oneself" which is implicit in this terminology. In Heidegger's ontology, the human being, or *Dasein,* is apprehended as a *being-in-the-world*, a *being-with* others. As Gendlin wrote:

> The world of Dasein is a with-world [*Mitwelt*]. Being-in is being-with others (BT 155).
>
> (Gendlin, 1978–1979/2018, p. 208)

Gendlin elaborates on this as follows:

> Our being, in Heidegger's view, is always being affected and that is how we find ourselves. We are the living-in events with-others, our being rides on the events, is dispersed in what happens, is the being-in what happens. Only in so finding ourselves can we constantly retrieve ourselves, so that there is a present in which our capacity to be is again and again our own. That is authenticity.
>
> (Gendlin, 1978–1979/2018, p. 214)

Just as we are situated as *being-in*, we are also *being-with* others. Therefore, to be more precise, the *Re-experiencing* mentioned in this chapter occurs upon our way of being *as being-in* and *being-with*, indeed a *co-explication* arising from *co-Re-experiencing.* It can thus be asserted that the undercurrent of the Experiencing Model is the ontological understanding of Heidegger and Gendlin.

In contrast to this ontological view, Gendlin articulates Focusing as a skill that people can do on their own, in the book *Focusing* (Gendlin, 1981/2007).

> The purpose of this book is to tell you what they [successful psychotherapy clients] do and how you can do it. For this uncommon skill, this internal act, not only is useful in the psychotherapist's office, it is a useful way of approaching any problem or situation.
>
> We have taught this skill to large numbers of people not in therapy in subsequent years. Now it seems anyone can learn it.
>
> (Gendlin, 1981/2007, p. 4)

The presentation of Focusing as a skill has undoubtedly been a valuable contribution to self-help across the globe. Gendlin did write that the relationship is important in Focusing, but in this book, he emphasized Focusing as a skill. In therapy however, he did explicitly write that the relationship is of first importance.

> In therapy the relationship (the person in there) is of first importance, listening is second and focusing instructions come only third.
>
> (Gendlin, 1996, p. 217)

Friedman (2007, p. xii) questioned the appropriateness of the name given to Gendlin's therapy. Why would it be "Focusing-Oriented Psychotherapy," not "Relationship-Oriented Therapy," when the relationship comes first and Focusing comes only third? As a therapist who had been a client of Gendlin, Friedman was impressed by the relationship that Gendlin's therapy created. Thus, Friedman wrote that he was "not entirely happy with Gendlin's name for this new brand of therapy." As Ikemi (2008) commented, it is somewhat paradoxical that Friedman, who had raised such a question, had also named his book *Focusing-Oriented Therapy*. It therefore seems as if both Gendlin and Friedman highlighted the process that was happening within the "person in there," although they both thought that the relationship is of primary importance.

It is interesting to note that Gendlin had added in parenthesis, the expression "the person in there" in the quote above. Rather than the process of *co-explication*, Gendlin seems to be more focused on helping to explicate the *client's felt sense* in the relationship. In fact, in the last page of the book *Focusing-Oriented Therapy*, Gendlin defines FOT as follows:

> 'Focusing-oriented therapy' is not therapy that includes brief bits of focusing instructions. Rather, it means letting that which arise from the *focusing depth within a person* define the therapist's activity, the relationship, and the process in the client.
>
> (Gendlin, 1996, p. 304, emphasis ours)

As beautiful as this statement is, we cannot help but to notice the part that we emphasized in italics, that the "focusing depth" comes from "within a person." In this book, Gendlin elaborated on the different psychotherapeutic strategies ("avenues") with which to bring about the Focusing process *in the client*. However, the Focusing process occurring "in the client" must not be misunderstood as an "intrapersonal" or "intrapsychic" process.

> Focusing is sometimes, quite wrongly, thought to be an exclusively "intrapsychic" therapy. There is no such thing. Interaction is always a

vital dimension of therapy, and as I have already said, focusing goes on within the wider context of the ongoing interaction.

(Ibid., p. 108)

"There is no such thing"; Gendlin strongly refuted the "intrapsychic" view of Focusing. Moreover, in the last page of *Focusing-Oriented Therapy*, a few lines below the previous quote, he wrote:

Currently there is a great deal of concern about the body, but most people have not yet discovered that special kind of bodily sense that is the sense *of* a situation.

(Ibid., p. 304, emphasis Gendlin)

The *of* points to intentionality, of how we as embodied beings are situated, how we are embodied being-in-the-world. Perhaps, Gendlin's emphasis of valuing the Focusing process occurring "within a person" may have overshadowed his ontological assumption that "the person" of whom he refers is a being-in and being-with. The process occurring "within a person" is *occurring within a relationship.*

The Experiential Model as presented in this paper addresses the relationship aspect of Focusing which occurs "within the person, within a relationship." In sum, this model is about "saying what WE mean" in the context of psychotherapy.

Notes

1 *Kizutsuku* in Japanese, meaning hurt or wounded.
2 *Majimé* in Japanese can be translated as "seriously," "genuinely," "honestly," "earnestly."
3 *Kokoro*. An exact translation of this word does not exist in English. It may be translated approximately as psyche or heart.
4 A technical term introduced by Eugene Gendlin in his article, "A theory of personality change" (1964).
5 I use this word with a capital R to distinguish it from the ordinary meaning of the word which signifies "to experience again."
6 Gendlin does not explicitly use the term *Nacherleben* here, although it is clear that he is referring to this as he is commenting on Dilthey's reference to "understanding the author better than he understood himself."

References

Casey, E. and Schoeller, D. (Eds.) (2018). *Saying What We Mean: Implicit precision and the responsive order—Selected works by Eugene Gendlin.* Northwestern University Press.

Cooper, M. and Ikemi, A. (2012). Dialogue: A dialogue between focusing and relational perspectives. *Person-Centered and Experiential Psychotherapies* 11 (2): 124–136.

Dilthey, W. (1927). *Der Aufbau der geschichtlichen Welt in den Geisteswissenschaften* (Gesammelte Schriften. 7. Bd.). B.G. Teubner.

Dilthey, W. (2002). *The Formation of the Historical World in the Human Sciences* (edited by R. A. Makkreel, & F. Rodi) (Selected works/Wilhelm Dilthey, Vol. 3). Princeton University Press.

Friedman, N. (2007). *Focusing-oriented Therapy: A Contribution to the Practice, Teaching and Understanding of Focusing-oriented Psychotherapy.* iUniverse, Inc.

Gendlin, E.T. (1964). A theory of personality change. In P. Worchel & D. Byrne (Eds.), *Personality Change*, pp. 100–148. John Wiley & Sons.

Gendlin, E.T. (1973). Experiential psychotherapy. In R. Corsini (Ed.), *Current Psychotherapies,* (pp. 317–352). F.E. Peacock.

Gendlin, E.T. (1978–1979/2018). Befindlichkeit: Heidegger and the philosophy of psychology. In E. Casey & D. Schoeller (Eds.), *Saying What We Mean: Implicit Precision and the Responsive Order—Selected Works by Eugene Gendlin,* (pp. 194–224). Northwestern University Press.

Gendlin, E.T. (1981/2007). *Focusing.* Bantam Books.

Gendlin, E.T. (1986). *Let Your Body Interpret Your Dreams.* Chiron Publications.

Gendlin, E.T. (1990). The small steps of the therapy process: How they come and how to help them come. In G. Lietaer, J. Rombauts & R. Van Balen (Eds.), *Client-centered and Experiential Psychotherapy in the Nineties,* (pp. 205–224). Leuven University Press.

Gendlin, E.T. (1996). *Focusing-Oriented Psychotherapy: A Manual of the Experiential Method.* Guilford Press.

Gendlin, E.T. (1997a). *Experiencing and the Creation of Meaning: A Philosophical and Psychological Approach to the Subjective.* Northwestern University Press. (Originally published in 1962 by the Free Press of Glencoe).

Gendlin, E.T. (1997b). How philosophy cannot appeal to experience and how it can. In D. Levin (Ed.), *Language Beyond Postmodernism: Saying and Thinking in Gendlin's Philosophy,* (pp.3–41). Northwestern University Press.

Ikemi, A. (2005). Carl Rogers and Eugene Gendlin on the bodily felt sense: What they share and where they differ, *Person-Centered & Experiential Psychotherapies,* 4 (1): 31–42.

Ikemi, A. (2008). Focusing-oriented therapy: A contribution to the practice, teaching and understanding of focusing-oriented psychotherapy. *Person-Centered and Experiential Psychotherapies,* 7: 147–148.

Ikemi, A. (2014). Sunflowers, sardines and responsive combodying: Three perspectives on embodiment. *Person-Centered and Experiential Psychotherapies,* 13: 19–30.

Ikemi, A. Ed. (2016). *Update Your Listening with Focusing.* Nakanishiya Publications [In Japanese].

Ikemi, A. (2017): The radical impact of experiencing on psychotherapy theory: An examination of two kinds of crossings. *Person-Centered & Experiential Psychotherapies,* 16 (2): 159–172.

Ikemi, A. (2019a). A portrait of a person seen through the four dimensions of focusing. *Journal of Humanistic Counseling,* 58: 233–248.

Ikemi, A. (2019b). The creative encounter of the sense and gives of expression: The interplay of art and experiencing. *Studies in the Clinical Applications of Drawings,* 34: 64–85 [In Japanese].

Ikemi, A. (2022). The experiencing model: Explications from a focusing session. *Japanese Journal of Humanistic Psychology*, 39: 131–141 [In Japanese].

Lietaer, G. and Gundrum, M. (2018). His master's voice: Carl Rogers' verbal response modes in therapy and demonstration sessions throughout his career. A quantitative analysis and some qualitative-clinical comments. *Person-Centered & Experiential Psychotherapies,* 17 (4): 275–333.

Makkreel, R.A. (1975*). Dilthey: Philosopher of the Human Sciences.* Princeton University Press.

Mead, G.H. (1932/1980). *The Philosophy of the Present.* The University of Chicago Press. (Phoenix edition, 1980).

Mead, G.H. (1934). *Mind, Self, and Society: From the Standpoint of a Social Behaviorist* (edited by C.W. Morris). University of Chicago Press.

Rogers, C.R. (1951). *Client-Centered Therapy.* Houghton Mifflin Company.

Rogers, C.R. (1957). The necessary and sufficient conditions of therapeutic personality change. *Journal of Consulting Psychology,* 21 (2): 95–103.

Rogers. C.R. (1980). *Empathic: An Unappreciated Way of Being. A Way of Being.* Houghton Mifflin Company.

Rogers. C.R. (1989). Reflection on feelings and transference. In H. Kirschenbaum & V.L. Henderson (Eds.), *The Carl Rogers Reader,* (pp. 127–134). Houghton Mifflin Company.

Chapter 5

The responsive order, oppressive order, and *disorder* in human growth

Challenging and carrying forward postmodernism

Robin R. Chalfin

The responsive order, oppressive order, and disorder in human growth: Challenging and carrying forward postmodernism

In 1997, philosopher and psychologist Eugene Gendlin hosted a pivotal conference entitled "After Postmodernism," in which he aimed to cultivate language beyond the "end point effect" of deconstruction (Gendlin, 1997). In this bold critique of the philosophical predicaments of our era, Gendlin recasts the human being as having an organic nature rather than a genetically fixed, socially conditioned, or inherently indeterminate condition. While humanists have emphasized the force of personal potential, and constructivists the significance of cultural patterns, Gendlin offers a vital philosophical critique of the perennial binary and any position or practice that divides, privileges, or fixes body over culture or culture over body. He helps us out of this polarization and illustrates how we can work with the interaction—think and speak *with* the inseparability (Chalfin, 2021). He articulates the human subject as a radically non-dual process formed and reformed through continual organism-environment interaction. As such, Gendlin recenters the potentiality of the lived body within a philosophical and psychological tradition that simultaneously avoided and overdetermined the body, challenging biological and cultural determinism. From this growth-oriented understanding of an indivisible human being, Gendlin makes his most practical philosophical contribution: he explicates, in exquisite detail, an embodied psychological interaction that characterizes and further guides the process of growth and therapeutic transformation.

Gendlin effectively taught philosophers and psychotherapists alike to practice this regenerative way of thinking about and engaging with human growth processes, or what Gendlin termed the responsive order in his later writing. This formulation and fresh way of accessing and working with implicit experience has been invaluable in a divisive landscape. Still, as Gendlin would agree, it is by nature incomplete or always already implying the next step. In this chapter, I consider the next step. I reflect on Gendlin's

DOI: 10.4324/9781003296706-6

bridging influence in my life and work and illuminate the point at which his conceptualizations and praxis imply a need for more specific articulation of how human growth occurs in contexts of systematic dehumanization.

Indeed, I find it most generative to draw on Gendlin's reclamation of an organic human nature alongside a more specific analysis of powerfully alienating cultural contexts and conditions that form and even foreclose embodiment. Conversely, I find that cultural critiques are enlivened and resist reductivity when grounded in bodily meaning-making processes. Thus, in this chapter, I elucidate how Gendlin has been indispensable in recognizing the inseparable yet irreducible power of nature, body, and situation in human growth, bridging dualities in the field and long-standing dualities in my life and practice as a psychotherapist. I also *carry forward* his work, centering the concern of bodily situated power in contexts of oppressive sociopolitical power. In doing so, I aim to bring Gendlin's concepts present to consider not only the therapeutic practice of attending to the responsive order but also the practice of attending to what we can call the *oppressive order* and even *dis*order.

As a therapist who works specifically with interpersonal, intergenerational, and structural trauma, exploring how Gendlin's *bodily felt sensing* could involve attention to all three dimensions is vital in a complete account of human growth and change. To be sure, the individual does not simply unfold but grows in dynamic and disruptive relation to the sociocultural situation, constituting subjective and somatic experiences alike. I play with his notion of order as always organically organizing alongside the realities of order as oppressive and the possibilities of order as productively disruptive. As such, my reflections throughout this chapter will consider three orders: the responsive order, oppressive order, and disruptive order in my work as a psychotherapist trained in feminist, relational, and deconstructive practices.

A postmodern feminist therapist finding Gendlin

I am neither a specialized Gendlin scholar nor a Focusing therapist. Yet, I sense that he would appreciate my using his philosophy, as he was interested in developing ways of thinking and models for working that could be extracted and applied across theoretical approaches and disparate disciplines. My training as a psychotherapist is grounded in postmodern and psychodynamic theories and had entirely bypassed Gendlin, his mentor and collaborator, Carl Rogers, and the humanistic/existential movement. I encountered his work some years into the field when I joined a group of therapists to write about and teach non-reductive ways of practicing psychotherapy and being-in-the-world; the joint consideration of psychoanalytic and existential hermeneutic philosophy was radical for me. This mode of thinking brought a fresh way to hold the tension between the idealistic humanism of my countercultural upbringing and the rigorous critical lens of my feminist academic training.

During our ongoing studies, we read Gendlin's essential writings and found a particular way to live in (rather than resolve) often-conflicting theoretical and literal homes. Foremost, Gendlin helped me maintain the tension between the human subject's potentiality and forces that render the same as an object; he fostered a resistance toward the polarities of biological and cultural determinism. Indeed, I have described this agentic position as an "entanglement" of being indivisibly both body and culture (Chalfin, 2021). Furthermore, Gendlin explicated the process of growth born out of this very tension in a fresh and finely tuned embodied language. Here I found the most vital aspects of Gendlin's philosophy with which I wrestle and carry forward.

It was particularly evocative to read his highly acclaimed paper on Befindlichkeit, meaning "where we find ourselves," expanding on Heidegger's conceptualization of the human capacity for authentic attunement and response to the conditions of our existence. For Heidegger, we—dasien—find ourselves there (da) being (sien). For Gendlin, this happens in a bodily way—we can always find a knowing guide in the body. As a feminist and trauma-oriented therapist, I struggled with Gendlin's optimism in this paper, and dove deep into the *befindliches*, or bodily felt meaning states of trauma, in a piece titled *Being Broken and Unbroken* (Chalfin, 2016), in which I argued that under traumatic conditions, the felt sense is not readily accessible. To even approach it, we need more specific formulations and language that first articulate the predictable patterns of traumatization and human vulnerability. This involves careful attention to implicit power and what is language-able, speakable, and livable in our social surroundings. We need critical consciousness, not just faith and optimism, in organic human nature. This was certainly clear in my own experience.

Born in the heyday of Gendlin's time in the 1970s, my first childhood home was literally in the countercultural intentional communities of the human potential movement, wherein the commitment to and faith in the wholeness of human beings was paramount. Yet, even here, implicit biases concerning race, gender, class, ability, and more delimited our very sense of freedom. As I came of age and entered academia, I engaged with critical consciousness theories and practices. Dismantling the presumptive background order—the constitutive matrix of social restraints and regulations—exposed dearly held yet reductive modes of thinking, being, and becoming central to humanism. However, for me, it was never a complete surrender to the deconstructive project, but rather, a tension between humanism and postmodernism, experience and intellect, self and non-self, certainty and uncertainty; between a certain holistic optimism and rigorous criticism, irreducible and irresoluble. I was living in an unreconcilable duality; here,

Gendlin is exceedingly helpful, but it was not until later that I encountered his work. When I did, his radically non-dual articulation of human nature through a rigorous philosophical and psychological account was quite useful for me.

With intellectual precision and infectious confidence, Gendlin characterizes human nature as an organic self-organizing process constantly moving toward growth and healing. His unapologetic and meticulous reclamation of human instinct or innate knowing—an organically ordered human life structure—is noteworthy in our deconstructed postmodern context. He asserts that there is a *responsive order* to human life; I find myself both drawn to this notion and averse to it. This return to human potentiality is comforting in a familiar way and yet I know there must be more and for it to hold true it must be interrogated. It is this unsettling tension that, interestingly, Gendlin encouraged us to attend to as it is in this interaction—or even friction—that forward movement is generated. This growth occurs between what feels most vital and unfinished in Gendlin's work, which I examine here regarding psychotherapy and human growth.

Trusting the felt sense

When psychotherapy, often referred to as "talk therapy," works well, it is much more than talk or words—it is, in Gendlin's view, a movement generated via *sensing, experiencing,* and finally *formulating* through language wherein the pain is lived in a new way out of the direct relating to it. During extensive research on the therapeutic process, Gendlin found that therapeutic movement successfully occurs when *focus* is on felt meaning in the core of the body, that is, the practice of attending to the *felt sense* and the interpretive skill of languaging that sensate experience. Moreover, he found that bodily sensation is always and already constituted in meaning or sense-making. Understanding this circular process illuminates the therapeutic process and challenges the philosophical dualities of body, language, and environment attending to the interactive whole that precedes and exceeds these conceptual parts. As such, Gendlin understood psychotherapy's linguistic and somatic phenomena as a radically nondual and indivisible interaction of experience and language (by which he referred to the whole context, culture, pattern, etc.; Gendlin, 1978). From this perspective, we can understand psychotherapy and living as, first and foremost, an interactive movement of organicity, meaning-making, and world-building, wherein growth occurs hermeneutically betwixt body and world. This, indeed, is Gendlin's direct challenge to the determinism of biologism and postmodernism alike.

The human being is neither predetermined nor indeterminate, rather an implicit knowing. Gendlin reminds us that it is the nature of living things, including human beings, to implicitly anticipate a next step (for example, sprouting seeds imply the stem and leaf; honeycomb implies the hive; and human infants already infer relational connection, language, and culture). What Gendlin termed an implicit intricacy or responsive order is always more than, yet simultaneously shaped by the environmental situation. In this regard, language, culture, history, and concepts—all together—develop from the body and are carried forward, revised, refused, and wrestled with*in* this implicit organic knowing. The process of living is simply an ongoing interaction, an inseparable movement between the implicit knowing of the organism—the body—and language (by which Gendlin means culture or one's environment). While Gendlin believes this implicit knowing is inherently there, it is habitually overlooked. He shows how to access the implicit intentionally and directly through a *felt sensing* and to further embody it in a fresh formulation in self-reflective or psychotherapeutic practices. Because this sensing and this kind of thinking are richer than any preformulated concepts or habitual modes of being, it holds the potential of *re*forming the next step, of developing entirely new conceptualizations, and of even reconstituting deeply embedded cultural ways of being; this process forms bodies, culture, and worlds.

Against this background, we can understand the subtle force of the felt sense that gives rise to new possibilities. In attuning to and languaging our implicit bodily felt situation, the psychotherapeutic process *re*constitutes the whole of our living—the meaning-making *and* matter of our existence. The body is a knowing or intuitively organizing system. This does not suggest, however, that movement happens effortlessly for human beings. We often become rigid, stuck, and destructively repetitive, and how we respond to our life problems can further reify and reinforce them. We can foreclose our very own growth.

Gendlin was interested in this *stuck-ness*—reductive negatively reinforcing loop—regarding the practice of therapy and, more broadly, philosophy. Here, it is most vital to activate the felt sensing, notice the implicit where words falter, fail, and frustrate the limits of our language. It is a murky yet potent place. We often access this by recognizing that we have gotten it wrong—we have misrepresented a bodily felt sense of more. We can sense it within uneasiness or even irritation. We say something, and it lingers in a flattening way. Our patient tells us "...no, that isn't quite right," and we remain there with the knowing that anticipates words. From this felt yet unformulated sensing, we can then speak and move on from the implicit yet always responsive order into a domain of more specificity and vitality. We know it in the "Aha! Moment," even when that knowing is disorienting or disillusioning. We identify it as movement even in subtle, imperceptible forms. Just as plants quietly form stronger stems in response to higher wind environments, so are our clients' minute expressions, shifts, or gestures—the very inhabiting of their bodies—formed implicitly in, with, and forward in their environments. Movement can flourish by attending to—in nurturing—the responsive order within the therapeutic process. We must also query what is missing here or what is at risk. In other words, how do we attend to the natural growth process while trusting and distrusting the felt sense? How do we recognize when the familiar or intuitively felt sense is our foreclosure?

Distrusting the felt sense

Gendlin's use of the term responsive order attests to a human nature, even in the postmodern era, when it has fallen out of fashion. Considering our nature as an interactive forward movement can be both freeing and frightening. He makes it clear that growth is continually linked to a process of putting new words to our felt knowing—moving from the unformulated to the formulated in a continual hermeneutic, circular yet forward progression. However, if we are already and always in interaction with our environment, then what happens to ever-present yet unlanguaged conditions of dehumanization, restriction, and control of the implicit living process? What happens when those strong cultural forces are powerful, although they operate in the background? What happens when the suppression of living is implicit, functioning out of the realm of awareness, and works toward a splitting or an explicit *not knowing*? I believe that we find something challenging to feel and formulate there, requiring more than an inwardly felt bodily sensing. Thus, and this is the main crux—the tension that I work with here—I would like to carry Gendlin's concepts further forward to consider not only the therapeutic practice of attending to the responsive order but also the practice of attending to what we can call the *oppressive order* and explore how a bodily felt sensing could involve attention to both. While Gendlin famously asked what is next after postmodernism, I ask what is generative in staying with the conflicting orientations of trusting and distrusting the notion of a felt sense of meaning.

We can then examine how we foreground implicit cultural norms—the internalization *of* and complicity *in* the already embodied oppressive order. In my observations, this involves accessing the bodily felt sense and articulating what can be considered the *unfelt sense*—that which has been systematically dissociated from the body politic. In simple terms, this is the work of comprehending bodily consciousness *and* cultivating critical consciousness. These two practices are typically polarized in different psychological and political spheres. For example, recently, in supervision, a supervisee and highly trained therapist shared her wish to include political dimensions in therapy with her clients, yet viscerally felt a sense of impropriety. To be sure, integrating the political into the therapeutic process requires astute skill and a counterintuitive movement. In truth, critical consciousness involves a strange counter-turn—a distrusting of our bodily sensing.

Furthermore, this statement may seem to undermine the notion of embodied therapy but consider this.

In recent therapy work with a heterosexual couple addressing a painful pattern of resentment, abandonment, and disconnection (not an uncommon cycle), my male patient expressed a persistent need for more space from his female partner. He felt an urgent need for solitude as a given in his body. He would often simply say that he was a different kind of person than his partner and did not need as much intimacy as she desired. As we delved further, we identified his intersecting experience of gender role conditioning away from his vulnerability, and racism that compelled him, as a man of color, to have no wants for himself—no felt yearning—but to flee from impossible demands upon him. We became curious about the bodily felt desire for space as a protective measure *and* a foreclosure of sensing, of feeling his longing (which, of course, would involve his vulnerability). Considering this broader perspective toward implicit oppressive orders, he began first to feel disoriented and then to feel an initially strange yet palpable aspiration for connection—he began to feel his hunger for sustenance. This involved risking his embodied vulnerability—his hope for care and connection. Staying with these counterintuitively felt senses, the relationship dynamic began shifting to a space of more vibrant and mutual involvement. This movement began with a distrust of the visceral desire for distance.

Thus, this questioning of a bodily felt knowing employs a conscious alienation from what we take as given, even in our most palpably felt certainties. While Gendlin attests that we can always access the implicit responsive order—a bodily felt sensing of the next step forward—we can also perceive in the inseparable interaction of body, culture, and power that our intuition and response can involve a great deal of complicity, conformity, constriction, and foreclosure rather than forward movement. We can also understand that our felt sense is often so flooded by states of fear, shame, or simply numbness that we sense more of a not knowing than a knowing. More broadly, we can witness the foreclosure of human living in situations of systemic and intergenerational constriction of growth. Despite this, we perceive human life as inexplicably and creatively continuing.

In truth, considering the persistent dynamism of human nature alongside the destructive forces that explicitly foreclose human flourishing does evoke a perpetual conundrum. Holding this conceptual conflict in mind produces a tension that we could call *productive tension*. I believe that we cannot resolve it and must rigorously resist privileging one over the other. I find that Gendlin's articulation of this tension calls for further explication of the cultural dimension. In this regard, I want to center the language of critical theory—the cultural or critical model, which insists that philosophy serves to illuminate and help transform the social systems through which being human is already regulated, restricted, and positioned. Gendlin most certainly addresses culture as an interactive phenomenon. He effectively addresses the body/culture conundrum, conceptualizing the human being as the interaction between the two. The human being is inseparable from body and culture. Indeed, to be animated is to be in movement, generated in the relationship between every organism and its environment, in which each is constituted by and reconstituted in the other.

Nonetheless, just as Gendlin pays necessary and particular attention to the problem of thinking with the implicit unformulated (the felt sense), I want to pay more attention to the problem of power in the implicit linguistic–systemic restrictions (the unfelt sense). While I do not believe that Gendlin addresses power directly, I do think that he offers a valuable way to do so. He says something particularly encouraging about problems: "What was a problem *could be a* power" (Gendlin, 2017, p. 94). As we address the power of cultural determinism, we can also consider this predicament a potentiality. This has been true for me in the experiential process of developing critical consciousness in life and psychotherapy.

Bodily consciousness—Critical consciousness

Indeed, an Irish American woman came to me for psychotherapy, grappling with telling her nearly adult children of the sexual and physical abuse she suffered at the hands of her parents (their grandparents). She had undertaken many somatically focused treatments but had never spoken about the abuse explicitly with anyone. We began to identify that, even within the well-intentioned trauma field, the cultural yet bodily felt sense that she was contaminated was reinforced. It was the horror from which she shielded her children, yet it persisted as a problem to cure. In articulating with words, together with grounded pacing—not only the direct impact of abuse but also the cultural context in which she could not speak of it—she was already reconstituting something in her body and our shared world: an implicit order that functions to protect perpetrators and condemn victims. Far more than the fact of the abuse, she needed to articulate to her children her bodily knowing about the implicit oppressive order we live in. From here, she found not only words but her reason to tell her children. As a survivor, she and now her children carry this intergenerational burden—this knowing—forward, and in so doing, something is already different. Trauma has been called the invisible wound. I would say that this is true, not simply because it is predominantly psychological but, more so, because it is inflicted and re-inflicted in the implicit and always complicit, unlanguaged, unspoken structures of power embodied in our collective living. Her trauma and many survivors' wounds are compounded because of the cultural compulsion not to articulate the experience with words. Despite this, trauma does more than compromise aspects of embodiment—it heightens our awareness of and attunement *toward* embodiment (Chalfin, 2016). Thus, trauma not only impedes life; in responding to trauma, there is a knowing about life as it is—a knowing that contends directly with violence and the realities of our shared vulnerability and responsibility.

In the light of systemic trauma, I am simultaneously drawn and averse to Gendlin's adamant belief in the capacity for direct reference—his presumption that we can always access a bodily felt sense that implies the next step forward of our living process—implies precisely what is organically needed. He is probably right, though it is important to remember how difficult it can be to access. For my client, this took nearly half a lifetime; to articulate words that named the implicit oppressive situation before she could carry it forward and before her body could become a useful guide. In the meantime, the directly felt sense accessed in her body recapitulated the shame, the silence, the stuckness, and the unfelt yet powerfully present oppressive order. We all want—often desperately—that direct protective and accurate intuition that could guide our lives. That would be so nice! Or would it be too nice? What could be wrong with that notion? Does it leave anyone behind, and whom does it unwittingly serve? What happens when the felt sense recapitulates and reinforces false presuppositions? Perhaps, it does leave behind those who (like my client) are gripped in the inarticulate personal shame of the implicit oppressive order. Indeed, first they must find more explicit language illuminating the complicit and powerfully oppressive sociopolitical context they find themselves in.

While I did not face overt abuse and violence like my client, I struggled with a similarly implicit, unformulated, yet ever so powerful sense of self as an object rather than an agentic subject, further compounded by an idealized humanistic view that I should feel limitless and whole. It was my Women's Studies (now called Gender and Sexuality Studies) advisor who invited me to relinquish my felt sense of individuality. Her critical, sometimes even pessimistic lens, however unsettling at the time, was a catalyst for growth far greater than any humanistic optimism I had inherited.

Set squarely in my cultural context and compelled to take a hard look at what had long been implicit, seemingly benign, yet stunningly powerful social conditioning, as we carefully read through the feminist canon from Beauvoir to bell hooks to Butler, it was interesting that in naming alienation, I somehow felt more myself and more connected. In articulating a deadness, I could already feel more alive. Yes, it was devastating, but exhilarating. I viscerally experienced the reductivism operating in the idealism of my upbringing giving way to new ground. Sometimes, this new ground was groundless. However, there was a sensation of my feet being more firmly planted, my body more intentionally moving, and my mind more engaged, despite being disoriented. Strangely, in considering myself a social construct, I was more aware of my place in the collective and agentic in my physical being. In articulating what felt *dehumanizing*, my classmates and I could access more humanity in ourselves and one another; this was humanity in which language and body, vulnerability and power, were inextricably linked and lived.

This circular unsettling and re-grounding movement is not necessarily comfortable. It was probably more bearable to have explicit language and rigorous relational support from my advisor to relinquish false securities toward a more consciously situated and critically aware embodiment. Indeed, she skillfully roused us with what she called the "walking power of talk" (Caruso, 1997, p. iii), shifting from the reductive power of "rhetorical language" to the mutually embodied, vulnerable, and powerful "poetics of conversation" (Caruso, 1983, pp. 104–106). Further, she explained that we do not simply use language—we walk it, wear it, or *are* it (Caruso, 1997, p. vi). Reckoning with my situatedness through this wider critical lens and connection was a medium for therapeutic growth equally transformative to any undertaking of formal psychotherapy. One can imagine how transformative critical and bodily consciousness is when cultivated together.

Indeed, it is potent alchemy to engage critical consciousness and bodily consciousness. I think it is necessary to point out different ways of understanding our felt knowing, sensing, and bodily dwelling in the world and consider what is obscured when we maintain a more singular view. If we place our trust entirely in Gendlin's direct reference, we risk reifying the implicitly biased and hierarchically based encoding of human nature. If we over-ascribe human experience to cultural determinants alone, we may miss the agentic nature of human growth. What more nuanced and productively intertwined ways of understanding invite us toward our embodiment? To further explore these questions, we can now consider three modes—three orders—(1) the complicit oppressive order, (2) the implicit responsive order, and (3) (what I think we can call) the explicit disruptive order or *dis*order. Attending to the complicit oppressive order engages a deconstructive mode of dismantling supremacist systems surrounding human nature, belonging, and becoming. This is the work of critical theory and the praxis of critical consciousness. Attending to the implicit responsive order activates a somatic mode of bodily sensing in meaning-making. This belongs to Gendlin's reclamation of human nature as an implicit and organic interaction between body and environment, always generating movement forward. Finally, attending to the disruptive order or disorder engages constructivist dimensions of critical theory and queer theory that center disordered multiplicity as fundamental to existence, embodiment, and world-building. I want to consider these differential potentialities of growth specifically within contexts of alienation.

The oppressive order

While human beings develop resiliency in interactive friction, akin to plant stems thickening in winds that evoke more durability, winds that are chaotically or systematically too destructive hinder rather than foster the flourishing of life. Indeed, a growing body of research demonstrates the sociobiological impact of systematic subordination in foreclosing and foreshortening the human lifespan. The aptly termed phenomena of "weathering" evokes the cumulative effects of systemic oppression, particularly the foreshortening of Black women's lives, irrespective of the material conditions of economic advantage or disadvantage. In this regard, the morbid intersection of implicit racism and sexism is so forceful that it transcends the materiality of financial progress and protections (Geronimus et al., 2006). Indeed, the implicitly operating oppressive order conditions the entire body–environment interaction and, to be sure, forecloses human potentiality. Thus, I want to consider philosophers alongside Gendlin, who come from the phenomenological tradition yet demonstrate that it is insufficient to examine the role of the body in human meaning-making without also examining the totalizing nature of the implicit social shaping, the naturalized oppression, and subsequent suppression of not only subjectivity but also of objective embodiment.

Thus, I now turn first to Simone de Beauvoir and then to Frantz Fanon, both icons of the French existential-phenomenological movements—each an influential progenitor of gender and critical race studies, offering constructive possibilities for theorizing the particularities of the gendered and raced body in repressive contexts of patriarchal and colonial power. While they are decidedly not the final word on these subjects, they set the stage for particular attention to implicit cultural power alongside Gendlin's philosophy of the implicit. While phenomenologists have broadly critiqued the domination of consciousness in terms of the subject/object divide, these two theorists brought attention to the effects of literal, yet paradoxically implicit, dehumanization of bodies such that the lived body becomes exploitable and disposable.

Beginning with Beauvoir—a white female philosopher and writer who carved out a voice in an almost entirely male-dominated field, publishing the seminal *The Second Sex* (2009/1949) in 1949, just three years before Fanon's timeless *Black Skin, White Masks* (2008/1952) in 1952—we see that, as a phenomenologist trained to examine embodiment, Beauvoir turns her attention to exploring questions of freedom and introduces the notion of gender as a social construct. She examines gender as a system of power relations wherein women are alienated from their full humanity, subject to survival through complicity in the disavowal of their freedom. Beauvoir offers, in detail, a material account of women's *unfreedom*, explained in terms of unequal social positioning through subordination to and dependence on men. She illustrates that not only are women unfree in a material sense, having fewer resources and fewer opportunities than men, but on a more ontological level, women are unfree as "Other." This existential Otherness fuels women's complicity in their unfreedom. To be Other in this existential sense means to be the passive object to man's active subject. Where man embodies the human Subject, woman is considered the *Object* and *Other* even unto herself. The male-bodied subject transcends his immanence, while his disavowed corporeality is projected onto the female body, which absorbs associations with birth, mothering, death, animality, nature, and vulnerability. Thus, woman as eternal matter, materially defined by her bodily reproductive capabilities, is narrowly idealized and implicitly, if not explicitly, debased. As Other—and, to be clear, less than human—women's agentic living is circumscribed on mythical and mundane levels.

The dehumanizing and internalizing effect of the concept of the Other, whether fetishized, romanticized, pathologized, or reviled, becomes critical in theories analyzing the experiences of marginal bodies—colonized, enslaved, or systematically alienated human beings across matrices of oppression. To be the Other is to inhabit the non-human, the negative: it is *not-to-be* or *to-be-an-object* of gratification and exploitation. To be the Other is to be an object—reduced to materiality, to immanence. If classical phenomenology is centered on movement expressed in the hopefulness and power of transcendent agency, then critical gender and race phenomenologists have had to highlight the bodily and social experience of restriction, mystification, precarity, violation, and literal or social death. Indeed, human living and flourishing require both imminence and transcendence—body and language in a constructive process of living. Beauvoir (2009/1949) attests that "in truth, all human existence is transcendence and immanence at the same time; to go beyond itself, it must maintain itself; to thrust itself toward the future, it must integrate the past into itself" (p. 443). In this regard, she accounts not only for the conditions of repression in women's lives but for the ingredients of regeneration—of reclamation and what would become the women's revolution. Indeed, Beauvoir argues that women's exploitation is historical and amenable to change. Existentially, however, such transformation requires that women are responsible for rejecting the temptations of comfort and discovering the pleasures alongside the risks of freedom.

Similarly, the beloved liberation philosopher and psychologist Frantz Fanon, born in the colony of Martinique and trained in the ivory towers of the French academy, furthers our understanding of the conditions of bodily experiences of non-being and the cost and urgency of embodying freedom. As a black man inhabiting the bourgeois academic world, fluent and prolific in his oppressors' language (French), Fanon still finds himself forever marked as flawed and feared as the debased Other. He writes that for the racially disinherited, the world over, "life [is] not a flowering or a development of an essential productiveness, but a permanent struggle against an omnipresent death" (1965, p. 128). This omnipresent death looms large, regardless of educational and economic efforts to enter life's opportunities. Indeed, Fanon speaks to white imperial colonial conditions that construct a codified world in which black existence is rendered a "living death." Furthermore, he theorizes that in embodying a negation, the Other, the oppressed, no longer acts, extends, or moves as himself in the world; instead, it is as if he is amputated, losing his very own sense of bodily agency (Fanon, 2008/1952). In classical phenomenology, wherein the body is experienced as "successful," as being "able" to extend itself, acting on and in the world, Fanon exposes this agentic "success" not as a measure of competence but the bodily form of privilege itself; the ability to move through the world productively is an advantage, not a personal achievement. For bodies cast as the Other, bodily knowing and literal movement cannot escape the totalizing project of the oppressive order.

In particular, Fanon highlights the phenomenological conditioning of language and the effect of bodily alienation in contexts of dehumanization. One cannot learn and speak a language without embodying the embedded equations of purity with whiteness and malevolence with blackness: to be white is simply to be, while to be black is to be bad. European humanism, namely its racism and sexism, has severe psychological costs contributing to complicity and fragmentation of consciousness such that addressing this alienation requires what Fanon calls no less than an "inner revolution" (2008/1952, p. 175). This inner revolution or regenerative process requires explication. We can see that this process engages a direct reference to the felt sense and yet requires particular attention to complicity and agency. Like Gendlin, Fanon postulates that this potentially revolutionary process does reside in the body-language interaction. Fanon reflects that in employing the colonizing language as a black subject, he already embodies the disruption of purity (whiteness) at its core. Consider Fanon's prayer to his body even in the face of disembodying racism: "Oh my body, always make me a man who questions!" (2008/1952, p. 206). Fanon asks of his body not to be seduced by forms of being-in-the-world that normalize violence and dehumanization—not to be seduced by illusions of safety secured through subordinate belonging. To do so is to question the bodily felt sense that seeks protection through complicity; it is to distrust and trust the body again as a source of knowing.

Fanon and Beauvoir attune to a paradoxical trust and distrust of bodily sensation and situation, cultivating a particular resistance toward the familiar. In reckoning with the entanglement of complicity and freedom, language and body, and most importantly, power, they already embody a different kind of agency—a capacity to make use of their otherness and imagine a world otherwise, one that draws on the ability to look critically and beyond what appears to be given. The response to the problem becomes a source of power. This explicit articulation of the implicit oppressive order evokes a response. Is this a part of Gendlin's implicit responsive order as well? I think so, but it must be carried forward explicitly. Distrust is as crucial as trust in directly accessing the felt meaning in the body beyond cultural conditions. Indeed, what feels organic must become strange and suspect. This is the beginning of disrupting complicity.

Like Gendlin, Fanon and Beauvoir seek to regenerate Western Humanism in a vitally specific way. While Gendlin seeks to wrestle western philosophy from its reductive tendencies and dualities, Fanon and Beauvoir seek to wrestle it from racism, sexism, and, more broadly, imperialism, and in the process, from the psychological grip of complicity. To do this is to resist the oppressive order, turning everything upside down through rethinking re-embodiment out of dehumanized existence. This is, first and foremost, to recognize that these oppressive systems are not givens but are historical constructs felt in the body as a natural order long before they are dissonant.

The responsive order

In life, and particularly in the work of psychotherapy, it becomes evident that critical consciousness alone is not enough to sustain growth and healing; a full critical consciousness requires bodily consciousness. While wholly naming the constitutive force of social constructs is essential, in doing so, it is easy to fall into cultural determinism bypassing the inseparabilities and possibilities of the body. Here, Gendlin is beneficial and, in this section, I will highlight the points at which bodily consciousness crosses, connects, and enlivens critical consciousness. Indeed, Gendlin's philosophy infuses critical and cultural theories with bodily wisdom and draws them closer to emancipatory purposes. Attunement to the implicit responsive order is a crucial corrective to the ever-seductive pull toward reductivity. Gendlin continually evokes a circular hermeneutic of being that resists all forms of determinism. It follows from within the responsive order; the language, the logic, and the structures of domination are of our human design. Therefore, surely, we must then be able to recreate something in response and resistance. Gendlin is positive that we *already* are. He reminds us that "we are not passive entities ruled by theoretical energy forces" (Gendlin, 2017, p. 104). We actively created these very cultural structures, and we can recreate them.

Further, he would say that we are this very interaction; a human being is this circular forward, moving interaction. "We *are* our next step (our *next stepping*)" (Gendlin, 2017, p. 104). In this spirit, both Beauvoir and Fanon identify the body as a site of oppression and a source of consciousness and change. This, too, reminds me of my college professor, who continually alerts us that we are "walking our talk." Our bodies imply the language that shapes our cultural patterns, which we then carry further. Gendlin also understands that however growth-oriented the human organism may be, we would certainly die without enough environmental sustenance. For socially wired human beings, this sustenance is chiefly experiences of belonging to the collective.

Nevertheless, even when the collective is corrosive, Gendlin attests that in response—this is fundamental to therapy—we can always attune to this problem as a source of new meaning-making. We can engage the bodily felt sensing that calls for something other, that "knows with a gnawing, like something forgotten, but what it knows may be new in the history of the world" (p. 283) how to live out of even the most dehumanized contexts. The movement may be slow. Even as we attune to and expand our conception of human nature in the face of restricted cultural norms, we wrestle with our tendency to disavow our full embodiment; this wrestling continues pushing our expression and languaging of human nature further. It is a slow, circular, and iterative process; we sometimes need to catch up with the language because it is dynamic. For example, we can no longer speak simply from or for the category of women without reinforcing or consciously dismantling its implicit exclusionary and reductive power: we now speak of the lived body, of living our gendered body. We no longer speak simply in black and white as a natural given; we speak of racial caste systems, coalitions, and constructed dimensions of race, ethnicity, and racialized embodiment.

This is an uneasy, persistent generative existence of the corporeal and cultural body. Even while reconceptualizing and living forward, we are aware that we risk foreclosing something. For Gendlin, working with this circular problem involves, first and foremost, attending to the implicit movement that is always already there. He insists that the responsive order "is more determinative than explicit [cultural] forms" (Gendlin, 2017, p. 304), and that even for the most socially constricted, the most traumatized, the innermost feeling will continue to imply its next step and what is needed, sometimes repeatedly. Here, we arrive at perhaps his most generative of observations. Gendlin perceives that "the human being prefers the openness even when it is difficult—prefers this to easy next steps" (p. 94). We are not born whole (contrary to the ethos I was raised within)—we are born in the implicit, and we grow with interaction.

The human being grows specifically in generative friction, with and within its environment, and withers in overly protected or alternately precarious situations. Perhaps, this helps us understand the high rates of resiliency in marginalized communities, where relational and meaning-making capacities strengthen like plant stems facing strong winds buffering the stress of the environment. Perhaps, it also helps us understand the rising rates of hopelessness, desperation, and even what is termed *deaths by despair* (referring to increased deaths by suicide and overdose) in more seemingly protected communities, for example, white working-age male populations facing increasing job insecurities (Case and Deaton, 2015) in contexts of deindustrialization. Here, we see how power and advantage do not necessarily equate to or sustain growth. Growth follows responsive embodied interaction with life, not illusory or temporary positions of security.

Of the responsive order, Gendlin (2017) writes, "Something continues where the words stop. We reach an edge where we sense more" (p. 205). For Gendlin, we comprise that "more." It is helpful to remember here that Gendlin had an interesting cross-cultural experience with language when he entered elementary school in the United States as an English language learner after he and his parents fled Nazi Austria. At this early age, he already began to access a sensing—a felt knowing—independent of one conceptual, linguistic pattern or another, yet simultaneously entangled in these same patterns. Meaning and sense-making operate beyond what words can articulate and yet language constitutes how we think. He writes about this very linguistic, somatic conundrum of living:

> So far, it has been understood only as a problem. I will turn it to advantage. What seems like a problem becomes a power...Since we always think with both [the pattern and the felt sense], we can do so deliberately. We can employ their inseparable togetherness...
>
> (2017, p. 195)

In this way, Gendlin challenges philosophical dualisms, the binary splits, and reversals of philosophy, privileging discourse over materiality, language over body, and becoming over being. He writes eloquently and emphatically challenging postmodernism attesting that "[w]here others see indeterminacy, we find intricacy an always unfinished order that cannot be represented but has to be taken along as we think" (2017, p. 81). Rather than settling with the arguably thin endpoint of not-being, of "nothingness," Gendlin argues for an intricate "something." This "something," this more, is neither reified nor rendered immaterial. Rather, it is felt as movement; it can be observed as a living forward, an ever-evolving relationship with the embodied and meaning-making necessities definitive of being-in-the-world. Gendlin's reformulation of the problem of language and body is grounded in the hermeneutics of being, in a circular forward movement rather than a resolution of opposites. While the ability to access one's bodily felt sense is perhaps not always a given, as he posits, we can observe that somehow, it is never fully repressed. Engaging with this tension enlivens and restores critical and cultural theories with creatively subversive rather than reductive purposes.

When the (aforementioned) young man in couples' therapy reflects with me upon his taken-for-granted preference for distance and reconsiders, indeed reconfigures, the possibility of a relationship wherein his heretofore unfelt vulnerability is felt, we are in the productive tension of the implicit responsive and oppressive orders. Indeed, one can understand this as Gendlin's instinctual responsive order that animates the capacity to critique the cultural patterns we create and then experience in a totalizing way. Thus, the problem that becomes a power is not powerful because we can use it as a tool to be entirely free from the conundrum, but because the problem is powerful in our very act of living it, even when we cannot reverse, resolve, or transcend it. This attention to tension is a necessary antidote to false comforts and polarizations, whether one exists in the "somethingness" or "nothingness" of existence.

The same phenomena were operating in the disillusioning yet exhilarating experience during my time in Women's Studies. As I named the totalizing impact of the implicit oppressive order and grappled with the unfelt bodily sense of not-being in my body, I felt a disorienting yet enlivening movement in naming the problem. Is this the sensing forward of Gendlin's human nature? I think so; however, it also included the sensation of disillusionment involved in any genuine critical consciousness or growth process. It should be remembered that Gendlin asserts we can only truly understand the human organism and the cultural environment as "one interaction" (Gendlin, 2017, p. 222), as "body-environment interaction first" (p. 232) and before they are perceptually separated.

This lived interaction and life energy is described somewhat differently and quite aptly by Gendlin scholar and existential psychotherapist Greg Madison (2014) as both *"potential* and *pessimism* released by an acknowledging of how things *really* are" (p. 5). The naming of the negation of being as an affirmation of being? The body knows what it cannot say or even feel. When the unfelt sense of despair, social death, and literal death is named, this languaging and critical consciousness animates the body with life energy to live more through its knowing, question its situation, and connect in sustaining generativity. We are alive then, not because we have changed the implicit oppressive order but because we have changed the terms that disavow our capacity to know it. Therefore, we pay more attention to our alienation. In naming it, there is already movement—let us remember that to be alive is to be animate rather than inanimate.

Beauvoir and Fanon are acutely alive in their languaging of their alienation. The question of how to live in our finite situation enlivens us even in its impossibility. Heidegger's resolute *question* of how to be toward our finitude (Heidegger, 1962) evokes this very "exhilarating pessimism" that we can understand not as an answer but as an experiencing forward (Madison, 2014). Indeed, I posit here that holding critical consciousness alongside Gendlin's bodily consciousness fosters continual questioning and attending to the implicit body and culture, which, in turn, reconstitutes, or what Gendlin would say regenerates, the very same situation.

The disruptive order

Questioning as a mode of being, even as definitive of being, is undoubtedly an existential and phenomenological concern. Feminist and critical race theorists further orient this questioning mode toward the implicit and oppressive background order. Recall Fanon's appeal to his body to live in the question of his existence—to resist the given conditions or governed responses to these conditions. This questioning as the basis of resisting complicity is foundational to critical consciousness and the shift from reactive to a regenerative lived embodiment. Queer theorists take this questioning—the very sensation of disorientation—in a fresh manner. Indeed, bare attention to questioning, *dis*order, and disruption can evoke movement (although not always what would be considered forward or linear development). I want to conclude this chapter by attending to this third dimension of movement as it is particularly dear to my non-linear growth and constitutes the bedrock of how I have come to understand therapeutic action.

While not explicit in Gendlin's theorizing, I see the implicit connections and want to highlight the richness in considering disorder alongside order. Queer theory, in particular, positions disorientation as a situation not of certain desperation but of radical concern, possibility, and aliveness. So too, as psychotherapists, we know that disorientation and disorder are not only quite distressing but also, with relational attunement, fruitful: with questioning, searching, and feeling the possibilities of just where life feels the most impossible, our suffering serves as an opening to further possibilities. For queer theorists, attending to Gendlin's "more," excess, or that something beyond what language can say fuels a potential *reorienting* of the living process and disorienting of the oppressive order. For example, in the experience of affirming a sexual orientation, gender expression, or relationship outside the lines of heteronormativity, the givens that construct our notion of human nature are unsettled. It is an attunement toward the bodily sensibilities beyond language structures; it is to live in the spaces between the unspeakable and speech, and to walk and talk out of socially delineated lines. It is to step out of line with what is given and what we have adhered to in our most habitual, constricted, and self-protective states. Again, this reminds me of my advisors' summons to a path of "walking our talk," however far out of line.

Queer phenomenologist Sarah Ahmed notes that to be oriented is to be in line. It is to follow a map that others have already drawn and that others already follow. She posits that "we are 'in line', when we face the direction that is already faced by others. Being 'in line' allows bodies to extend into spaces that…have already taken shape" (Ahmed, 2006, p. 15). We could say that being in line is related to being connected and assured of a livable place in the world. To be oriented is not only to have ease and freedom of movement but also to move in social connection—to have kinship as the necessary ingredient that sustains human life. In Gendlin's terms, it is to have the regenerative human organism and environment interaction supported. Unfortunately, this socially sustained movement is foreclosed for many worldwide, and the image of the closet where one's disavowed embodiment is safely sequestered out of social sight is still apt. This closet or cultural constriction often operates implicitly and pervasively. We may not even notice that we are operating from within this closet, that we are oriented in this way until something collides so that we become aware of our implicitly constricted movements and narrowly programmed orientations. Only in this rupture or disruption can we begin to open possibilities and reshape the course of conditioned complicity. Something slips out and opens a door— and now, of course, it feels as if we are talking about psychoanalysis and the uncanny slips of the tongue, dreams that highlight what could not be said, associations that reflect what has not yet been felt—the movement between the unconscious and the conscious, the bodily felt unknown or psychoanalytically what we now call the *unthought known* (Bollas, 2018).

While Gendlin challenged any reified notion of the unconscious, he beautifully articulated working with the implicit regenerative process or movement between unformulated, formulated, and reformulated experience (Gendlin, 1997/1967). Carrying this same exquisitely detailed process forward, I urge us to focus on how we formulate implicitly operating social orders. In psychotherapy, we then attend to these socially delineated lines and each person's implicit disorientation and sensations out of line, outside their habitual modes of speech and belonging. We can consider the psychic costs of closets, other forms of social constriction, and the social gains of maintaining norms. We can name the risks of more authentic belonging. We can linger there in the disarray of implicit orders, the disordering vulnerability, sensing the darkness for vitality and visceral connection. This queered understanding of human growth is certainly not just about sexual orientation or gender identification. It is about bearing the disruptive truths—the full breadth of our felt knowing—even as we confront life's unknowability and live into its real possibility. Indeed, when attending in particular ways to sensations and meaning-makings that disrupt the natural order, we may come even closer to embodying Gendlin's sense of promise in the power of focusing on the felt sense. Within Gendlin's framework of the responsive order, we can find a skillful commitment to staying with the unsettling sense of the yet unlanguaged, unformulated, the next step in living, etc. With a queered understanding, this attunement to organic order can be sensitive to organic disorder or disruption as constitutive of living, of vitality itself.

Bodily and critical consciousness is evoked when we actively seek to live from the disjunction between organism and environment while questioning the implicitly operating social rules. In this disruptive or disordered questioning, we expose, dislodge, and resituate our material and existential possibilities. Consider Beauvoir, who was "free" of marriage (having no dowry) and supported herself by training in philosophy and then teaching the subject in high schools, eventually establishing herself as a philosopher and an icon of the feminist movement. In Beauvoir, we see a woman who lived in the disruption and reformulated the constrictions of her existence. She embraced the financial and social precarity of her gendered social role, defying notions of spinsterhood, and lived this situation; she lived her work passionately, boldly explored her sexuality, taking lovers of the same and opposite genders, and freely enjoyed a lifelong romantic and intellectual companionship (with Sartre) outside the strictures of marriage. This movement must involve material and existential vulnerability, yet it evokes an embodied vitality. Indeed, however filled with anguish, one can take pleasure in living the truth of one's unfolding questioning.

By living into our questions (however disruptive) and bearing their consequences and unanswerability, we cultivate critical consciousness, embodied resistance, and the capacity for knowing and not knowing. There is an inescapable tension or circularity between turning to and away from bodily cues—or we could say trusting and distrusting human sensing and meaning-making. In bearing tension, we find, hermeneutically, movement and connection forward and Gendlin's regenerative responsive order. I experienced this "rapturous" questioning of my situatedness in gender and sexuality studies—I experienced the heightened embodiment in querying the conditions of my social positioning. In the work of psychotherapy, I observe the disruptive role of attending to one's felt sense that, however unsettling, stirs a further knowing that opens toward generative and connective movement.

Conclusion

What did we learn about Gendlin's human nature, psychotherapy, growth processes, and power? More specifically, what is the responsive order? How does it work? Gendlin insists that we can know how it works. It works with the implicit at organismic and environmental levels. We come from an unformulated organic inwardly felt sensing, and we also come from cultural forces operating in highly formulated yet unfelt ways. Both are inherently implicit; thus, I argue that both require phenomenological "analysis." As they are bodily and culturally obscured, unformulated, and unfelt, any movement toward an embodied knowing thus requires a *critical phenomenological* analysis in which we consider the whole interaction—the human condition in all its yearnings. This movement forward must then involve an exercise of disorientation, vulnerability, and culpability. Working within this productive tension and attending to the inseparable power of language, body, and situation fuels the hermeneutic movement of therapy—in fact, growth of any kind—forward.

Alongside Gendlin's exquisite attention to the implicit responsive order, a complete account of and reckoning with the oppressive order allows for a regenerative engagement with disorder, disruption, and the destruction of norms that foreclose human flourishing. When the state of questioning, critiquing, and living the unanswerability is shared, it allows us to move from alienation—from the unfelt—to exhilarating embodiment and openness, which, in turn, animates a more truthful and vibrant world. Disorder and disorientation then become a useful reconstituting of the implicit order. Questioning the otherness of being is thus embodied as ontological and necessary disorientation. In closing, I invite you to turn toward your unfelt sensations; linger in unfamiliar encounters; contemplate points of tension; language your disorientation; live your questioning body; reconstitute your world wherein human nature is indeed generative, necessarily disruptive, and abundantly life-giving.

References

Ahmed, S. (2006). *Queer phenomenology: Orientations, objects, others*. Duke University Press. https://doi.org/10.1515/9780822388074

Bollas, C. (2018). *The shadow of the object: Psychoanalysis of the unthought known*. Routledge.

Caruso, B. (1983). The difference between poetry and rhetoric. *Earlhamite: Magazine of Earlham College, 104*(1), 18.

Caruso, B. A. (1997). *The words we wear: Talking and walking* [Baccalaureate address]. Commencement ceremony, Earlham College, Richmond, IN. Available from: https://earlham.edu/media/445737/1997address.pdf

Case, A., & Deaton, A. (2015). Rising morbidity and mortality in midlife among white non-Hispanic Americans in the 21st century. *Proceedings of the National Academy of Sciences, 112*(49), 15078–15083. https://doi.org/10.1073/pnas.1518393112

Chalfin, R. R. (2016). Being broken and unbroken: Trauma, Heidegger, and Befindlichkeit. In E. R. Severson, B. W. Becker, & D. M. Goodman (Eds.), *In the wake of trauma: Psychology and philosophy for the suffering other* (pp. 99–118). Duquesne University Press.

Chalfin, R. R. (2021). The entanglement of being: Sexuality inside and outside the binary. *Studies in Gender and Sexuality, 22*(1), 28–39. https://doi.org/10.1080/1524 0657.2021.1883847

de Beauvoir, S. (2009). *The second sex* (C. Borde and S. Malovany-Chevallier, Trans.). Alfred A. Knopf. (Original work published in 1949.)

Fanon, F. (1965) *A dying colonialism* (H, Chevalier, Trans.) Grove Press. (Original work published in 1959).

Fanon, F. (2008). *Black skin, white masks* (R. Philcox, Trans.). Grove Press. (Original work published in 1952.)

Gendlin, E. T. (2017). *Saying what we mean: Implicit precision and the responsive order* (E. S. Casey and D. M. Schoeller, Eds.). Northwestern University Press. https://doi.org/10.2307/j.ctv7tq4qc

Gendlin, E. T. (1978). *Focusing*. Everest House.

Gendlin, E. T. (1997). *Experiencing and the creation of meaning*. Northwestern University Press. (Original work published in 1967.)

Gendlin, E.T. (1997, November). On cultural crossing. Paper presented at the Conference on After Postmodernism, University of Chicago, Chicago, IL.

Geronimus, A. T., Hicken, M., Keene, D., & Bound, J. (2006). "Weathering" and age patterns of allostatic load scores among Blacks and Whites in the United States. *American Journal of Public Health, 96*(5), 826–833. https://doi.org/10.2105/AJPH.2004.060749

Heidegger, M. (1962). *Being and time* (J. Macquarrie & E. Robinson, Trans.). SCM Press.

Madison, G. (2014). Exhilarating pessimism: Focusing-oriented existential therapy. In G. Madison (Ed.), *Theory and practice of focusing-oriented psychotherapy: Beyond the talking cure* (pp. 113–127). Jessica Kingsley Publishers.

Chapter 6

Liberating language

Gendlin and Nietzsche on the refreshing power of metaphors

Sigridur Thorgeirsdottir

I belong to the type of philosophers who always felt that philosophy was not only something one learns by going through a standard curricula but also something that is intricately connected to one's own life and experiences. One of the benefits of engaging with Eugene Gendlin's philosophy is not only the thrill of getting to know a process ontology that offers a richer understanding of our place and being on this earth, with ourselves and others. Gendlin's philosophy also gives one the hope of becoming more oneself in thinking by offering methodological tools that strengthen one in thinking for oneself. His focusing-based methodology of Thinking at the Edge that he developed with Mary Hendricks and Kye Nelson fills a gap in philosophical education and research training in general. I wish I had been introduced to this methodology while I was studying philosophy since it captures how ideas emerge not only by reading and writing but also through our experiences and living.

I am the sort of philosopher who has always held that philosophy is not just something one learns through some standard curriculum, but always intricately connected to one's life. Finding Gendlin's philosophy was therefore nothing short of a life changing point in my philosophical life and career. Until then, I had adhered to the type of philosophies that emphasize what I have come to call embodied critical thinking. Nietzsche's philosophy of the body and embodied thinking, phenomenologies of embodiment and feminist philosophies of situated knowledge are foundational aspects of my own philosophy embodied critical thinking.[1] I have come to see these approaches as the path that led me to Gendlin's philosophy. They continue deepening my own ideas about embodied critical and creative thinking within philosophy, not the least when explored in light of Gendlin's methodology of embodied thinking that opens one's eyes to potential implicit features of a methodology of embodied thinking in theories of embodied cognition. Radical advances in philosophy of embodied cognition like Gendlin's can show the past and present of philosophy in a different light and allow to unearth possibilities there that one was not aware of before. I was therefore quite surprised when I found out that Gendlin himself as well as a few other contributors to the collection of articles in *Language Beyond Postmodernism: Saying and Thinking in Gendlin's Philosophy*, edited by David M. Levin (1997), present

DOI: 10.4324/9781003296706-7

Nietzsche as antipode to embodied thinking. They view him as the pioneer of a Neo-Nietzschean, postmodernist representationalism according to which our knowledge of reality is reduced to linguistic and symbolic signification. In their depictions, Nietzsche is the opposite to Gendlin's efforts to state the body as an order of its own that partakes in linguistic articulation of reality.

The goal of this paper is to show that Nietzsche's philosophy of embodied expression offers a needed missing link in the "Neo-Nietzschean" representationalist theories under critique by Gendlin and other co-authors of *Language Beyond Postmodernism*. I contend that Gendlin and Nietzsche are allies rather than antipodes when it comes to renewing our understanding of philosophical thinking and its linguistic expression. This becomes evident in Gendlin's theory of metaphoric thinking which is very much a dialogue with Nietzsche's philosophy of metaphors. Gendlin develops further Nietzsche's theory of metaphoric thinking further by explicating how:

> Classically, metaphor was said to be a crossing between two single situations. My **first modification** of the theory is to argue that there is only one single situation, the new one. The so-called old situation is not actually a single situation, but rather the whole use-family. The word brings all of its many, many old uses into this new situation. What crosses are not two situations, but a use-family and a situation (Gendlin, 1995).

Critique of representationalism

Gendlin (1991) acknowledges that Nietzsche was a philosophical pioneer with his idea "that the body has a reason of its own, superior to reason. He lauded the 'wisdom of the body,' and spoke of tending it like a garden." He furthermore states that Nietzsche "also called the body a primordial disorder on which order must be forced from outside. At most, one can choose what sort of work of art to make of oneself and others. In Nietzsche's work the self-creation has no feedback" (Gendlin, 1991).[2]

> also called the body a primordial disorder on which order must be forced from outside. At most, one can choose what sort of work of art to make of oneself and others. In Nietzsche's work the self-creation has no feedback.

Gendlin describes what he means by feedback here:

> The experts tell you not to be fixed in your thinking, but they don't tell you how to become free and open. If you pay *direct attention to your sense of anything*, that opens you up. Start reading, for instance, and stop at any point. Stay with what you're feeling right then, even if it seems vague or blank at first. Just know that you may have a sensation of something opaque, uncomfortable for a few seconds. But then you'll find the texture—it's always there.
>
> (Gendlin, 1979)

From a Gendlinian perspective of embodied linguistic expression, there is more at stake in this description than a critique of representationalism or of what is lacking in social constructivist understanding of knowledge and meaning-making. The need for language to get "beyond postmodernism" is driven by an ethical and emancipatory impetus to liberate ourselves from a disembodied understanding of knowledge and language that permeates in Gendlin's view modern philosophy from Kant to Nietzsche and Freud: "Lacan emphasizes in Freud what comes from Kant and Nietzsche: The 'id' has no order; therefore order can only be something that is externally imposed. What is imposed upon is not capable of meaningful feedback" (Gendlin, 1991). The embodied sources of individual self-constitution are blocked out with this philosophical-psychoanalytical idea, making Gendlin (1993) further claim that after Nietzsche, the Western hope for free individuals:

> was viewed as mere "ideology"—inherently impossible. Individual experience was thought to have no role to play. What is not primitive in the individual was considered to be the creation of past domination. Only new domination—imposed social engineering—seemed possible to those who sought political "liberation."
>
> (Gendlin, 1993)

Even though Neo-Nietzschean thinkers referred to by Scharff in *Language beyond Postmodernism* may largely or partly be understood as proponents of representational understanding of language and meaning, Nietzsche's philosophy of self-creation and embodied linguistic expression is overlooked. It seems to me that with this understanding of Nietzsche's philosophy, Gendlin mainly read Nietzsche through the optical lens of Foucault, because he only refers to Foucault's text on "Nietzsche, Genealogy, History" (1977) when placing Nietzsche under the heading of postmodern theories and a psychoanalytical model of oppression. This tradition of Western philosophy is hence in a negative sense a historical point of departure for Gendlin's own philosophy of embodied and emancipatory expression. Placing Nietzsche's position under "Neo Nietzscheans" like Scharff (1997) explicitly does in *Language beyond Postmodernism* does not do justice to Nietzsche's philosophy of embodied and embedded being. Nietzsche was a thinker of personal liberation and self-creation precisely by means of one's embodied way of thinking as opposed to dominance of moralistic discourses, sterile, one-sided rationalistic thinking and cliché-expressions of those lost in conceptual abstractions. The parallels in Gendlin's and Nietzsche's philosophies are far greater than their differences in terms of their epistemological, ontological and ethical understanding of the human subject. As a critic of morals, Nietzsche contributed to a philosophical and psychological model of oppression that is central to theories characterized as Neo-Nietzschean. His reflections on self-creation and thinking for oneself, creatively and critically, is no less significant for his philosophy, although it has been neglected within the Neo-Nietzschean theories Gendlin and his co-authors criticize in *Language Beyond Postmodernism.*

As for Gendlin, Nietzsche's philosophy of language, his understanding of the embodied basis of linguistic and symbolic expression, has a foundation in his philosophy of metaphors. In his early text on "Truth and Lies in a Nonmoral Sense" (1873), the metaphor displays the generation of articulation from an embodied sentiment that leads to an image that in turn is translated into a word or a concept. Gendlin's philosophy of metaphors in his article on "Crossing and Dipping" (1995) displays similarly, metaphor as a crossing between the embodied, felt sense and a linguistic articulation. In the following, I will discuss the parallels in Nietzsche's and Gendlin's theories of metaphors to display how Nietzsche's philosophy of language should not be falsely interpreted as mere representationalism, and that leads further to a rejection of Scharff's (1997) understanding of Nietzsche's perspectivism about truth and knowledge as relativist in the strong sense of representationalism. That everything is an interpretation means for Nietzsche that an interpretation is an embodied expression of a will which is relative to a place and time. The fact that man is as embodied a part of the natural environment in Nietzsche's philosophy shows striking parallels with Gendlin's own philosophy of living- and thought processes. I hence interpret Nietzsche's philosophy as a proto-phenomenological, pragmatic theory of embodiment and embodied experience and philosophical expression. This interpretation shows that there are richer resources of embodied thinking in the modern philosophical tradition for embodied thinking than acknowledged by Gendlin and his co-authors in *Language Beyond Postmodernism.*

Liberating thinking

The deeper underlying goal of this interpretation is something that goes beyond a mere comparison of two seminal thinkers on the topic of embodied linguistic expression. The comparison serves to work out the liberating potential of embodied thinking that, like Gendlin and several of his co-authors in *Language Beyond Postmodernism* point out, is missing in Neo-Nietzschean theories of representation that have among other things been quite important for gender studies within philosophy.

As a feminist in philosophy, I have always struggled with a male-centric tradition of academic philosophy, apparent in a narrow, disembodied understanding of rationality and language, a canon of philosophers that has excluded most women thinkers of the past, and exclusive structures and styles of philosophy as an academic institution. Therefore, Gendlin's intervention to bring together experiential thinking and logic, like is his stated goal with his theory of metaphors found in "Crossing and Dipping," speaks directly to my longing to practice and train philosophical thinking in a more embodied way. Gendlin elaborates modes of thinking that take lived experience more seriously as means to become more human in the sense of being better able to understand oneself and one another despite our differences in the way we practice philosophical thinking, dialogue and exchange. Gendlin's concept of crossing as metaphor is an important if not groundbreaking discovery of contemporary philosophy, not the least since Gendlin accentuates the *inter*subjective dimension of it and thereby adds something missing in Nietzsche's philosophy of metaphors that is more *intra*subjective. I therefore want to try to understand crossing as a liberating and humanizing force of philosophical practice of thinking, listening, sensing and speaking. We can perform crossing in our own thinking as well as with others, hence the method of crossing is a tool for generating understanding between people, groups and cultures. Having been socialized as a student at a time in academic philosophy in the 1980s and 1990s of the last century where a competitive and even combative style of philosophical dialogue was ubiquitous, an embodied manner of philosophical thinking is a transformative, liberating, empowering and a humbling force.

Feminists and queer theorists have conveyed an understanding of how the personal is political. Embodied, personal thinking is part of philosophical thinking and not subjective or mere solipsistic thinking as thinkers like Daniel Dennett and Hilary Putnam, misjudge experience-based methodological approaches like phenomenology to be (Zahavi, 2017, p. 10). Embarking on an understanding of philosophical thinking as embodied thinking therefore requires that one shows how the personal is or becomes philosophical, how a personal as embodied and a felt sense for an issue or a problem can become a conceptualized, abstract, generalized and universalized idea.

The problem is that drawing on "the personal" to become philosophical, universal and political counters a sharp distinction between introspection as mere subjective thinking and philosophical reflection as the proper universalizing thinking about essential structures (Zahavi, 2016). The problem is paradoxical, for how can something that is subjective, personal become universal like philosophical propositions are insofar they are generalizations about something about the human condition? We can pose the question negatively: how can a philosophical proposition not have a source in some felt meaning or lived experience? If one claims that it does not need to have any connection to experience that amounts to saying that there is no experiential base to that idea, that it comes out of the blue. The experience of getting an idea often feels like it comes out of the blue when we least expect it but nevertheless it is most often preceded by long periods of brewing, digesting and reflecting the problem or some issue related to it.

As philosophers, researchers and scientists, we have mostly been trained in understanding and learning about theories and concepts, but less so about how an idea emerges, like Claire Petitmengin discusses (Petitmengin, 2007). Gendlin's novelty of approach consists in illuminating how one comes to formulate a generalizing, philosophical statement, and, on that basis, he develops a methodology of embodied thinking that can guide one through steps of formulating a key sentence toward constructing a theory. The scheme of philosophical moves introduced with the Thinking at the Edge methodology is clearly also reflective of Gendlin's own accumulated experience of thinking philosophically as well as displaying a keen perception of the process of zigzagging between a felt sense and logical operations of thinking. He sheds a light on the process of conceptualizing and theory making that is mostly taken for granted or silently presumed within academic philosophy without an effort to dissect, analyze and categorize it like Gendlin, Nelson and Hendricks do by working out and schematizing the moves of a Thinking at the Edge methodology.

Models of oppression

For purposes of clarifying and underscoring the liberating and emancipatory potential of embodied thinking, Gendlin and Scharff are intent on criticizing theories they categorize as "postmodern" for a lack of an embodied base of thinking by reducing thinking to verbal and symbolic expression. When read through the lens of Foucault's (1977) text that focuses on how Nietzsche's genealogical method implies that interpretations can never be traced to a definitive origin, Gendlin is bound to react to Nietzsche in the following way:

> I disagree with the Nietzschean saying "There are only interpretations, there is nothing to interpret." That saying attacks but still also depends for its punch on the old perspectival notion that reality is something that is just there. Then we perceive and interpret it only from different angles or with different interpretive schemes. The Nietzschean saying points out that we can never get at anything like that; that would just sit in the middle and be interpreted. So there are only the interpretations.
>
> (Gendlin, 1993)

Gary Brent Madison (1997) in his paper at the "After Postmodernism" conference held in conjunction with the book on *Language Beyond Postmodernism* takes issue with Nietzsche in a similar manner as Gendlin when he asks:

> Is there anything to be found in Nietzsche's legacy ("Let us abolish the real world") other than the most abysmal of nihilisms? What are we to do when there is no more Truth and no more Reality--and no more Philosophy (Science) to tell us what Truth and Reality really and truly are? How are we to cope with this situation which defines our postmodernity?... In other words, as Nietzsche would say, when the value of (representational) truth is called into question, everything becomes

(mere) *interpretation* ("There is *only* a perspective seeing, *only* a perspective 'knowing'"). The world itself becomes nothing more than a "sign-world," i.e., merely a semiological construct, a mere signifier signifying only itself.[3]

The charge of nihilism does in my view not sit well with Foucault's critique of biopower and biopolitics as ruling governmentalities of contemporary societies. Foucault's critique is "negativistic" in the sense that the analysis and disclosure of oppression are understood to be a precondition to resisting it and not resigning to it which is certainly nihilistic.[4] Gendlin nevertheless rejects the "negativistic" Foucauldian approach when he explicitly states the following:

> But many of us are now tired of negative ways of saying that there is more. Abyss, rupture, tragedy, loss, nothingness, negativity, void, limbo, flux, fluidity, looseness, these deny what we try to affirm: that when the culture-forms and conceptual distinctions break, we find more precise meaning and order, not less
>
> (Gendlin, 1997a, p. 251)

This "more" is precisely the space out of which feedback comes. Crossing as a metaphorical way of thinking and speaking is a core means of reviving and creating fresh meaning from a place of felt sense that is for Gendlin a point of departure for a sense for an issue that has greater precision (is more than logic) and can enable to think it further. How is such feedback visible in Nietzsche's theory of conceptual metaphors?

Nietzsche's and Gendlin's theories of conceptual metaphors

It is quite clear that Gendlin relies on Nietzsche's early text on "Truth and Lies in a Nonmoral Sense" that contains his theory of metaphors. Nietzsche sets out with how language has become tired or drained, likening concepts to metal coins that have lost their embossing, i.e., whose images and signs have become vague due to long usage. A metaphor has precisely the same function for Nietzsche as for Gendlin as the intersection at which felt meaning and words cross and generate new meanings because "creativity depends on the willingness to let go of the usual, trite ways of seeing anything" (Gendlin, 1981). The creation of new meanings within natural language is hence not only a renewing force within language but nothing less than a potential force against oppressive and inhibiting structures toward a renewal of culture.

Nietzsche's philosophy contains a passage from a model of oppression to a model of embodied experiencing as the feedback-point of departure for liberating language toward cultural renewal. Paul Ricoeur continues this line of thought with his idea that the metaphor is living because it revives our perception of the world with the capacity of language to extend itself, forever discovering new resonances within itself (Ricoeur, 2003). Metaphors are words that are used creatively by recasting their meaning by making them refer to something new. Computers can neither create metaphors and theories nor recognize metaphors (Gendlin, 1997a; Dreyfus, 1979). There are no metaphors in dictionaries but only words because metaphors come into being in an unpredictable way by giving a word a new referent like Shakespeare does when he writes that Juliet is the sun.

Gendlin addresses the difference between words and metaphors when he writes: "If words were only discursive forms, then they could not say something new, nor something that does not follow from their established patterns. Then what words new say has to be considered only a contradiction and a rupture" (Gendlin, 1997b). Metaphors have a special power for good or for bad. The "glass ceiling" has, for example, been a metaphor with much critical impact and emancipatory force. In Nietzsche's texts, we find an abundance of misogynistic metaphors about women (as well as some derogatory statements about men as a sex), although his philosophy of embodiment with its implications for theories of gender has also been of great importance for feminist and queer philosophy.

In "Crossing and Dipping," Gendlin defines crossing as the metaphor that is generated when one attempts to formulate and describe something in a fresh way. Within a natural language crossing is for Gendlin the interface between a bodily sense for meaning and its linguistic articulation. With this idea, Gendlin takes up and reacts to George Lakoff's and Mark Johnson's theory of metaphoric language according to which conceptual metaphors are more than linguistic phenomena as is common to view them, for example in analytical philosophical theories of metaphoric use within sentences and along the lines of semantic and syntactic structures. In *Metaphors We Live By* (2003), Lakoff and Johnson, as theoreticians of embodied cognition, argue that metaphors are grounded in our bodies and lived physical experience, with some fundamental concepts thought to develop in infancy as a means of orientating oneself and finding a bearing in the world. Along these same lines, Claire Petitmengin articulates well how "in... gestural, pre-discursive, embodied structures of our experience... meaning is to be found: not only linguistic meaning, but *meaning* in its wider sense" (Petitmengin, 2007, p. 67).

With his theory of crossing, Gendlin partakes in this novel theoretical development of connecting embodiment and metaphoric language which has a precursor in Nietzsche's early theory of metaphors. There Nietzsche asks himself what a word is and replies that it is a "copy in sound of a nerve stimulus" and that every word that becomes a concept has a source in a unique and individual experience (Nietzsche, 1992, p. 81, 83). He further goes on to describe the embodied sources of metaphors in the following way:

> To begin with, a nerve stimulus is transferred into an image: first metaphor. The image, in turn, is imitated in a sound: second metaphor. And each time there is a complete overleaping of one sphere, right into the middle of an entirely new and different one.
>
> (Nietzsche, 1992, p. 82)

When Gendlin remarks that Nietzsche does not ascribe any order or form to the level of nature to which the body connects us to as part of nature he refers to a passage in Nietzsche's text on "Truth and Lies in a Nonmoral Sense" where there is a reference to the Kantian idea of the thing in itself as something unknowable and beyond human categorization:

> … whereas nature is acquainted with no forms and no concepts, and likewise with no species, but only with an X which remains inaccessible and undefinable for us. For even our contrast between individual and species is something anthropomorphic and does not originate in the essence of things; although we should not presume to claim that this contrast does not correspond to the essence of things: that would of course be a dogmatic assertion and, as such, would be just as indemonstrable as its opposite.
>
> (Nietzsche, 1992, p. 83)

This passage may also have led Gendlin (1991) to trace the origin of postmodernist philosophy of language all the way back to the Kantian foundation of modern philosophy by lumping Kant-Hegel-Nietzsche together as a series of Western thinkers who systematically overstate the role of form: "Nothing is considered to have an order of its own. Everything is taken as ordered by imposed forms, patterns, and rules." Gendlin finally concludes that most "modern philosophers have utterly lost an order of nature, human nature, the person, practice, the body" (Gendlin, 1991).

Gendlin takes up this early formulation of Nietzsche about a formless nature to criticize what he claims is his lack of attention to the body that can give feedback. It is also precisely for this same reason that Gendlin rejects Lakoff's and Johnson's sharp distinction between a preverbal and a verbal level of expression for he purports that there are patterns of experiencing that verbal formulations touch and hence language and felt meaning are part of the same responsive order where bodily interaction functions in language and is prior to perception and interpretation (Gendlin, 1997a, 1992). In his later reflections on philosophical thinking and its linguistic expression, Nietzsche does not uphold the strict division between the verbal metaphorical and formless nature from his early text on metaphors. It is quite clear that Gendlin does not take note of Nietzsche's later modifications of his position.

In his later philosophy, Nietzsche deconstructs the distinction between the real world and a world of appearances and merges both into this one and real world (see the passage on "How the 'true world' finally became a fable" from his late work, *The Twilight of the Idols*). In fact, he comes to question the distinction between the presymbolic and the symbolic or the inner and the outer side, the "visible organic life" and "the invisible creative... thinking," making him ask to what extent thinking and logics can be seen as the outside and symptom of a much more inner and thorough happening.[5] Nietzsche's early theory of language as presented in his text on "On Truth and Lies in a Nonmoral Sense" does in fact depart from the tradition of viewing the natural origins of language as formless like Gendlin assumes. One has to look deeper into Nietzsche's text and its background in other theories and authors of his times to get a fuller picture.

Nietzsche's reading of F. A. Lange's *History of Materialism*[6] that was influential for his early theory of natural, metaphoric language contains explanations of the transition from sensorial stimulus and sense perception to abstract thinking. Lange is a thinker who combines materialism (in opposition to Hegelian idealism) and Neo-Kantianism thus aiming for a non-reductionist materialist position by giving due respect to Kantian transcendental idealism about knowledge as a product of our a priori cognitive capacities for ordering sense perception. Lange's materialist position is further more supported by novel findings in the up and coming physiology of his day and it succeeded in instantiating a psycho-physics movement. Nietzsche was part of that movement by later on rebranding his philosophy as "physio-psychology" (Nietzsche, 2002, p.23), and by discussing how there is a continuous interplay between the bodily and the mental, claiming that the "physiological center" also may be the "psychic center."[7]

As a philosopher in the tradition of sensualism, Nietzsche describes the body as a body-organization ("Leib-Organisation") with the mind as the seat of mental states that have a bodily basis. For that reason, Claudia Rosciglione has argued that Nietzsche's theory of the mind-body problem resembles Antonio Damasio's work on embodied cognition and on the neural basis of language (Rosciglione, 2013, p. 51). For Nietzsche, the range of our mental representations is therefore much broader than their conceptual content that is a mere "symptom of a much more inner and thorough happening."[8] Nietzsche describes this level of "inner and thorough happening" not as formless nature but rather as vibrating rhythms and tensions that precede symbolic and verbal expressions and articulations. In fact, even in the early text on metaphors, Nietzsche writes about "intuitive metaphors" that he opposes to a hierarchical, strictly ordered conceptualizations. In his later writings on the topic, he does not hold on to the bleak idea of a worn out or drained language but rather continues to develop in much more detail the potential of creating new meanings. For that purpose, he views verbal expression from the perspective of patterns of rhythms, gestures and music because metaphoric language creation is for him an artistic practice, just like crossing and metaphors create for Gendlin fresh meanings. Among the rules of styles of writing that Nietzsche lists is this one: "The richness of life reveals itself through a *richness of gestures*. One must *learn* to feel everything *like gestures*, the length and brevity of sentences, inter-punctuations, the choice of words, the *pauses*, the sequence of arguments."[9]

Rhythms in thinking

In his reflections on what he calls the "sudden impressions" and "intuitions" in his early text about metaphors, Nietzsche claims that these intuitions are individual (Nietzsche, 1992, p. 84). Therefore, they elude any form of recording or, literally, of registering into a game of truth that is like a game of dice where "truth" means using every dice "in the designated manner, counting its spots accurately, fashioning the right categories, and never violating the order of caste and class rank" (Nietzsche, 1992, p. 85). Such ordering is juxtaposed by Nietzsche to a more apperceptive ordering of reality. For that purpose, he takes up, originally influenced by his studies in classical rhetorics and metrics, the concept of rhythm which is a manifestation of human beings as embodied, affective and temporal beings. In the context of embodied naturalized being, he talks about the rhythm of "organic life" and an "elementary rhythm" in the conditions of sensation, and he even speaks about how the life of the young child is determined by shorter rhythms making the child more restless.[10] With all this, he suggests that rhythms are physiological universals, and with them he denotes the intensity of sensations, their time dimensions and their bodily extension (like breath, heartbeat, fatigue, energetic tension, density). For Gendlin, felt sense is similarly not something in us, but rather a bodily process that comes to us when we tune into and "listen" to the body by allowing the rhythm of bodily processes.

Like Eldridge has remarked, rhythms in Nietzsche's philosophy are simultaneously a phenomenon of fixed, organizing form and one of dynamic, changing flow (Eldridge, 2018). With his idea of rhythms, Nietzsche furthermore presents the human being as an interactive instance within a responsive order, to use the Gendlinian term. Gendlin defines the responsive order as a "reality" (...) to check against. We can check each approach (procedure, performance, set of experiments, measurements) against the feedback of an equally precise "reality" (Gendlin, 1997a). Yet, in his text on "The Responsive Order: A New Empiricism," Gendlin reiterates his interpretation of Nietzsche as a thinker that does not acknowledge the body's feedback, and he even accentuates it further by situating Nietzsche's stand as restricted to the sense perceptions in the same manner the empirical sciences are:

> With the percept comes the whole familiar problematic of interpretation (and Nietzsche's puzzle: there are only interpretations; nothing to interpret). This problematic will surely arise if one takes perception as the basic model of experience (events, situations [...]). The world presented by science is made along the lines of percepts.
>
> (Gendlin, 1997a)

I doubt that Gendlin would have categorized Nietzsche's perspectivism as postmodern representationalism if he had considered that Nietzsche discusses how we are affected by rhythms, be it in music or in texts, and that he also discusses how rhythms of individuals affect culture. Nietzsche, for example, vividly describes how the rhythmically in Wagner's music (that he came to criticize after his early infatuation with it) affects him in an embodied way, his stomach, his heartbeat, breathing, degenerating the feeling for rhythm.[11] The rhythmic bodily response to a rhythmic occurrence is not to be understood solely as an imprinted and culturally conditioned response based on the cognitive content of the affect that triggers or generates it. That would be reductionistic because the response is both driven by an affect with a cognitive content as well as an individual felt sense for the issue at hand. Given Nietzsche's idea of the individuality of affective expression, it is therefore more adequate to speak in Gendlinian terms of the rhythmic bodily response as an individually informed felt sense for the object, making Nietzsche's position in tune with Gendlin's conception of bodily feedback. Rhythms are therefore a kind of elementary sensations or expressions of affects that can be distinguished from emotions that contain a greater amount of cognitive content. For Nietzsche, all these forms of emotions are part of parcel of embodied philosophical thinking, and not mere perceptions like Gendlin wrongly holds. "We philosophers," Nietzsche begins:

> are not free to separate soul from body as the common people do; we are even less free to separate soul from spirit. We are no thinking frogs, no objectifying and registering devices with frozen innards—we must constantly give birth to our thoughts out of our pain and maternally endow them with all that we have of blood, heart, fire, pleasure, passion, agony, conscience, fate, and disaster.
>
> (*The Gay Science*, Preface to the second edition, 3)[12]

Nietzsche even speaks of how he and embodied thinking philosophers of the future think by taking "walks in us" ("*in uns* spazieren gehen") (*The Gay Science,* 280)[13] and he discusses how we cannot understand a metaphor like "love" unless we recall a personal memory of an emotion in order to guide our understanding of love.[14] Again, this does not imply that philosophical knowledge that has an experiential and affective base merely offers a subjective perspective. Nietzsche's critique of objectifying knowledge needs to be understood against the backdrop of his physiologically informed and Neo-Kantian conception of embodied knowledge. Any product of knowledge is relative to the time and place of its origination but that does not mean that Nietzsche abandons ideals of objectivity for an anything goes or post-truth type of relativism. In fact, he advocates extending objectivity by accounting for a plurality of (embodied) perspectives. The more affect we express over a thing, the more different eyes for the same thing we train, the more complete will our knowledge of that thing or issue be.[15] What Gendlin adds to this notion of extended objectivity in the context of his philosophy of crossing is a thicker notion of the intersubjective dimension of it. When practicing the step of crossing when doing Thinking at the Edge, a listener supports the one thinking and speaking with reflecting remarks that assist the speaker in expressing, articulating and formulating a thought more precisely.

Crossing and interaction

When I introduce the Thinking at the Edge step of crossing to my students, I always point out the novelty of this concept by discussing how crossing adds an embodied involvement to conventional, disembodied argumentative and logical operations of comparing and contrasting. Gendlin himself points out that constructivism "reduces everything to comparisons," and that interaction is hence "reduced to comparisons" (Gendlin, 1997a). It is precisely by way of the interface between the instances, situations, phenomena, topics, ideas, concepts, tropes or issues that are crossed that the specific objectivity of each of them is understood because only by way of the interaction or the interface does the objectivity of each become apparent. As a scholarly method, comparison, on the other hand, loses sight of this interface and then "the empirical disappears and we lose the objectivity of both" according to Gendlin (1997a). When something is compared to another, the difference may be accentuated or something similar may be made alike. In comparison, we do not acknowledge the one who does the comparing as opposed to crossing where we become aware of and activate our first person relationship to the subject matter. Like Petitmengin has researched, we have closed our eyes to the deeply pre-reflective dimension of the first person experience of scholarly and scientific thought. She furthermore claims that this dimension of "felt meaning" is rhythmic and gestural and plays an essential role in the emergence of all thought and understanding:

> A precise observation shows that a felt meaning has precise sensorial submodalities—essentially form, intensity, rhythm and movement—which

have the common characteristics of being 'transmodal', i.e. they are not specific to a particular sense, but can be transposed from one sense to another.

(Petitmengin, 2007, p. 64)

The micro-phenomenological elicitation interview method that Petitmengin studies and develops aims at collecting precise descriptions of the lived experience associated with a cognitive process. The interview consists in assessing the interviewee's level of felt meaning to extrapolate the knowledge stored or emerging in it (Petitmengin, 2006). The fine-grained descriptions that come out of it yield insights that can lead one to formulate generalizing, philosophical propositions.

Gendlin articulates such a process with his idea of the interface in which meaning is created when we cross a conceptual or linguistic metaphor, bringing the word's old situation into a new situation. "Something new is formed when the two situations are crossed" (Gendlin, 1986, p. 150). Like Akira Ikemi writes, "in contrast to conventional theories of metaphor where the similarity of the situation and the metaphor is assumed to be primary, in Gendlin's metaphor theory, the similarity is found after the carrying forward" (Ikemi, 2017, p. 9). Again, one may think that with this idea of crossing, a mere subjectivistic idea of kind of a random comparison, for that is what metaphors often are, is being presented. However, as a Wittgensteinian philosopher, Gendlin always assumes that any meaning-making by way of metaphors is situated in a use-family of words. Furthermore, what is and crossed. A and B, are not fixed parts once and for all, but rather the work of understanding consists in a crossing where the "'parts' can always be further reprecisioned" (Gendlin, 1997a).

What is most important about crossing as a conscious and deliberative methodological step of Thinking at the Edge is the very experience of performing it when dealing with a philosophical problem, question or an issue. For practitioners, an exercise in crossing, yields results that give them a sense that they employ *"thinking that employs more than conceptual logic, rules, or distinctions"* because they *"become able to think with the intricacy of situations (experience, practice, ...) (Gendlin, 1997b)*. Even though the instances or concepts that are crossed may seem random and hardly fit for comparison, the process is productive in yielding greater understanding. Crossing is also much more than a particular methodological step of the Thinking at the Edge methodology. Crossing happens all the time in our thinking, such as when we are grappling with a problem and by coincidence or out of the blue witness or come across something totally different that may give us a fresh perspective on our problem and allow us to use a word for it in a fresh way. The interface where crossing takes place is a reality check, a space where the personal and the universal touch, allowing us to refresh a philosophical thought and find ways of articulating it. Crossing is therefore a powerful and sometimes quite a playful tool of bringing the personal consciously and deliberately back as a jumping board into the philosophical, where it has always been. Let me finish with a quote from Nietzsche that has usually often been misunderstood as a sarcastic critique of philosophers' blind spot. After crossing the following quote with Gendlin's philosophy of crossing, we can understand this quote as proclaiming that what is special about philosophy as a discipline is that it has a deep personal core:

> I have gradually come to realize what every great philosophy so far has been: a confession of faith on the part of its author, and a type of involuntary and unself-conscious memoir; in short, that the moral (or immoral) intentions in every philosophy constitute the true living seed from which the whole plant has always grown.
>
> (Beyond Good and Evil, I, 6)

Nietzsche does not mention the ability to critically reflect the "living seed" of the first person perspective but that is something that Gendlin does with his methodology of crossing, and with it the capacity of understanding oneself and others more deeply in the liberating practice of embodied philosophical thinking.

Notes

1 The research for this paper is part of the Embodied Critical Thinking project and the Erasmus+ funded European program Training Embodied Critical Thinking that I founded with Donata Schoeller at the Department of Philosophy at the University of Iceland in cooperation with the Micro-phenomenology Lab in Paris, the Landscape Architecture Department at Technion in Haifa, the Network of Mindful Universities in Germany, the Bernoulli Institute for Mathematics, Computer Science and Artificial Intelligence at the University of Groeningen and the Center for Cognitive Science at the University of Ljubljana. See www.trainingect.com, also Schoeller and Thorgeirsdottir (2019).
2 Most of the quotes from Gendlin's texts are take from *The Gendlin Online Library*. The online texts do not have page numbers. The page numbers of the texts in books or journals where they were originally published are given but page numbers do not appear in their online version because there are not separate pages in online texts. Therefore, the page number cannot be given but only the link to the text in *The Gendlin Online Library*.
3 Gary Brent Madison, "Coping with Nietzsche's Legacy: Rorty, Derrida, Gadamer," *After Postmodernism Conference*, http://previous.focusing.org/apm_papers/madison2.html.
4 Even though Judith Butler's work, inspired by Foucault's philosophy, is not mentioned in *Language Beyond Postmodernism*, her early book on *Gender Trouble* (1990) offers a deconstruction of biologically and socially essentialist gender binaries by describing how gender identities are performative by reiterating symbolic and linguistic categories. Butler, like Gendlin, interprets Nietzsche as a forerunner of her deconstructive approach with his idea from the *Genealogy of Morals* that there is no doer behind the deed to suggest how culture and language are constitutive of a person's (gendered) identity. Butler nevertheless goes

a step further than Foucault by discussing how such categories can be resisted by subversive gender performances which have since the publication of *Gender Trouble* become increasingly visible through the LGBTQ movement. Yet, also in Butler's *Gender Trouble* the feedback as the incentive for resistance is not explicitly accounted for.

5   Friedrich Nietzsche, Posthumous fragments, Fall 1885–Fall 1886, *Kritische Studienausgabe der Werke Nietzsches* (KSA), KSA 12, 2[146], 139. My translation. "Inwiefern Denken, Schließen und alles Logische als *Außenseite* angesehen werden kann: als Symptom viel innerlicheren und gründlicheren Geschehens?."

6   Friedrich Albert Lange, *Geschichte des Materialismus und Kritik seiner Bedeutung in der Gegenwart* published in *1866*.

7   Friedrich Nietzsche, Posthumous fragments, Fall 1885 – Beginning of Janary 1889, KSA 12, 5[56], 206.

8   Ibid.

9   Letter from Nietzsche to Lou Salome from August 8/24, 1882, translatation is mine. *Kritische Studienausgabe der Briefe Nietzsches (KSB), KSB 6,* 244.

10   Friedrich Nietzsche, Posthumous fragments, summer 1875, 9[1], KSA 8, 148.

11   See Friedrich Nietzsche's *The Case of Wagner* and *Nietzsche Contra Wagner.*

12   Friedrich Nietzsche. *The Gay Science,* Cambridge: Cambridge University Press, 2001, 6.

13   Ibid., 160.

14   *Friedrich Nietzsche, Posthumous fragments, summer 1875, 9[1], KSA 8,154.*

15   Friedrich Nietzsche, *Genealogy of Morals* (Book III, 12).

References

Butler, J. (1990). *Gender Trouble. Feminism and the Subversion of Identity.* New York: Routledge.

Dreyfus, H. (1979). *What Computers Still Can't Do: A Critique of Artificial Reason.* Cambridge: MIT Press.

Eldridge, H.V. (2018). Towards a philosophy of rhythm: Nietzsche's conflicting rhythms. *Journal of Literary Theory,* 12(1), 151–170.

Foucault, M. (1977). Nietzsche, genealogy, history, in Bouchard, D.F. (Ed.), *Language, Counter Memory, Practice* (pp. 139–164). Ithaca, NY: Cornell University Press.

Gendlin, E.T. (1979). Gendlin: Experience is richer than psychology models. *Brain-Mind Bulletin,* 4(10), 2. http://previous.focusing.org/gendlin/docs/gol_2131.html

Gendlin, E.T. (1981). Focusing and the development of creativity. *The Focusing Folio,* 1(1), 13–16. http://previous.focusing.org/gendlin/docs/gol_2062.html

Gendlin, E.T. (1986). *Let Your Body Interpret Your Dreams.* Wilmette, IL: Chiron Publications.

Gendlin, E.T. (1991). Thinking beyond patterns: Body, language and situations, in B. den Ouden & M. Moen (Eds.), *The Presence of Feeling in Thought* (pp. 25–151). New York: Peter Lang. http://previous.focusing.org/gendlin/docs/gol_2159.html

Gendlin, E.T. (1992). The primacy of the body, not the primacy of perception. *Man and World,* 25(3–4), 341–353. http://previous.focusing.org/gendlin/docs/gol_2220.html

Gendlin, E.T. (1993). Human nature and concepts, in J. Braun (Ed.), *Psychological Concepts of Modernity* (pp. 3–16). Westport, CT: Praeger/Greenwood. http://previous.focusing.org/gendlin/docs/gol_2060.html

Gendlin, E.T. (1995). Crossing and dipping: some terms for approaching the interface between natural understanding and logical formulation. *Minds and Machines,* 5(4), 547–560. http://previous.focusing.org/gendlin/docs/gol_2166.html

Gendlin, E.T. (1997a). The responsive order: A new empiricism. *Man and World,* 30(3), 383–411. http://previous.focusing.org/gendlin/docs/gol_2157.html

Gendlin, E.T. (1997b). Preface to the paper edition. In *Experiencing and the creation of meaning: A philosophical and psychological approach to the subjective* (pp. xi-xxiii). Evanston, Illinois: Northwestern University Press. http://previous.focusing.org/gendlin/docs/gol_2152.html

Gendlin, E.T. (2004). Introduction to "Thinking at the Edge", *The Folio, 19* (1), 1-8. http://previous.focusing.org/gendlin/docs/gol_2160.html

Ikemi, A. (2017). The radical impact of experiencing on psychotherapy theory: An examination of two kinds of crossings. *Person-Centered and Experiential Psychotherapies,* 16(2), 159–172. DOI: 10.1080/14779757.2017.1323668

Lakoff, G. and Johnson, M. (2003). *Metaphors We Live By.* Chicago, IL: University of Chicago Press.

Levin, D.M. (Ed.) (1997). *Language Beyond Postmodernism. Saying and Thinking in Gendlin's Philosophy.* Chicago: Northwestern University Press.

Madison, G.B. (1997). Coping with Nietzsche's Legacy: Rorty, Derrida, Gadamer, After Postmodernism Conference. http://previous.focusing.org/apm_papers/madison2.html.

Nietzsche, F. (1992). On truth and lies in a nonmoral sense, translated and edited by Daniel Breazeale, in *Philosophy and Truth. Selections from Nietzsche's Notebooks of the Early 1870s* (pp. 79–91). Atlantic Highlands, NJ: Humanities Press International.

Nietzsche, F. (2002). *Beyond Good and Evil: Prelude to a Philosophy of the Future,* translated by Judith Norman. Cambridge: Cambridge University Press.

Petitmengin, C. (2006). Describing one's subjective experience in the second person. An interview method for a science of consciousness, *Phenomenology and the Cognitive Sciences,* 5, 229–269.

Petitmengin, C. (2007). Towards the source of thoughts the gestural and transmodal dimension of lived experience. *Journal of Consciousness Studies,* 14(3), 54–82.

Ricoeur, P. (2003). *The Rule of Metaphor: The Creation of Meaning in Language.* London/New York: Routledge.

Rosciglione, C. (2013). A non-reductionist physiologism nietzsche on body, mind and consciousness. *Prolegomena,* 12(1), 43–60.

Scharff, R.C. (1997). After Dilthey and Heidegger: Gendlin's experiential hermeneutics, in Levin, D.M. (Ed.), *Language Beyond Postmodernism* (pp. 190–226). Chicago: Northwestern University Press.

Schoeller, D. and Thorgeirsdottir, S. (2019). Embodied critical thinking and its transformative aspects. *Journal of Continental Feminism,* 9(1), 92–109.

Zahavi, Dan (2016). The end of what? Phenomenology vs. speculative realism. *International Journal of Philosophical Studies,* 24(3), 289–309.

Zahavi, D. (2017). *Husserl's Legacy: Phenomenology, Metaphysics, and Transcendental Philosophy.* Oxford: Oxford University Press.

Chapter 7

Missing the felt sense

When correct political arguments go wrong

Ole Martin Sandberg

Have you ever had a discussion where the other person states a position that you know is factually wrong, but when you present all the counter-arguments – the relevant empirical data and the logical and rational explanations – it still does not work to persuade the other party? It might be because they don't accept your arguments but, even more frustratingly, they might acknowledge all of them and still hold on to their initial conclusion. You have convincingly shown that the reasons they gave for their position are incorrect but now they've come up with new reasons to support it, or maybe they still feel it to be true despite not having any arguments for it – or rather, not being able to articulate their arguments.

One possible reaction to this situation is to simply conclude that their beliefs are unreasonable and irrational and that the person, by implication, is irrational. After all, it is hardly a hallmark of rationality to hold on to a belief without any supporting reasons and despite overwhelming arguments against it. The conclusion would then be that there is no further reason to continue the conversation; the other person is a "lost cause." Another possible reaction is to suspect that the initial arguments in favor of the position, the arguments that have now been debunked, were not the real reasons for the belief. In that case, the debunking was inefficient and left the belief intact because it never actually touched the deeper causes of the belief. These causes might not have been articulated by the person, perhaps not even to themselves, and are thus very hard to engage directly. The conclusion would then not be to close off the conversation but allow it to develop to find out what is really at stake.

This essay is about conversations that go wrong in this way. I believe they are a widespread part of our contemporary experience and that interrogating them can help make sense of many topics in the political and social landscape. I argue that beliefs and dispositions might not always be derived from "facts and reason," as contemporary popular discourse would like to have it (Hong, 2020), and thus cannot be refuted with a superficial application of those tools. Instead, their cause is more akin to what the psychiatrist-philosopher Eugene Gendlin calls the "felt sense" or "felt meaning" which

DOI: 10.4324/9781003296706-8

a bodily felt experiencing of the environment. The body, he says, implies "a whole vast maze of behaviors and the environmental circumstances in which the behaviors would occur" (1973, p. 273). This interactional awareness is not like the cognitive knowledge that can be differentiated into logical pieces and articulated as arguments but rather comes as one a "great, rich, complex experience": the felt sense (1981, p. 39).

Gendlin also differentiates the felt sense from emotions, although it can be an occasion for emotions to occur. An emotion, he says, "is often sharp and clearly felt, and often comes with a handy label by which you can describe it," while the felt sense is more complicated and unclear (1981, p. 40) – until, that is, we focus on it, which is a process that can generate a shift in the body and its emotions (1981, p. 119). The felt sense is thus the "bodily sensing of the whole situational context" (1973, p. 397) which has not yet been articulated. As such, it can give rise to many different sensations, emotions, and beliefs, some of which may be unconstructive or harmful. My claim is that addressing the different manifestations is not going to be helpful if the felt sense is left untouched and unchanged. I further argue that in some cases, this process of "debunking" can be downright counter-productive and result in the "opponent" becoming hostile to the argument and doubling down on the initial beliefs. In other words, showing why a belief is wrong is not enough; we must also find out and address the reasons for why it felt right. This requires taking account of the whole situation.

Debunking in "the post-truth age"

In 2016, the Oxford Dictionaries chose the Word of the Year to be "post-truth." This word, they wrote, is an adjective "relating to or denoting circumstances in which objective facts are less influential in shaping public opinion than appeals to emotion and personal belief" (Oxford Languages, 2016). This was not a new word – already in 2004, the author Ralph Keyes published a book with the title *The Post-Truth Era* (Keyes, 2004) anticipating coming trends – but as they noted, the frequency of its usage in public media exploded in 2016 "in the context of the EU referendum in the United Kingdom and the presidential election in the United States." This was a period where standard epistemological terms were severely challenged. The administration of the newly elected US president, Donald J. Trump, became so known for its relaxed relationship with reality that the president's counselor, Kellyanne Conway, coined the term "alternative facts" (NBC, 2017), and his attorney, Rudolph Giuliani, boldly declared that "truth isn't truth" and that the "truth is relative" because it's always "somebody's version of the truth" (Viebeck, 2018). A charitable interpretation might see the latter statement to imply an almost Nietzschean perspectivism where the idea of "knowledge in itself" is rendered absurd as "the only knowledge we have is knowledge from a perspective" (Nietzsche, 2009, p. 98). A less charitable interpretation, offered by the philosopher Daniel Dennett, also lays the blame on Nietzschean-inspired "postmodernism" which he decries as "truly evil" (Cadwalladr, 2017).

The media responded by committing itself to fact-checking the president and his administration: every statement the president made was to be investigated and any lies or misinformation had to be exposed and debunked. This quickly became an impossible task. Not because the lies were sophisticated and difficult to entangle – quite the contrary, they often took the form of a blatant disregard for the truth – but simply because there were so many of them. Toward the end of Trump's presidency, the fact-checker for the New York Times described the work as "exhausting" (Gabbatt, 2019) and The Washington Post reported that their fact-checking team "cannot keep up" as the president was "averaging more than 50 false or misleading claims a day" (Kessler et al., 2020). All the fact-checking made little impression upon the president, though, as he consistently responded by calling them "fake news" – a term that soon became a mantra among his followers. Trump's strategy seemed to be that if you state a lie boldly and confidently, it does not need to be wrapped in the layers of deception that other politicians might use, and when you are called out on your falsehoods you never admit or explain anything, instead, you attack the messenger. More importantly, it made little impression upon his followers. Since Trump had vilified the media as "the enemy," all the journalists' attempts at exposing his falsehoods were perceived by his loyal base as merely slanderous attacks.

The epistemological assaults did not just come from the US president or other political actors for that matter. The period was – and still is – characterized by multiple simultaneous media-induced waves of panic about what we can and should believe and how beliefs can be manipulated. The Internet, which was once upon a time hailed as the technology that would make information accessible to the world, became a profitable tool for spreading misinformation about everything from political events to basic health and nutrition, and social media, rather than uniting the world in a global community, actively pushed people into so-called "bubbles" where beliefs and world-views were shared and reinforced among those on the inside who might be epistemologically disconnected from those on the "other side" of the bubble. This process of polarization even became an entirely new academic field, "bubblestudies" (University of Copenhagen, 2015), and was frequently described as a threat to democracy itself (Hendricks & Hansen, 2014).

Besides the US administration, the potential sources of misinformation were numerous, and neither political party was innocent, nor was the "mainstream media" despite its claim to be the valiant defenders of Truth in an Age of Lies. The quite real Russian informational warfare exercise that used social and standard media to sow discontent and distrust among the

American populace quickly blew out of proportions and became the fantastic story about how Russia "hacked the US election" (Justice & Bricker, 2019). This story was peddled particularly eagerly by the host of MSNBC's sensationalist entertainment program *The Rachel Maddow Show*, which according to a court ruling, "no reasonable viewer" would expect to be factual (*Herring Networks v. Maddow*, 2021). A similar ruling was made concerning Fox News' host Tucker Carlson who also protected himself from legal liability by insisting that no reasonable person would think his show was actual journalism (*McDougal v. Fox News*, 2020). These are two of the most prominent and influential media figures in the US, catering to two different political consumer demographics, both insisting in court that they are in fact "fake news." This situation does not exactly help the media's epistemic reputation or their campaign against other peddlers of misinformation. If the felt sense is the implicit bodily awareness of the situational context, then epistemic mistrust is not entirely unreasonable reaction in a media-context where truth is indeed devalued in favor of the production of emotional engagement. This cements the general feeling that nothing can be trusted which unfortunately extends to other sources who might have higher epistemic integrity such as medical experts.

In both court cases, the ruling relied on the judges' opinions about what a "reasonable person" would believe. This fictional concept of "the reasonable person" does a lot of work in legal theory and practice as well as in philosophy. For example, throughout the philosophical works of John Rawls, we find references to "reasonable people," "reasonable disagreements," and "reasonable doctrines" (Young, 2006). These concepts work to stabilize the political theory by narrowing the set of preferences, opinions, and beliefs to be considered and agreed upon down to a set that can indeed agree with the theory, and, as such, they are concepts meant to exclude certain reasons (and people) from political consideration (DePaul, 1998). While this might work within "ideal theory," real political theory has to contend with the empirical fact that a substantial number of actual people, who are active members of our societies and have full rights of democratic participation, have opinions and beliefs that deviate from what Rawls and other liberals consider "reasonable" (Klosko, 1993). Likewise, I suspect that the US district courts might have excluded a substantial number of actual American viewers who do get their political beliefs from entertainers like Maddow and Carlson from their definition of "reasonableness." In law, the "reasonable person" is often defined as a hypothetical person who is "in the same situation" as an actual agent (typically the accused) and has the same "knowledge of circumstances" (Nottelmann, 2007, p. 13). This definition makes me recall what might be my first philosophical contemplations when other kids in my preschool would say something like "I wouldn't have done that if I were you" which always made me think "but if you were me, then you would have the same beliefs and motivations and everything else as me so, of course, you would do the same as I did." This applies to the legal definition too: a hypothetical person in exactly the same circumstances with the same knowledge, etc. is likely to be indistinguishable from the actual person and is thus likely to perform the exact same action, *unless* the defining and blameworthy difference is the content of their beliefs (an argument also made by Nottelmann, 2007).

The relevance of this legal definition to the discussion about political and other arguments is that we often tend to assume that if we merely provide the other person with all the same information about a topic that we possess, then that person would also come to have the same opinions and beliefs about the topic as we do. And when that fails, the only explanation might seem to be that the other person is simply "unreasonable" – or in less polite terms: "stupid." What we might forget to consider, both in legal practice and in political debates, is that *nobody* is literally in the same situation and has all the same knowledge of circumstances as another person. Yes, we might be able to present the arguments and facts that on a surface level seem to be all the relevant information that should determine an epistemic attitude, but this approach relies on what I believe is a fundamentally mistaken view of human cognitive behavior. When we – including those who have the "correct beliefs" – assess the information about a topic, there is always a lot more going on in our cognitive processes: background beliefs that influence what kind of information we find more trustworthy, our lived experience that influences the degree to which we can relate to an interpretation, and many other factors. These factors are also part of a person's situation, and they shape what Eugene Gendlin calls "the felt meaning" of the situation. This felt meaning can of course "go wrong" – i.e. become articulated incompletely and be associated with destructive beliefs and behaviors. When that happens, the goal is to step back and listen to the felt sense and take account of the whole situation to examine what might have let to the mistaken articulations. Rather than simply dismissing them, focusing on their source – the felt sense – can cause a shift that creates new articulations which are hopefully better at addressing the situation. In other words, from a Gendlidian perspective the problem of our time is not that people are too driven by emotions and gut feelings, i.e. but rather that we do not take the time to truly listen to our bodily feelings. Or, we must add, to the feelings of each other.

From truthiness to felt meaning

The idea of "post-truth politics" is not new. The book that introduced the concept of "the post-truth era" was written under, and partially about, the presidency of George W. Bush. The author, Ralph Keyes (2004, p. 183), wrote that "Bush is partial to the notion that facts were whatever you say they are" and that "with his reliance on language games, George W. Bush has been our most postmodern president." This is not just political banter. Bush described himself as a "gut player" who relies on "instincts" rather than "textbooks" (Woodward, 2002, p. 118) and was criticized by prominent members of his own party and administration for getting rid of people who confronted him with "inconvenient facts" (Suskind, 2004). Among the results was one of the biggest lies of the 21st century, a lie that required the collaboration of several governments and was presented to the world at the highest diplomatic stage, the United Nations Security Council: the lie about the Iraqi weapons of mass destruction that led to the invasion of that country by a multinational force and reconfigured the global political landscape for decades. If "post-truth politics" describes the current age, it is an age that was created by the world order based on that lie. That the experts assigned with the task of investigating the issue found no evidence of WMDs in Iraq (Ekéus, 2016) meant little: Saddam Hussein was a dictator, so starting a war felt right regardless of the soundness of the articulated justifications. It was a war started on a "gut feeling" but obviously not as a result of carefully focusing on the felt sense. Bush might have reacted on instincts and guts but he did not spend time examining them: "We must not blink"[1] was his motto. But listening to the body requires no less time than listening to experts; it is a slow process that requires self-examination and involves bodily gestures such as blinking.[2]

The then-president's reliance on instincts and gut feelings over other epistemological tools was brilliantly satirized by the comedian Stephen Colbert who, in the first episode of his show, *The Colbert Report*, coined the phrase "truthiness." Truthiness is distinct from "truth" and "facts" which Colbert's satirical persona mocked as elitist concepts for people who think too much. He described the world as being divided between "those who think with their head and those who know with their heart." Truthiness does not rely on whether a claim is supported by empirical evidence or textbooks but on whether it *feels* right. This feeling of truthiness comes from the gut, he claimed, which is the most reliable epistemic source. The segment ended with the words "anyone can read the news to you; I promise to feel the news at you" (Colbert, 2005). As said, the fictional persona was created to mock the political era of George W. Bush but, as others have noted (Zhang, 2019), it also describes the cognitive attitude of Donald Trump, who has repeatedly declared his gut instincts to be more reliable than the carefully examined information from various experts.

Despite being satire, I think this word, "truthiness," describes an important element of the human condition and one which should be taken seriously. And I think it describes something related, though certainly not identical, to Gendlin's "felt sense." It is a central element in Gendlin's works that the body stores and processes information that is not always directly accessible to the conscious brain. In *Focusing*, he writes "Your body knows but you don't" and "You can feel that huge vague something with your body but you can't touch it with your mind" (1981, pp. 44, 41). This "large, vague feeling" is what he calls the "felt sense" (Gendlin, 1981, p. 20). Compare Gendlin's statement that "your body knows much that you don't know, much that you cannot possibly figure out" (1981, p. 46) with Trump's claim that "I have a gut, and my gut tells me more sometimes than anybody else's brain can ever tell me" (Washington Post, 2018). Of course, Gendlin is also careful to say that "focusing is not just getting in touch with your gut feelings" (1981, p. 80), but clearly, these are important and necessary elements.

To help us see what he is getting at by these statements, Gendlin (1992) uses the example of walking home at night and sensing a group of men walking behind you. This causes you to feel a sense of alarm and urgency. The "body-sense" is not just your awareness of the situation but also includes past experiences and implies a series of potential future actions such as running, hiding, and shouting (1992, p. 346). Some of these are deliberate cognitive processes, while others are more akin to gut feelings, emotions, and quick intuitive associations and thoughts, all of which together form the "felt sense" (1992, p. 346). He is explicit that this process is a bodily function: your body is simultaneously running different scenarios and potential courses of action, sensing how they feel and what other actions and scenarios they might imply, and it does this must faster than you could do consciously. You then get a bodily feeling that a certain action does not "feel right," although you are not in the moment aware of why that is. Gendlin advises you to trust that gut feeling; not instead of a rational analysis of the situation but such an analysis should not ignore the bodily feeling because your body might know something that will lead you to safety.

I do not intend to disagree with Gendlin on this. There is no doubt that vast amounts of information and processing take place in our body, instinctively and unconsciously, all the time. This is critical for our survival and thus for biological evolution. For example, we do not consciously calculate the angle, velocity, and trajectory of a ball when we raise our hands to catch it – somehow this process takes place in our body and, with practice, our hands just know where to go. The neuroscientist António Damásio has demonstrated how important emotions and bodily processes are for human cognition and behavior. For example, test subjects were able to behave as if they knew the rules of a certain game after a few rounds without being able to articulate the rules simply because their bodies had picked up the pattern assisted by the positive or negative feelings that occur when they did the right or wrong thing (1995, p. 212). Meanwhile, patients who suffered from brain damage that inhibited this emotional learning were not able to rely on this "gut instinct" and they made poor decisions not just in the experimental game but also in life.

Surely this "body-sense" is a crucial part of our lives, and Gendlin is right to advise us to trust the felt sense in a situation of potential danger. But that does not mean it is always right. Yes, in a situation where you are gripped by sudden fear or even panic, you should take the relevant cautionary measures, but afterward, there can be reason to reflect and ask questions like "what was I afraid of?", "what background experiences have caused this reaction in that situation?" and "was it – in hindsight – a justified, reasonable, and good reaction?" I for one, know from personal experience, that there have been situations where I have been overcome with anxiety in situations like the one Gendlin describes, where I have felt the rising panic in my body, while my more conscious brain knew that it was unjustified and was getting annoyed with my body because there was actually nothing to be afraid of. I do believe that, as important for our survival as it is, the felt sense can still sometimes "go wrong."

In Gendlin's example, your body-sense draws on past experiences while it quickly goes through all the potential sequences that might happen in the near future. This is good, but there is also reason to be critical of our bodily feelings. For example, what are the past experiences implied in the felt sense? Are they personal experiences of having been assaulted in similar situations in the past or perhaps the experience of a lifetime of absorbing too much sensationalist and fear-mongering media that greatly exaggerates the rates of violent crime? Gendlin says you are not merely perceiving the men behind you but rather sensing them – the bodily sense comes before actual perception. This is true, but our bodily sense is still produced by having picked up various sensory data that our brain has not yet processed.

Might it be that the sense of anxiety was at least partially formed by having picked up that the group of men seem to have a different skin color than you do? Or that they speak a different language or have some other cultural behavior that seems "foreign" and "strange" and therefore causes the sensation that something is off and not as it should be? They could be following you for nefarious reasons, but they might also just be going the same way. Let's say that they call out and you panic and run, but perhaps they were trying to inform you that you had lost your wallet. You could be greatly misjudging the situation.

Misjudging the situation is not a big problem in that particular situation – after all, you could be right, and then it would have been much worse if you hadn't listened to your body. But I hope we can all see the problem of being a "gut player" who doesn't listen to critical voices when your guts tell you to invade another country, as in the case of George W. Bush, or start a trade war as in the case of Donald Trump. This is of course why Gendlin says it is not "just" a matter of getting in touch with your gut feelings (1981, p. 80) – focusing is about listening to them carefully and letting them develop so a "felt shift or bodily release" (1981, p. xvii) can occur. This felt shift cannot occur if we don't take the bodily feelings seriously, but that does not mean we should simply blindly trust them.

Embodied Critical Thinking (Schoeller & Thorgeirsdottir, 2019) explores this point. The theory states it is not just about a return to the body as a tool for critically engaging with the "rational" but also about a critical engagement with the bodily feelings themselves. When taken seriously and articulated they can change. Gendlin too is careful to state that we "cannot—and should not—trust any single set of words, any one feeling, any one body message that comes" (1981, p. 88) but rather accept them as steps in the process that carries us forward. This process might involve some bad feelings and we tend to avoid those, but the bad feelings "evidence that your body knows what is wrong" (1981, p. 86). The way to know that the process is working is that there is a change which *feels good* (1981, p. 9). The bad feelings are the body's way of moving toward a "more right way of being," which can only be achieved if we give it space (1981, p. 86). If we don't give ourselves and each other that space, we get stuck in the bad feelings.

Thus, the problem of miscommunication and anger that characterizes our current age might be less about people not being "rational" or "too emotional" and more about a culture that discourages the bodily and emotional side of our lives. If these sides are ignored, they are not allowed to develop and change, but they will still be present as active forces. Even when the felt sense is wrong – especially when it is wrong – we need to listen to it because otherwise, it will dominate our discourse and decision-making without us being aware of it or having any tools to change it. And that, I think, is relevant for the topic of debunking in the age of post-truth: we can provide all the logical arguments and empirical evidence we want against a false belief, but if we don't take seriously the reasons why it "feels right," as Steven Colbert says, then we'll miss the truthiness of it. And truthiness can be powerful. Thus, the first step toward a process of changing believes, if that is what we want, is to give them the space to be articulated – not in order to accept them as equally true in a postmodern relativistic sense, but precisely so that they might change. In *Focusing* (1981), Gendlin gives several examples of such a process, where felt convictions and emotions suddenly shift merely by being articulated in the presence of an active listener (e.g., pp. 12–36 and 51–57).

Reasonable false beliefs

Let us start with a semantic assumption: being reasonable means simply having reasons. The reasons a person has for believing something might not be reasons you think are valid, they might not be reasons that have any logical relation to the particular belief, and they might not even be consciously articulated by that person as the reasons for the belief. They are nonetheless *reasons* for the belief. If the belief feels right, it is not helpful to debunk the surface articulations of the belief; and then call the person "irrational," "unreasonable," or "stupid," for still holding on to them. That is more likely to backfire and cause resentment. We have to address, and take seriously, the reasons for why they feel right. And those reasons might be more reasonable than we assume.

In a French study (Barrera et al., 2020), scientists examined the effects of misinformation and of debunking it. They presented a group of test subjects with so-called "alternative facts" – deceitful statements about immigrants by the right-wing populist politician Marine Le Pen. Another group was presented with accurate statements on the same topics from various scholarly sources, and a third group received both the "alternative" and the official facts. The third group thus received the "fact-checking treatment" where they were exposed to harmful and hateful lies and then the debunking of those lies. The groups were then tested for both their belief in the factual statements and their degree of support for Marine Le Pen.

Unsurprisingly, the misleading statements alone both increased the belief in the statements and the support for the politician who made them. The interesting result is that although debunking did indeed change the subjects' beliefs concerning the factual statements, it did not reduce their support for the candidate who had made the false statements. Both the group who was exposed to the "alternative facts" alone and those who had also received the official facts and corrected their knowledge, experienced an increase in support for the candidate. Thus, the false statements worked even when the participants knew they were false. The scientists conclude that "fact checking is completely ineffective in undoing the persuasion effect of populist arguments." An even more troubling result is that even those who were only exposed to the official facts without the false statements also reported a small increase in voting intention for Marine Le Pen, which supports the conclusion that the mere exposure to the topics makes them more salient as factors in political decision-making, regardless of the epistemic beliefs concerning the topic.

I think "salience" here can work as a stand-in for "it feels right." Even when the participants received correct information and updated their factual beliefs accordingly, they were still pulled in the direction suggested by the false statements. This might be because they feel that even though the statements they received seem harmless there must be a reason for why they are suddenly brought up – and that feeling brings up associations to other potential facts as well as suspicions about what the correct statement is not saying. In other words, the truth can sometimes create a contradictory sense of "truthiness." This effect can be exaggerated when the initial lies – as the most efficient ones do – contain a grain of truth, which is instrumentalized to make the lies feel more right. In that situation, the mere debunking of the lies is likely to feel like a denial of the core of truth they are connected to and in that case, the debunking is likely to backfire and have the opposite of the intended effect.

I suspect this was the case for some people in the 2016 US presidential election. The Republican candidate, Trump, ran an aggressive campaign relentlessly criticizing everyone and everything that represented the American establishment as well as outsiders. He entered his political candidacy after having spent years promoting the racist dog-whistle conspiracy theory casting doubt about Barack Obama's place of birth, and thus presidential legitimacy, but the dog-whistle was replaced with openly racist rhetoric in Trump's first speeches and videos as an official candidate. The speech where he announced his candidacy became notorious for his description of Mexican immigrants as drug dealers, criminals, and rapists (Time, 2015), and the first campaign videos were exclusively centered around keeping foreigners out and "making America safe again" by banning Muslims and building a border wall.

But the messaging took a turn during the campaign as his staff tried to widen the potential audience: the final advertisement, called "Argument for America," was not only focused on outsiders but described the entire American and global political establishment as corrupt, having brought about disaster and destruction on the American people. Mixed with subtle antisemitic messages – as when the Jewish billionaire George Soros was shown while the voice-over mentioned "global special interests" who "control the levers of power" – the video described a nation in decay where a small elite has "robbed our working-class" and "put that money into the hands of a handful of large corporations" (Hodges, 2016). This was not just an attack on some of the least powerful people in the country – immigrants and other marginalized people – but on the most powerful people and the structures they uphold.

Meanwhile, his opponent, the Democratic candidate Hillary Clinton, ran a campaign that in comparison can only be described as conservative. Much of her campaign speeches and advertisements were focused on showing the most reprehensible clips and quotes from Trump to mobilize outrage, but as the French study shows, repeating false claims – even when accompanied by their refutation – is not politically effective, and the intended outrage is likely to only work on those who are already disposed to it. The rest of the campaign's messaging centered around her vast experience as a member of the very political elite Trump was attacking and defending an image of America as "already great" (Roberts & Siddiqui, 2016). Her final advertisement video, named "Tomorrow" (Hodges, 2016), contained a small acknowledgment that "we've come through some hard economic times" (which she most certainly had not, as all viewers must have been aware of) but insisted that "our best days are still ahead of us" if we just have faith in the political system and its core values.

In other words, the "liberal" campaign was solidly in defense of the status quo, while the "conservative" campaign called for an overturn of the economic and political establishment. The irony of these political positions aside, it is relevant to ask what "felt sense" in the population they were speaking to. Of course the millionaire tycoon-cum-politician Trump had no actual intention of overturning the economic or political structures, nor doing anything that would benefit the American working class, and of course, closing the borders for Muslims and Mexicans would not fix the problems average Americans were facing, but we need to look beyond the explicit articulations, which are easy to dismiss as irrational and empirically wrong, and find the kernel of truth that could make them "feel right."

I am convinced that a crucial difference between the two campaigns is that while he may not have provided any real solutions to the problems, Trump – unlike Clinton – clearly *acknowledged people's pain and suffering.* From the perspective of a policy analyst, he of course did not offer any solutions and being swayed by the rhetoric can thus be seen as "irrational." But that critique would miss a crucial fact about human existence. The campaign clearly and explicitly told people: I see your pain, it is real, you're not wrong to feel the system is not benefitting you, you're right to feel your situation is unfair, we should fix that somehow. That is the felt sense millions of Americans have been having and if you start by acknowledging people's felt sense, it is much more likely that anything you say after that will "feel right" no matter how nonsensical it is. In that context, the claim that America is "already great" and just needs a little push in the same direction will feel to many as gaslighting (McKinnon, 2017).

What is the reality that I think Trump implicitly addressed and Clinton brushed over? It is among other things, a reality where despite a global reduction in poverty rates over several decades, in "advanced economies" like the US poverty has been on the rise since the 1990s, despite the general economic growth of those economies (Dabla-Norris et al., 2015, p. 14). The lower income brackets have been "left behind" and in many OECD countries "as much as 40% of the population at the lower end of the distribution has benefited little from economic growth." This means the so-called "American dream" where you could expect that if you work hard your children would be likely to have a materially better life than you did is dead, as social mobility in the US has "fallen from approximately 90% for children born in 1940 to 50% for children born in the 1980s" (Chetty et al., 2017). This is not just some temporary "hard economic times" as Clinton implied but a long-term systemic trend that cannot be corrected by simply restoring faith in that system. As researchers from the OECD (2015, p. 21) conclude: "When such a large group in the population gains so little from economic growth, the social fabric frays and trust in institutions is weakened," and it is that mistrust populist politicians like Trump can tap into and channel to their own benefit. Now, economic hardship is of course no excuse for racism and building border walls is an absurd "solution" to the problem of a political and economic system that is ruled by a tiny elite who fly on private jets and have privileged access to cross international borders. But it is a reason to feel insecure, anxious, and angry, and pointing out the irrationality of the response does not help remove those general feelings. We can laugh at voters in, say, Iowa, who think building a wall in Texas would help them, when their problems are not caused by poor people from South or Central America, but perhaps we could also ask what "The Wall" signifies at a symbolic level – might it not represent some idea of security, of being in control in a world where you feel powerless? Trump's fans repeated the chant of "build the wall" at every rally all over the US which should give us reasons to suspect that it became a "floating signifier" (Laclau, 2005, p. 131) that for every individual in the different geographic locations could stand in as an imaginary solution for whatever anxieties – justified or not – people might have had.

During Trump's presidency, this wall was never completed, although having made it his central promise, he had to make some efforts toward it. But not completing the thing that has become the symbol of people's desires is an essential part of the demagogic project. In the terms of the psychoanalyst Jacques Lacan, desire always leaves a lack, or a gap, and is constituted by that gap (Lacan, 2005, p. x). The raison d'être of desire "is not to realize its goal, to find full satisfaction, but to reproduce itself as desire" (Zizek, 2008, p. 53). In other words, if the wall was finished, Trump's voters would find that their problems were still unresolved, but the point is precisely to have the problems unresolved in order to maintain the desire that drives them to demand solutions that will not work. Right-wing demagogs are not alone though, in using imaginary outsiders to generate affect and divert attention away from systemic problems. As Jesse Cohn writes, "US liberals have clung to narratives of Russian electoral hacking, attributing the present explosion of racist and misogynist violence to 'bots' and 'troll armies' rather than homegrown, endemic, institutionalized evil. Liberals thus shore up their belief that fascism is fundamentally unreal, a passing tangent in the long arc of a history that bends incrementally toward ever greater justice and inclusivity" (Cohn, 2020, p. 454). Both imaginaries leave the real problems unresolved and thus keep the desire in perpetual motion.

My argument is that both political camps tend to use arguments that are unpersuasive for the other because they miss the felt sense or the felt meaning of the others, and – perhaps equally important – they might not even be aware of their own felt sense. I further claim that the felt sense, when left unattended, unexamined, and unresolved, can result in articulations, emotions, and behaviors that are unconstructive and even harmful to oneself and others. Although these articulations and behaviors can be irrational, they are not "unreasonable" in the sense that they do not have *reasons* although the reasons might not be articulated. These unexamined reasons can give a sense of "truthiness" to various ideas: they "feel right" because they somehow connect to an underlying and implicit felt meaning in the body. That does not necessarily make them right – we should not simply trust our guts – but it does mean that simply dismissing or criticizing them is not going to work; that might just result in more anger.

Gendlin on anger

In "A Phenomenology of Emotions: Anger" (1973), Gendlin distinguishes emotions from "felt meaning." The latter concerns the bodily awareness of its situation and environment – both the "given whole complex situation" (p. 370), i.e. everything that is currently going on, and "the body's implying of sequences not now going on" (p. 377). Such a felt situation gives rise to various emotions, but the emotion is not the same as the feel of the whole situation, it is one possible "emotion sequence in a situation" (p. 383); just like in the example of you walking home at night and suddenly being swept by fear, anger might be the right response in a given situation, by which I mean that it implies a sequence of behaviors that are appropriate to the situation and can help it carry forward. Also as in that example, it might not be – perhaps the anger is appropriate to something in the situation but misdirected at the wrong thing in it. The specific emotion comes out of the felt sense of the complex situation, but it does not necessarily focus on that situation. Gendlin writes that if you focus on the anger, "you will get madder and madder" (p. 374) and you might lose the connection to why you are mad. Likewise, in the other example, if you focus on your fear, you might become more and more afraid and lose track of why you have that reaction: is it really caused by the strangers on the street or is it something else in your bodily situation that includes your past experiences and much else?

The potential disconnection between the emotional response and the bodily situation is, according to Gendlin (1973), a unique human capacity. Animals have fight-or-flight reactions too, but they have them in the situations that cause them. Humans, on the other hand, "can behave in reaction to situations they are not physically in at a given time" as well as "live in a situation and yet not behave in it" (1973, pp. 374, 375). This means we can suppress our emotional response in the situation that caused it but also have the capacity to "take situations along, to take them home, to be in many situations not present" (1973, p. 374). We can "nurse our anger, have it every time we put ourselves gesturally into the situation, although it isn't present" (1973, p. 376).

This ability can be quite useful because it enables our bodies to recognize a pattern in a situation that shares traits with a previous situation, which caused a certain reaction, and then reproduce the bodily response from the previous situation. For instance, if you've suffered pain, injustice, humiliation, etc. in a given situation or from a given person, your body now knows the cues which can enable it to anticipate and avoid or prepare for similar experiences: the muscles might tighten, the breathing and pulse might change, the body might go stiff, etc. This is not because you have analyzed the new situation rationally and empirically but because it contains something that reminds you of something in the past which triggered such strong bodily reactions that they were stored as templates for future use. A benign example from my own life is that after I had twisted my ankle several times, which can be excruciating, my whole body simply developed the instinctive reaction to go limp and collapse at the slightest unexpected twist rather than continue the planned step. This protected the weak ligaments and gave them time to heal. A more annoying example is when my acrophobia, which causes unpleasant bodily reactions when I am confronted with a steep drop from some height, is triggered by a visual cue in a perfectly safe situation.

The body notices something in a situation and reaches for a whole template of reactions and behaviors which could have been appropriate in the previous experience but might not be the right toolkit for the current one. This doesn't mean it is "irrational" because it is this instinctual habit-formation that enables us to learn and to adapt quickly to new situations and environments much faster than if we were rationally analyzing and calculating everything. But it does mean that it can sometimes make mistakes because the situation might not be identical to the previous one. Furthermore, it can be hard to know what aspect of a situation it is that causes the patterned reaction.

Perhaps you have tried, as I have, to be walking somewhere and suddenly you get a song in your head or remember a particular conversation? At first, you don't know why but then you remember: you were at this exact spot when you heard that song last or had that conversation, so the audible memory is triggered by the visual or spatial input. Memories and experiences are not compartmentalized in separate units but organized into whole experiential patterns, which is how the whole pattern of bodily reactions can be activated when just one of the elements is present.[3] This means that a subject that is in some way associated in the bodily unconscious with a different subject – perhaps because they share certain characteristics or because they happened in the same geographical area or temporal period – can activate the neurological and emotional reactions that might more appropriately "belong" to the associated subject. This process can be highly individual, or it can be shared among people who draw from similar cultural histories. And, importantly, those who do not have the same experience and therefore lack this affective association – or have a completely different one – are likely to fail to comprehend it unless they engage in serious attempts at active and sympathetic listening where the associative thoughts and feelings can be explicated, and if we fail at that we are likely to see the others as irrational.

To take a non-US-based example, during the UK campaign on the referendum to leave the EU in 2016 a friend of mine sent me a pro-Brexit meme (i.e. a piece of internet propaganda in favor of leaving the EU) that she wanted to share for a laugh because she considered it stupid. It was a post from a senior citizen describing a conversation with a young waitress telling her the reasons the EU had been bad for Britain and why it was desirable to "take back control."[4] The author claimed that when he was young, it was easy to get a job despite not having an education, working conditions were better, and even with a low-wage job you could make enough money to save up to buy a house, give your children an education, etc. These sentiments are all pretty standard conservative nostalgia that paint a romanticized picture of an idealized past and point to a specific cause for the loss of that past. Likewise, it is the EU and the free movement of labor between the member countries, with the implied message that if we just get rid of that cause, we can regain the good things from that past.

On the surface, this message seems ridiculous – firstly, because life in Britain before joining the European Common Market in 1973 (a year characterized by several bombings and assassinations within the UK and multiple UK wars abroad, a stock market crash, and massive strikes) was far from the idyllic fantasy the post was intended to evoke; and secondly, because leaving the EU and closing the borders would never bring back any elements of a long-lost era even if those elements had been real. My friend showed me this so we could share the mutual joy of expressing our contempt for the Brexit campaign's lack of arguments. I did not share the laughter though. Instead, I felt troubled because the post probably did express and connect to a real sentiment that is shared among a lot of people – namely, the "felt sense" that some things have gone wrong. It is a fact that it costs more, relative to the average income, to buy a house in the UK (Lamont, 2021), and it is a fact that social mobility has halted so that those born at the bottom of the income distribution have less chance of improving their occupational status and earnings than they did in the 1970s (OECD, 2018, p. 3).

As the OECD (2018, p. 24) document, people with a deteriorating economic situation are less likely to feel that their voice counts in the political process. The desire to build walls and to take back control comes from genuine feelings of insecurity and disempowerment that have real causes. These feelings are not "irrational" although they might be canalized into false explanations when hijacked and manipulated by those promising false solutions. Border walls and anti-immigration policies are not likely to alleviate the real experiences of pain and distress, but neither is the dismissal of these experiences. They come from a felt sense which must be taken seriously and addressed. Now that is not to say that the other side of the political issue does not have real experiences and affective reasons for their views. My friend who drew my attention to this Brexit message was herself an immigrant to the UK and has a background as a refugee from a country that disintegrated in civil war due to nationalist rhetoric and emotional hijacking of a kind not unlike that of the Brexit campaign. Her aversion to this rhetoric, and to the political proposal which would take away her rights in her new home, also comes from a lived reality, and the demand that this is taken seriously goes both ways.

The point is that when people have different lived experiences and histories which produce different bodily and cognitive meanings, it can be difficult to have a conversation because we might talk past each other. The idea that we can, or should, disentangle political topics from lived experiences is misguided though. These experiences will always be present – as implied affects and felt meanings – and if ignored or suppressed in the political discourse, they are easier to misdirect and become articulated in problematic ways.

"Trust the science" is not a neutral slogan

Felt meanings do not have to be grounded in individual experiences. Within the same country, different groups of people have had different histories, resulting in intergenerational memories and traumas, which means the present will be interpreted differently. This can affect the level of trust in various institutions and create division on topics that in other circumstances might not be "political." For some, vaccinating their children against a potentially serious childhood disease like measles or getting themselves vaccinated against the deadly COVID-19 virus might be a fairly straightforward decision of weighing potential pros and cons based on the available evidence or – more likely – simply trusting the medical experts to have done these calculations before recommending the vaccines. For them, politics are not part of the consideration.

At the start of the COVID-19 pandemic, vaccine hesitancy was highest among the Black and Hispanic population in the US and among people of African and South Asian descent in the UK (Nguyen et al., 2022; Razai et al., 2021). A report conducted in partnership with the civil rights organizations UnidosUS and NAACP concluded that the strongest predictor of whether Black and Hispanic Americans trusted the vaccine to be safe was the degree to which the respondents had general trust in the institutions involved in producing and distributing the vaccine from local medical institutions to the US government: negative trust correlated with higher hesitancy (Langer Research Associates, 2020, p. 11). This was thus not a matter of looking at the scientific evidence and then making a political decision to ignore it – the epistemic process was political from the beginning.

Slogans like "trust the science" are insensitive to the reality of US, and global, history, which still disproportionately affects people today. From the Tuskegee Experiment where the medical authorities of the US government injected hundreds of Black men with syphilis to the medical industry using the inhabitants of Puerto Rico and South America as unwilling test subjects, there is a list of cases going back centuries where there was every reason not to "trust the science" (Spigner, 2007). Not everyone is aware of these historical atrocities, but many minorities have experiences of explicit discrimination or unconscious biases in their encounters with health-care professionals, which in itself is a cause of reasonable medical mistrust (Bajaj & Stanford, 2021) and a reason to put "trustworthiness before trust" (Warren et al., 2020), i.e. prioritize demonstrating that the health-care system is committed to trustworthiness and equity rather than blaming the victims of structural discrimination for their hesitancy (Corbie-Smith, 2021). It is not just maltreatment and discrimination in healthcare that causes mistrust, though. Studies show that experiences of racial discrimination from other institutions such as in housing or employment and negative encounters with the police all have spillover effects resulting in a broader cultural mistrust, including mistrust in medical authorities and higher predispositions to seek alternative treatment and alternative information (Alang et al., 2020; Shippee et al., 2012; Whaley, 2001).

In other words, rather than thinking of mistrust as existing within individuals or communities, it is "a phenomenon created by and existing within a system that creates, sustains and reinforces racism, classism, homophobia and transphobia, and stigma" (Jaiswal & Halkitis, 2019). The manifold experiences engender a felt sense of generalized insecurity and mistrust, originating from what Gendlin calls the "bodily feel of the whole situation." For the particular emotional response – such as the medical mistrust or the vaccine hesitancy – to be addressed, it is necessary to pay respect to and address this whole situation. One does not rebuild a sense of safety and trust by shaming, stigmatizing, and attacking people who already feel stigmatized and under attack.

Conclusions

I have given different examples of how political arguments can go wrong even though they are technically correct because they focus on the surface articulations but miss the implicit felt sense that gives rise to these articulations. Debunking, criticizing, or dismissing these articulations is not going to move the process further if the felt sense remains unexamined. Such articulations can be anger or mistrust, both of which can be directed at targets that are not necessarily complicit in the situation causing these emotions. Focusing on the articulation can get us stuck in a behavioral pattern. As Gendlin says, emotions are "specifics" – they have recognizable patterns, they are "always the same" (1973, p. 370). Focusing on the felt meaning, on the other hand – the whole situation implied in the body and its environment – can result in many possible behaviors and thus open "alternative ways of acting and speaking" that take account of all the facets of the situation (1973, p. 373).

This is why dismissing the explicit articulations as irrational, hateful, or misguided is not helpful. This dismissal does not open any alternative articulations; it merely suppresses the existing ones. In *A Process Model*, Gendlin writes that to let new concepts emerge, "we must permit exactly what has emerged, and we must tell ourselves carefully just how we have it so far" (2017, p. 24). This is hard if what has emerged is hateful and hurtful. But the goal is not merely to accept whatever comes from the body. We should listen to the body, but we can be critical listeners. The goal is to start a process that can move forward through a series of shifts that make the situation feel different. That involves not only allowing what comes but also always asking "is there more" to get to the "fuzzy edges, the unclear part of the whole situation" (Gendlin, 2017, p. 210). This is obviously not a task we can demand of everyone. It is not the job of marginalized people, for example, to take abuse and listen sympathetically to racist tirades to guide the abuser toward a new perspective. It is though a necessary element in the broader cultural and political process if we want this process to move forward rather than being gridlocked in fixed behavioral patterns where opposing parties are merely shouting at each other with neither of them getting to the core of the issues.

These cores, the felt sense of the whole situation, are always more than what is articulated, but it is implied in the articulations. Merely looking at the explicit neglects the implicit meanings and thus fails to understand the epistemic function of "truthiness." Meanings and their articulations are never isolated. In formal logic we can take a statement, "P," and examine its truth conditions and its causal relation to another statement, "Q." Felt meaning does not function like that. It is a process, and no part of a process functions as itself or "as an individuated 'it'" (Gendlin, 2017, p. 39). Thus, from the perspective of formal logic, there might be no relation between the brutal killing of a Black man, George Floyd, by a White police officer, and skepticism about the safety of the vaccine against COVID-19, and there might be no logical connection between wage stagnation, growing inequality, and decreasing social mobility on the one hand and support for building border walls or leaving the EU. But on the level of the bodily processes, these issues might be related. Any bodily articulation, or "occurring," always implies the environment it occurs into (2017, p. 42), and when the environment is one of precariousness, insecurity, and disempowerment, it is going to be part of the felt meaning that is implicit in various articulations: the different processes "imply each other in the same occurring" (2017, p. 24).

Rather than seeing the popularity of conspiracy theories, scapegoats, "alternative facts," and other elements of the "post-truth era" as evidence of a decline in rational thinking, we might interpret them as attempts to grapple with the felt sense that the social environment is not functioning the way we are expecting it to or the way we are told it does. Our bodies feel that our needs are not being met but we are not paying attention to the body. This creates articulations that are disconnected from the lived experience, and the task for those who want to ameliorate the situation must be to help guide us back to our felt sense, the place that is in pain, and allow it to be articulated in a way that feels better and carries us forward.

Notes

1 A prohibition against blinking is mentioned no less than thirty four times in the public speeches of George W. Bush in the first half of 2002 (Bush, 2002).
2 One of Gendlin's key discoveries was that a successful therapeutic process involves bodily gestures. Micro-phenomenologists, such Claire Petitmengin, have developed this research further and examined the bodily micro-gestures involved in thinking more generally (Petitmengin, 2007, 2019).
3 From a neuroscientific perspective, Damásio (1995, p. 100) argues that memories are not stored as facsimile pictures of things in separate brain regions but are rather attempts at replication of patterns that were once experienced and strengthened particular dispositions of synaptic structures; when we recall a memory, we thus rely upon several aspects of that experience. Similarly, from the perspective of microphenomenology, Claire Petitmengin (2007) notices that the beginning of a recollection, which she compares with Gendlin's "felt meaning," is sensorily transmodal, i.e. not specific to a particular sense but can be transposed from one sense to another.
4 For the sake of privacy, I am anonymizing both the original post and its critic here.

References

Alang, S., McAlpine, D. D., & Hardeman, R. (2020). Police brutality and mistrust in medical institutions. *Journal of Racial and Ethnic Health Disparities*, *7*(4), 760–768. https://doi.org/10.1007/s40615-020-00706-w

Bajaj, S. S., & Stanford, F. C. (2021). Beyond Tuskegee—Vaccine distrust and everyday racism. *New England Journal of Medicine*, *384*(5), e12. https://doi.org/10.1056/NEJMpv2035827

Barrera, O., Guriev, S., Henry, E., & Zhuravskaya, E. (2020). Facts, alternative facts, and fact checking in times of post-truth politics. *Journal of Public Economics*, *182*, 104123. https://doi.org/10.1016/j.jpubeco.2019.104123

Bush, G. W. (2002). *Public Papers of the Presidents of the United States: George W. Bush, January 1 to June 30, 2002* (Vol. 1). Office of the Federal Register, National Archives and Records Administration.

Cadwalladr, C. (2017, February 12). Daniel Dennett: 'I begrudge every hour I have to spend worrying about politics.' *The Observer*. https://www.theguardian.com/science/2017/feb/12/daniel-dennett-politics-bacteria-bach-back-dawkins-trump-interview

Chetty, R., Grusky, D., Hell, M., Hendren, N., Manduca, R., & Narang, J. (2017). The fading American dream: Trends in absolute income mobility since 1940. *Science, 366*(6336). https://doi.org/10.1126/science.aal4617

Cohn, J. S. (2020). The fantastic from counterpublic to public imaginary: The darkest timeline? *Science Fiction Studies, 47*(3), 448–463. https://doi.org/10.5621/sciefictstud.47.3.0448

Colbert, S. (Director). (2005, October 17). *The Colbert Report.* Comedy Central. https://www.cc.com/video/w9dr6d/the-colbert-report-first-show

Corbie-Smith, G. (2021). Vaccine hesitancy is a scapegoat for structural racism. *JAMA Health Forum, 2*(3), e210434. https://doi.org/10.1001/jamahealthforum.2021.0434

Dabla-Norris, E., Kochhar, K., Suphaphiphat, N., Ricka, F., & Tsounta, E. (2015). *Causes and Consequences of Income Inequality: A Global Perspective.* International Monetary Fund.

Damásio, A. (1995). *Descartes' Error.* Avon Books.

DePaul, M. R. (1998). Liberal exclusions and foundationalism. *Ethical Theory and Moral Practice, 1*(1), 103–120. https://doi.org/10.1023/A:1009960532401

Ekéus, R. (2016). The lessons of UNSCOM and Iraq. *The Nonproliferation Review, 23*(1–2), 131–146. https://doi.org/10.1080/10736700.2016.1186875

Gabbatt, A. (2019, January 21). The "exhausting" work of factcheckers who track Trump's barrage of lies. *The Guardian.* https://www.theguardian.com/us-news/2019/jan/21/donald-trump-lies-factcheckers

Gendlin, E. (1973). A phenomenology of emotions: Anger. In D. Carr & E. S. Casey (Eds.), *Explorations in Phenomenology: Papers of the Society for Phenomenology and Existential Philosophy* (pp. 367–398). Springer.

Gendlin, E. (1981). *Focusing* (2nd ed.). Bantam.

Gendlin, E. (1992). The primacy of the body, not the primacy of perception. *Man and World, 25*(3–4), 341–353.

Gendlin, E. (2017). *A Process Model.* Northwestern University Press.

Hendricks, V. F., & Hansen, P. G. (2014). *Infostorms: How to Take Information Punches and Save Democracy.* Springer.

Herring Networks v. Maddow. (2021). *No. 20–55579.* United States District Court for the Southern District of California (July 27, 2021). https://cdn.ca9.uscourts.gov/datastore/opinions/2021/08/17/20-55579.pdf

Hodges, L. (2016, November 7). In closing ads, Trump goes dark while Clinton goes Cozy. *NPR.* https://www.npr.org/2016/11/07/501029170/in-closing-ads-trump-goes-dark-while-clinton-goes-cozy

Hong, S. (2020). "Fuck your feelings": The affective weaponization of facts and reason. In M. Boler & E. Davis (Eds.), *Affective Politics of Digital Media.* Routledge.

Jaiswal, J., & Halkitis, P. N. (2019). Towards a more inclusive and dynamic understanding of medical mistrust informed by science. *Behavioral Medicine, 45*(2), 79–85. https://doi.org/10.1080/08964289.2019.1619511

Justice, J. W., & Bricker, B. J. (2019). Hacked: Defining the 2016 presidential election in the liberal media. *Rhetoric & Public Affairs, 22*(3), 389–420.

Kessler, G., Salvador, R., & Kelly, M. (2020, October 22). Trump is averaging more than 50 false or misleading claims a day. *Washington Post.* https://www.washingtonpost.com/politics/2020/10/22/president-trump-is-averaging-more-than-50-false-or-misleading-claims-day/

Keyes, R. (2004). *The Post-Truth Era: Dishonesty and Deception in Contemporary Life*. St. Martin's Publishing Group.

Klosko, G. (1993). Rawls's "political" philosophy and American democracy. *The American Political Science Review*, *87*(2), 348–359. https://doi.org/10.2307/2939045

Lacan, J. (2005). *Ecrits: A Selection*. Routledge.

Laclau, E. (2005). *On Populist Reason*. Verso.

Lamont, D. (2021, March 15). What 175 Years of Data Tell Us about House Price Affordability in the UK. Schroder Unit Trusts Limited.https://www.schroders.com/en/uk/private-investor/insights/markets/what-174-years-of-data-tell-us-about-house-price-affordability-in-the-uk/

Langer Research Associates. (2020). Survey on coronavirus vaccine hesitancy in black and latinx communities: Covid collaborative. *COVID Collaborative*. https://www.covidcollaborative.us/resources/coronavirus-vaccine-hesitancy-in-black-and-latinx-communities

McDougal v. Fox News. (2020). *1:19-cv-11161-MKV*. United States District Court Southern District of New York (September 24, 2020). https://www.courthouse-news.com/wp-content/uploads/2020/09/McDougal-Opinion.pdf

McKinnon, R. (2017). Allies behaving badly: Gaslighting as epistemic injustice. In I. J. Kidd, J. Medina, & G. Jr. Pohlhaus (Eds.), *The Routledge Handbook of Epistemic Injustice* (pp. 167–174). Routledge. https://doi.org/10.4324/9781315212043-16

NBC. (2017, January 22). Meet the press 01/22/17. *NBC News*. https://www.nbcnews.com/meet-the-press/meet-press-01-22-17-n710491

Nguyen, L. H., Joshi, A. D., Drew, D. A., Merino, J., Ma, W., Lo, C.-H., Kwon, S., Wang, K., Graham, M. S., Polidori, L., Menni, C., Sudre, C. H., Anyane-Yeboa, A., Astley, C. M., Warner, E. T., Hu, C. Y., Selvachandran, S., Davies, R., Nash, D., ... Chan, A. T. (2022). Self-reported COVID-19 vaccine hesitancy and uptake among participants from different racial and ethnic groups in the United States and United Kingdom. *Nature Communications*, *13*(1), 636. https://doi.org/10.1038/s41467-022-28200-3

Nietzsche, F. (2009). *On the Genealogy of Morals: A Polemical Tract* (I. Johnston, Trans.). Richer Resources Publications.

Nottelmann, N. (2007). *Blameworthy Belief: A Study in Epistemic Deontologism*. Springer Science & Business Media.

OECD. (2015). *In It Together: Why Less Inequality Benefits All*. OECD Publishing. http://www.oecd-ilibrary.org/employment/in-it-together-why-less-inequality-benefits-all_9789264235120-en

OECD. (2018). *A Broken Social Elevator? How to Promote Social Mobility*. OECD Publishing. https://doi.org/10.1787/9789264301085-en

Oxford Languages. (2016). *Oxford Word of the Year 2016*. Oxford University Press. https://languages.oup.com/word-of-the-year/2016/

Petitmengin, C. (2007). Towards the source of thoughts: The gestural and trans-modal dimension of lived experience. *Published in the Journal of Consciousness Studies*, *14*, 54–82.

Petitmengin, C., Remillieux, A., & Valenzuela-Moguillansky, C. (2019). Discovering the structures of lived experience. *Phenomenology and the Cognitive Sciences*, *18*(4), 691–730. https://doi.org/10.1007/s11097-018-9597-4

Razai, M. S., Chaudhry, U. A. R., Doerholt, K., Bauld, L., & Majeed, A. (2021). Covid-19 vaccination hesitancy. *BMJ, 373*, n1138. https://doi.org/10.1136/bmj. n1138

Roberts, D., & Siddiqui, S. (2016, July 28). "America is already great": Obama urges US to back Clinton in DNC speech. *The Guardian*. https://www.theguardian. com/us-news/2016/jul/28/obama-hillary-clinton-convention-speech-trump

Schoeller, D., & Thorgeirsdottir, S. (2019, July 18). *Embodied Critical Thinking: The Experiential Turn and Its Transformative Aspects*. Philosophia.

Shippee, T. P., Schafer, M. H., & Ferraro, K. F. (2012). Beyond the barriers: Racial discrimination and use of complementary and alternative medicine among black Americans. *Social Science & Medicine, 74*(8), 1155–1162. https://doi.org/10.1016/j. socscimed.2012.01.003

Spigner, C. (2007). Medical apartheid: The dark history of medical experimentation on black Americans from colonial times to the present. *Journal of the National Medical Association, 99*(9), 1074.

Suskind, R. (2004, October 17). Faith, certainty and the presidency of George W. Bush. *The New York Times*. https://www.nytimes.com/2004/10/17/magazine/faith-certainty-and-the-presidency-of-george-w-bush.html

Time. (2015, June 16). Here's Donald Trump's presidential announcement speech. *Time.Com*. https://time.com/3923128/donald-trump-announcement-speech/

University of Copenhagen. (2015, March 2). *The Carlsberg Foundation funds Centre for Information and Bubble Studies*. University of Copenhagen. https://bubblestudies.ku.dk/news/the_carlsberg_foundation_funds_centre_for_information_and_bubble_studies/

Viebeck, E. (2018, August 19). 'Truth isn't truth': Giuliani weighs risks of possible Trump interview in Russia probe. *Washington Post*. https://www.washingtonpost. com/politics/truth-isnt-truth-giuliani-weighs-risks-of-possible-trump-interview-in-russia-probe/2018/08/19/61c11916-a3ca-11e8-a656-943eefab5daf_story.html

Warren, R. C., Forrow, L., Hodge, D. A., & Truog, R. D. (2020). Trustworthiness before trust—Covid-19 vaccine trials and the black community. *New England Journal of Medicine, 383*(22), e121. https://doi.org/10.1056/NEJMp2030033

Washington Post. (2018, November 27). President Trump's full washington post interview transcript, annotated. *Washington Post*. https://www.washingtonpost. com/politics/2018/11/27/president-trumps-full-washington-post-interview-transcript-annotated/

Whaley, A. L. (2001). Cultural mistrust: An important psychological construct for diagnosis and treatment of African Americans. *Professional Psychology: Research and Practice, 32*(6), 555–562. https://doi.org/10.1037/0735-7028.32.6.555

Woodward, B. (2002). *Bush At War*. Simon and Schuster.

Young, S. P. (2006). Rawlsian reasonableness: A problematic presumption? *Canadian Journal of Political Science, 39*(1), 159–180. https://doi.org/10.1017/S0008423906040741

Zhang, S. (2019, January 14). Trump's most trusted adviser is his own gut. *The Atlantic*. https://www.theatlantic.com/politics/archive/2019/01/trump-follows-his-gut/580084/

Zizek, S. (2008). *The Plague of Fantasies* (Second Edition). Verso.

Chapter 8

Toward a concept of "freedom to make sense"

Donata Schoeller

Introduction

In the following I sketch features of a freedom that plays out in conditions that allow us to sense the problems, dilemmas, and questions that arise from actual experience. This is not a trivial capacity. It needs training, support, and cultivation. And it needs a kind of focus that is not only result-oriented or pre-determined by a set agenda. The kind of freedom I mean implies time and practice-possibilities. It grants spaces and methods to find the right words that clarify matters that are meaningful in the contexts of everyday life.

Critical terms such as racism, sexism, speciesism, gender, or the banality of evil, sustainability, and resonance have grown from experiential grounds. These terms condense and make tangible basic patterns within cultural, political, and economic systems, habits, values, and ways of knowledge, which shape the lifeworld. Naming these entangled patterns is a vastly difficult affair. Not because they are hidden, but because they are the complex lenses through which one learns to see, feel, and experience the world. The sheer emergence of these terms changed the course of events: their meaning and implications have been tipping points of novel forms of understanding that have had the potential to change the very fabric of cultural possibilities from which they emerged. These tipping points do not just rely on knowledge and information. They rely on people that have the courage to take seriously the perplexities of experiencing their world. These are people who boldly explicate what feels wrong, even though it seems right according to shared values and frameworks of thinking; or what feels right, yet has no chance to be enacted due to customary ways of behaving and going about things.

"Freedom to make sense" is inspired by this kind of critical thinking. Latter is characterized by engaging with experience and formulating its complex structures in ways that convey a novel kind of clarity, together with new pathways of thinking and acting. If one grants each other conditions to engage with experience and find words to clarify the muddle and uncover

DOI: 10.4324/9781003296706-9

the relevant questions, dilemmas, cruxes, and intuitions, then the terms that emerge are highly transformative – not only to oneself. Obviously, para-digmatic changes do not happen on a daily basis. Yet, the kind of think-ing involved in a "freedom to make sense" grants a surprising openness and transformativity in the midst of the thick situations one strives to cope with and understand. Therefore, this freedom may begin small, personal, yet the personal cannot be separated from its interaction with a world. A continuity between the personal and the collective, the particular and the universal realm features in the freedom I mean. In the following, I hope to demonstrate this a little. Furthermore, I will characterize some conditions of such a freedom, and strive to reflect its consequences in terms of what it tells us about experience, meaning, and language. I will add three examples to convey a taste of the transformative quality of enacting a "freedom to make sense" on the scale of daily situations. All of this, of course, is deeply inspired by Eugene Gendlin's work. And all of this is still very much work in progress, so please bear with the rough edges and loose ends.

Approaching the terms freedom and felt sense

Freedom

Understanding freedom along the above-mentioned lines, changes some traditional implications. Let me begin by mentioning some of these.

Emmanuel Levinas and Corine Pelluchon (2019) have demonstrated that in European philosophy the concept of freedom is implicitly connected to the individual's power. The famous freedom of will, for example, builds on the tacit assumption of autonomy as an ideal. Autonomy in this sense stresses the individual's independence and capacity to do what it wants. Even Heidegger, who questioned so many tacit assumptions of Western philosophy, still seemed to consider the fact that we are born as a kind of violation of human freedom. After all, nobody has asked us if we want to be born. His term "Geworfenheit" indicates this primordial violation of the autonomous will as a trait of the human condition (Heidegger, 1967, p. 175). Pelluchon, carrying forward Levinas work, confronts such a view by acknowledging the fact that humans are beings that are in constant need of being nourished by the earth, by a world cultivated and developed by ances-tors, by inspirations, and by relationships. Additionally, Martha Nussbaum has made us aware of the specific cultural circumstances that grant or do not grant capabilities to make the best of our life, which goes hand in hand with dismantling an abstract concept of human freedom (Nussbaum, 2000). These philosophers rethink the meaning of freedom under the condition that every fiber of our being is deeply interdependent of environments, all the sensitivities that come along with that.

We can never leave behind our being in-the-midst, engaged, entangled, and involved within a lifeworld, this is the number one lesson of classical phenomenology (Merleau Ponty, 1976). This starting point is today strongly propagated within new developments of generative, critical, and engaged phenomenology (Stanier, 2022). Interactionality as the experiential, embodied, and factual ground from where we think and act is also at the center of Gendlin's process philosophy. Our organism is and implies interaction with the world on every chemical, biological, social, cultural, political, and economical level. Our embodied life processes affect and imply environments which were created by former and present living processes. As Gendlin poignantly says: "The skin-line is not the great divide" (Gendlin, 2018, p. 6).

Under this major condition, freedom is a processual affair: it emerges within the richness of entanglements of lived experience. "Freedom to make sense" thus indicates a process of being able to make sense within a highly complex web of living, which itself is affected by this very process of sense making.

Sense

Sense is a term in which disembodied tensions of European philosophy are tangible by the mere fact that it has been narrowed down for a long time in two respects. First, in sense perception, the term indicates mainly the input by the senses (what we see, hear, smell, taste, touch), while seeing traditionally occupied a main place. Second, experience as a whole has been identified with sense perception requiring the ordering categories of the mind to make sense. The Kantian conception of experience consisting of two components, of sense perceptions and the categories of the sense-making mind, has been the target of major criticism of feminist, hermeneutical, phenomenological, and pragmatist philosophy.

Gendlin's concept of a *felt sense* functions strongly in this traditionally loaded context by drawing together what has been chronically separated as: body and mind. As a notion, the felt sense also bridges other major dualism in a single stroke, conceptual cuts between subject and object, nature and culture, feeling and rationality. The provocation of this term consists in the fact that feeling was long considered as the "other" of mind and rationality which alone seemed responsible of conveying order, sense, and meaning to the world (Böhme & Böhme, 1985). Also, the *felt sense* locates the capacity to sense not only in the sense organs but in the experiencing body that enacts meaning by living a life in constant interaction with environments. Most importantly however, felt sense as a concept acknowledges a dimension of meaning that develops and unfolds according to how we interact and relate with situated, embodied experience. In this respect, it echoes the interactive characteristic of the freedom I touched upon above. One cannot attend to the felt sense without latter being affected by this attending. Epistemologically, this reciprocity is a major crux in dealing with the kind of knowing involved. Therefore, analogies of first-person experience and quantum mechanical epistemology are being drawn today by cognitive scientists (Kordeš & Demšar, 2019).

For now, let me tentatively say, a freedom to make sense implies engaging with experience in ways that transforms both the experience explicated and the meaning of the words used.

Conditions of a freedom to make sense

Making space for the experiential response

Eugene Gendlin's epistemological and rather abstract criticism of a model of reality build on steady explicit units of information and knowledge, reads to me as a culture critique on a basic level:

> The old model has only explicit structure, "information" that is attributable to space-time positions. Most of the parameters of our sciences are structured in just this fashion, so that it is no use denying these assumptions themselves, since they are not only general; they also inhere in how everything else is conceived and written down.
>
> (Gendlin, 2018, p. 49)

Yet, what is missing in such a model? What is wrong about supposing that information is everything and everywhere, on the micro- and the macro-levels of life? Every space-time position can inform us about something, of a physical, biological, social, and political situation. Everything that happens can be analyzed into units that participated and thus become reliable pieces of knowledge that can be connected. Nothing seems to be missing in this understanding of reality. It also proves highly functional for the human hope to construct algorithmic artificial intelligence, which can by now analyze complex situations in ways that allow predictions no human brain could ever achieve.

Nonetheless, what is missing in such a model one can name in three words: it is the *situated embodied experience*.

Phenomenology but also classical pragmatism and feminist philosophy have contributed greatly in describing the complexity of ordinary experience, in which we navigate pre-reflexively within a web of interconnected situational circumstances that exceed the explicit kind of knowledge (Barad, 2007; Jung, 2014).

Gendlin's work is a treasure trove of unfolding the complexity of situated experience:

> Since cultural situations are very complex, and each situation implicitly involves others too, which are also complex, a very great deal more is bodily lived and felt in this "in-action" way than is ever sequenced as such in those rather few "slotted" sequences we consider our feelings.
>
> (Gendlin, 2018, p. 200)

The term "situation" elaborates something elementary in human life that Dewey might have been the first to notice (Dewey, 1984). To make sense of a situation is not identical to knowing the facts or making a narrative about something or someone. To specify the term situation, Dewey began to spell out the function of a feeling that is not an emotion, yet a kind of tacit orientation that involves more than information, concepts, identifiable emotions, and data. Dewey also recognized that situations one is involved in are never only subjective, or private. A situation *is* a complex interconnectivity with other situations, people, circumstances, cultural settings, norms, rules, and environments. In line with William James, John Dewey, Wilhelm Dilthey, and George Herbert Mead, Gendlin elaborates what today feminist thinkers term situated knowing (Harraway 1988). This kind of knowing cannot be reduced and analyzed to pre-existing units. In his work, Gendlin describes the multi-schematic and nonnumerical characteristics of situated knowing and experiencing, which can lead to very different conceptualizations. This texture of implicit dynamic crossings of previous experiences, interpretations and learnings, is logically determinable and conceptually patterned only *after* it has been explicated (Gendlin, 1993, p. 197).

Acknowledging what Gendlin calls a pre-separated intricacy of the experiencing body has contributed greatly to the possibility of evaluating and unpacking the complexity involved.

> The intricacy you are now living vastly exceeds what cultural forms have contributed to you. (...) Direct access to this intricacy enables us to think-from much more than the usual concepts and assumptions.
>
> (Gendlin, 2003, p. 115)

The term "direct access" however is misleading if insinuating that one refers to some given, internal entity. Rather, this term indicates a possible shift of attention from *what* to *how* we experience. Focusing, the hermeneutical method Gendlin developed, can be regarded as a way to practice such "direct access" as a disciplined attention to the qualitative dimension of experience. As such, this is a practice for making a space for the complex web of situated experience. I like to compare Focusing to the skill of closely and carefully reading texts which opens up surprising layers of understanding and further thinking (Schoeller, 2019). Let me draw out this analogy some more.

In closely reading a text, our slow involvement makes us notice that our assumptions of what the text means do not work as presumed. The text confronts us with phrases and passages that get us off track of an understanding we thought we had. Puzzled by some passages, we thus become more receptive to look through the text, find clues, connections, and terms that become important. We discover more, after being puzzled. We start to look, read back, connect, pause, and become aware of decisive sentences we did not notice before. Only through our close engagement with the text does a lively process of shifting meanings happen. As the text begins to speak to us, it responds to questions that emerge through the clash of what we implicitly thought we understood and what we actually find in the text.

Focusing is a method to "read" slowly and dwell carefully with whatever aspect of situated experience one chooses to explore. This practice builds on one of the crucial findings of Gendlin's work: that words impact and affect the very experience of the situation described. Acknowledging this impact obviously creates a tension in relation to the phenomenological project of which Gendlin is part. In recent cognitive science the project of describing experience is considered as "non-trivial" and "precarious," because the description has an effect on the experience described (Kordeš and Demšar 2018). However, Gendlin's emphasis of the responsive relation between the explication and the explicated (or described) experience does not end in the acknowledgement of first person inquiry being precarious. Rather, this is a starting point of a new kind of very precise exploration that focuses on the interface, and what happens in the logically non-determinable transitions *between* propositions when we try to make sense of a situation (Gendlin 1963).

In Focusing, one practices exactly this. One does not just concentrate on propositions, but on the embodied experiential response to how one formulates something: what happens experientially, when you say it like this, or another way? With this method, one notices how what one articulates changes in *non-random* ways through the very act of being articulated in one way or another. We can feel what we say is not quite right, even though the grammar is correct and the words used would make sense in the context. Noticing such felt response is a strong bias control. What we mean to say very frequently proves different to what we conceptualized. Gendlin demonstrates throughout his work this amazingly precise and often tender responsiveness of situated experience (Gendlin, 1991, 1997). Noticing this was like discovering a new keyboard on my reflexive organ.

Thus, "a freedom to make sense" is very distinct to the act of fabricating some narrative or interpretation about experience in one's mind. That is why this kind of freedom is especially challenging for the complex creatures we are, responsive to others and to ourselves, responsive to every occurring, and responsive to how we speak about it. Slowing down to explore more closely this responsive fabric of experiencing a situation does not work from a position of detachment. So, a "freedom to make sense" is opposite to disengaging from experience to say whatever one likes. It is also different to jumping on an emotion and cannibalizing it to fuel an opinion. We have scarce methods when it comes to creating a space of transformative understanding in the engagement with actual experience. You might say: well, isn't that the role of art or therapy? So let me demonstrate in small examples why I think this kind of freedom should not be "disciplined" in this way. I rather believe it applies across the walks of life.

Courage to acknowledge

While hardly being able to sense our reactions, our outrage, perplexity, despair, or at times joy, within the speed of daily news, information, images we take in on social media, attending to the qualitative dimensions of experience seems very counter-culture. The only way to deal with the world that pours into our digital devices seems to be developing a thick skin, becoming cool and kind of numb toward what is going on beneath the skin-line. While our culture provides us with ample of means of delivering information, news, and bits of knowledge, there is a bewildering scarcity of means to integrate any of this with our own situations in a way that enables us to process the complex environments we inhabit.

In this kind of context, I consider the following account of Steven Hayes an enactment of a "freedom to make sense." After being informed about the Sandy Hook school shooting (Hayes, 2016), Hayes realized that he could not continue with the news as usual. Turning off the TV, he sat with what he just heard and thereby encountered his grief – the powerful felt response that he usually tried to ignore when watching news. Finding himself weeping alone in front of the TV, he began to realize that this really was the only way to intelligibly process what he saw and heard. Attending to this experience and the tears coming along did not wear him out, on the contrary. It started an engagement with the devastating information that otherwise would not have come about. This engagement gradually shifted his understanding. The ensuing in-depth research transformed his thinking about the whole situation in ways that exceeded the patterns implicit in the news, the powerful binary of good and bad, victim and perpetrator. Granting himself to be shaken by what he heard and saw, by acknowledging his own experience and the challenging embodied response, allowed resources of sensitivity, situated understanding, and felt empathy to thicken his approach and find his own stance. Not canceling and shutting down his own painful feelings and flood of tears, affected his reflections in ways to become capable of holding a wider situation of everyone involved, while unfolding the story behind every single child, including one more, the pale child that as a grownup turned deadly violent. This process shows how a "freedom to make sense" is distinct from constructing narratives or jumping on one emotional trigger to funnel one's thinking. Also, this kind of freedom involves even more than accessing different sources of news, and it goes beyond discussions about fake news or truths, as crucial as all of this is. The kind of freedom I mean grows from an engagement with something, in which the thinking is receptive to experiencing, and experiencing is receptive to thinking. Both stay in touch with each other to come up with an understanding that was not there before.

Let me add a personal example that is not as dramatic as the courageous account of Hayes. The example shows how acknowledging the experiential side of a "position" I held, opened my eyes to my own limited view. This enabled me to move beyond preconditioned alternatives that imprint social patterns of debates today.

The following happened during a COVID lockdown. Differing positions concerning the political and medical strategies to cope with the situation started to impact my relationship with a close friend. I had confidence in the system and followed its recommendations. The position of my friend was diametrical to mine, and in my eyes, lacked scientific foundation, and seemed annoyingly irrational. And even though we would both provide more and more sources for our positions and opinions, it would get us nowhere. Building on facts and narratives, the ground to understand each other had almost totally diminished. So, I chose to attend to this clash of positions more closely. I started to explore the experiential dimension of the situation, and I asked someone to accompany me while doing so. This is Focusing. It very often is done in a dyadic setting. The partner has the function of saying back what one formulates, so one can notice more clearly the experiential response to one's own verbal explorations.

Soon I noticed there is a qualitative side connected to my "position." I expressed this as a "confidence in the medical system," which my friend did not have. After being reflected back to me by my listener, I realized the term did not work well. Rather, the feeling seemed more like a "trust," a "personal kind of trust." Trust to a partner, who is a doctor, and trust to a daughter, who is becoming one – yes, that rang true. A slight pressure on my stomach became softer while repeating this term. Yet, there was also a fuzzy feeling of "belonging to a university context" professionally, that I needed to acknowledge. The "trust" and that latter feeling seemed quite "questionless." This made me curious. I gradually had to concede that this "questionlessness" really had no clear basis of knowledge. Neither did I fully understand the harmful workings of the virus nor did I exactly grasp the different forms of functioning of the vaccinations, and their different procedures of immunization, despite the explanations from my medical surrounding, which, at some point in the conversations regularly needed to admit they would not know exactly either, that one would need to ask a virologist.

During this Focusing session, I began to realize, it was not just trust, more of a "decision to trust," and that term rang very true and led to a deep breath. It made me see that the rational reasons I believed I had, which qualified my position as the one that seemed more sensible in comparison to hers, were not the foundation of my position. Discovering that I did not rely on facts, as I thought I had, yet on a pre-reflexive decision to trust, made me realize we are not so far apart after all: I pre-reflectively decided to trust, she pre-reflectively decided not to. In the ongoing process, I gradually noticed there was something deeper still. Again, it was the word "trust" that literally "resonated" with the experience in ways that shifted something, as if uncovering another level. There was a kind of vital "trust in life" as the bottom line, something I had never consciously felt as such, especially not in the troubled situations around me. Naming this tacit foundation immediately opened a novel channel of understanding. It shifted my perspective in ways I could not foresee. Even though I would always continue to trust in medical experts and their research, touching base with this deep layer of experiencing made me realize that the "positions" we both held need not separate us. Hannah Arendt came to mind, who used to toast to friendship after fierce debates. I now could see why. Differing positions, I vividly sensed in that moment, are indicators of something deeper, which was vague, not fully rationally founded, utterly difficult to explicate. Sensing a vital trust in life as a baseline made me understand that we fiercely cared in different ways. Holding on to that joint foundation opened up the realm of a surprisingly tender understanding that made the binary options of rational and irrational, true and false, less cutting.

Weeks after this process I read William James' (2022) *Will to Believe*. While being amazed about his bold intellectual honesty, I smilingly nodded while reading the following sentence:

> Our faith is faith in someone else's faith, and in the greatest matters this is most the case.
>
> (James, 2022, p. 26)

My process above did not result in ignoring the reasons for our different ways of thinking and acting. It rather opened my eyes to see that for understanding the situation more fully, reasons alone are not enough. Once more, this made me aware of the multi-stranded, intricate, and intimate experiential side involved that needs to be considered to overcome a partial kind of reflection, a term I borrow from Francisco Varela (Varela et al., 1983). Partial reflections are not thoroughgoing enough to consider the affective and experiential dimension involved in what we hold to be true – James called this the passionate dimension beneath the rational. Dominant reasons, facts, and narratives that lead to splits within families and societies blur the actual felt happening carrying the narrative. Attending to the felt dimensions of *what* we think opens and specifies the involvements, relation-ships, engagements, and implications of *how* we experience the issue. Only then do we know what exactly we are talking about.

"Freedom to make" sense thus implies conditions that allow us to real-ize the responsive plasticity in the very fabric of human situations. Things already change just by paying attention to this fabric more closely. In the toughness and scarcity of time characterizing daily situations today, this might seem a luxury and privilege. I believe the opposite is the case. Being unable to acknowledge and explicate the felt and experiential dimensions of our position in the context of debates, is a severe limitation of commu-nicative practices. Not granting each other conditions to spell out the com-plexity of embodied situated experience involved, is what makes our social discourse get hard and compressed to the point that the societal fabrics become explosive. A freedom to make sense thus involves a kind of stub-bornness that is directed toward what is beneath.

Stubbornness to connect with what's beneath

Gendlin writes:

> Experiencing is a myriad richness that exceeds any number of separated facets. There is vastly more than our conceptual structures can encom-pass. And experiencing moves—we cannot think all that just was. We feel more than we can think, and we live more than we can feel. And if we enter into what we feel in certain genuine steps, we feel more than before. And there is much more still. ...
>
> (Gendlin, 1971, p. 1)

In the fairy tale of the *Princess and the Pea* by Hans Christian Andersen, the princess can sense through all the layers of materials in which she is embedded, she feels and experiences something which she cannot identify yet. This image of someone not being able to say what matters to her, yet not giving up, is a vivid characteristic of a hopeful stubbornness that to me seems connected to a "freedom to make sense." This stubbornness indicates possibilities to get beyond habituated ways of saying something, beyond a powerful discourse that imprints how we approach anything. Layers of entanglements hinder the princess from saying what she means, and at the same time, they are the medium through which she can feel it as a prob-lem, puzzlement, or perplexity. Ordinary language, but also expert jargon, can become another disconnecting layer if covering up what one senses (Petitmengin 2007). Phrases, concepts, or theories may seem acceptable, but they do not connect to your point. In the fairy tale, the princess is ridiculed for being so sensitive, stubbornly holding on to her sense that something is wrong. Obviously, her receptivity will be the turning point of the story, a competence that marks her as free.

Carrying forward

If words finally work in saying what one thinks and means, the complexity of the happening cannot be underrated. Networks and backgrounds change in a way such that a system of further meanings and the experience of situations involved transform (Schoeller, 2019, Chapter 11).

A process of making sense of situated experience therefore is not graspable in terms of representation or construction. Gendlin uses the term "carrying forward" (Gendlin 2004b) which acknowledges a happening when we manage to say what we think, feel, or experience. If the princess can get to the point, the place where she sits is not the same as before.

Gendlin's writes:

> [W]e are likely to make many false starts and say many things that we don't quite mean. As we hear them, we say, "No, that isn't exactly what I mean," or "No, that's only part of it," or "No, it's sort of like that, but not quite." All through this process the felt meaning to be symbolized functions both as selector and as arbiter. We concentrate on (directly refer to) this felt meaning and words come to us (....).
>
> (Gendlin, 1997, p. 115)

Being absorbed in concentration on a content, such a linguistic process is usually but a means to an end. Usually, philosophers of language so focus on the results of the articulation process, propositions, and their truth conditions, that the process itself goes without further notice.

The subtlety of Gendlin's point arises from an awareness rarely practiced. His attention makes us notice *how* words come, uncovering something obvious and at the same time remarkable: the implicit precision at work when words "come" in a situated context:

> The coming of words is so clever! They come specifically and newly phrased to make just your point! The words come with their past uses taken into account. Much that you have read and know is taken account of, as well as the present situation, what you just heard these people say, what you know of them from other times, even the peculiar way in which *this* group uses certain words.
>
> (Gendlin, 1991, p. 104)

From his first work on, Gendlin carefully elaborates *how* language and situated experience need to be considered as interconnected systems, as a functioning-together, from which meaning emerges (Gendlin, 1997). Meaning of words have grown and changed throughout generations of living, and they grow and change again during the lifespan of an individual, collecting ever more aspects of meaning according to the situations in which they are used to work. Therefore, words and sentences do not just represent, they complexly *occur* into a situated context that is always also embodied, while implying language. Occurring words come along with experienced meanings, affecting the situated experience in ways that can carry it forward. We experience this on a daily basis, and also of course in creative work, in research, in therapy. *Having said this, I can now see that, and seeing that allows for new words to come, which again make me see the limitations of how I said it before, and recognize the implications that might not be quite right.* In this process, the meaning of the words shift while occurring into and carrying forward what they mean to convey (Gendlin, 1991).

In making sense of experience in this way, we engage in an interactive process of unconceivable plasticity. What we refer to in these cases are not clear-cut entities or states of affairs. Of course, set definitions, ordinary meaning of words, and explicit structures of thinking powerfully channel the flow of experience and felt meaning. Yet, these structures are also affected by this very flow. Again and again, dominant structures of thinking and public meanings of words transform due to the fresh happening of symbols interacting with the implicit precision of embodied and situated experience (Casey & Schoeller 2017). Thus, using language can – at times – get the "mattresses" to move, to stay in the metaphoric image of the *Princess and the Pea*. The mattresses stand for personal and collective backgrounds and structures in which the thinking moves.

Let me demonstrate the non-foreseeable transformative effects of such a process with another example, which I was granted the permission to use here. It happened when Angelica (her pseudonym) was almost at the end of a Focusing training consisting of six weekend modules. A difficult decision of whether she should operate her back after a car accident was her chosen starting point. She has been thinking about this decision for months now, and all the while she lives with an aching back that she learned to ignore. There is a big risk at stake. The back could become stiff if things go wrong. Thinking about the decision has always led in the same circular movement of telling herself she needs to trust, but not knowing how to. She is blaming herself for this. In fact, her mind keeps spinning while the pain in the back gets worse while being ignored. During the Focusing session, I invite her to notice the experience of her back right now, while talking. Angelica acknowledges that it needs a bit of a nudge to do so, as the pain is such a nuisance to her. Noticing her back, a feeling of "melancholy" arises. This is surprising to her. It does not seem to have to do with her back. Rather, it is about "something that does not have any space ..." She does not know what that is. After some moments she adds that there is "an insecurity deep down concerning decisions and the topic of trust." Having said that she recognizes a crux: "There is this paradox: I need to decide without being able to know the outcome. The outcome is just not in my hands." After a pause she silently concedes: "I need to bear the paradox. To decide what I can't control, makes me very fearful. You see, I am rather good in controlling things," she smilingly adds. "Now I have to seriously rely on someone, and I have to have confidence in him. The rest of my life is in his or her hands." After a pause, she muses: "The hurt of the pain has to do with not having the confidence. There is too much at risk ..."

At this point, however, her well-known circular movement begins again: "I am just not courageous enough. Maybe I just need to decide and live with the decision." And thoughts come that keep reoccurring since months. At this point, I suggest going back to the bodily experience right now and to be curious of the qualities she senses. Angelica says nothing, only gently places her hand to her heart. I ask her to sense into this gesture, which, as it turns out, she was not aware of. Angelica very slowly begins to describe: "It feels like ... something warm ... like ... something that connects me ... it feels like something rather foundational." And with a perplexed tone in her voice, she adds: "It is as if I have not sensed my heart for a long time. As if there was no space for that ..." At this point, the coming of tears surprises her, being a woman with a lot of professional responsibilities and self-discipline. While tears keep coming, she remains amazed, not knowing what they are about. After a while, she says: "Now it calms down a bit. It is as if it, something ... kind of ... seems to find its place ..." After another long pause, her expression changes once more, becoming very lively. She says with movement in her voice: "Something does not have any space, I do not grant it any space ... even if it hurts ..." She adds: "Acknowledging this now makes the breathing become deeper ... it is as if it ... something comes into balance." With an expression of amazement: "How this so suddenly ... so strange ... I cannot say what it is ... so intense, something moves so much, because it did not have any space!" After a further long pause she realizes: "There is a very different feeling of my body now ... the heart cares for the whole body! It is a different feeling of the body!" And then it dawns on her: "It does not have to do with confidence! Maybe I do not even need that. It is more the heart ... the feeling, to be closer to that ... the heart-feeling." A long pause, she has her hand on the same place, totally focused on what is going on right now in her embodied experience. She utters: "I am so amazed, how it feels with the heart. The confidence is in there!" She pauses and softly murmurs: "This is an utterly new experience." I suggest finding a word or symbol for this experience to not lose it, it seemed so tender and new to me. She disagrees: "This is not tender; it is so powerful! So new, overwhelming, and so confident." After a while, she says: "The heart is the anchor. And what's so impressive, I do not feel my back anymore that had hurt so when we began.

Then it was cramped. The space we created now has made a space also for the back. Let me continue to feel this. It's so strong."

This process did not end up in a decision. It did not serve helping her to know which of the dual options to take: to operate, or not. And it did not solve the problem in the way she set it up: to finally have confidence in the person operating her even though she did not have anything in her hands. However, the process changed the situated place from where she thought about the decision. Staying attentive to the experience that was going on *now* while she talked about her situation changed her situation in a way she could not envision before. It was not about the crux around confidence and not-knowing anymore. Making space for the embodied experience involved in thinking about the decision, and becoming more aware of the experiential responses, resulted in the emergence of a kind of confidence that she did not need to "make" or force herself to.

A "freedom to make sense" thus implies allowing symbols and experiencing to do their interaction-work more responsively, more precisely, and more effectively.

Meaning as a transformative environment

Such transformative process of making sense calls for new overall concepts that open our eyes to the sensitive plasticity of experiencing and meaning. The sequence above was neither determined only by the implications of the words Angelica used nor by the feelings. Angelica's attending and describing the subtle feeling in her body so affected and transformed her entire sense of the situation. What kind of overall concept of meaning would make sense of such a process?

What if we consider attending to the embodied, experiential sources of meaning like an act of caring for a living environment. Gendlin's concept of the body as environment opens such a perspective. In the first chapter of *A Process Model*, he writes:

> The bloodstream is often called the environment of the cells it feeds. The many processes in the body have various parts of it for their environment.
> The skin-line is not the great divide. (...) The body *is* an environment *in which* body-process goes *on further*. The body was made from an embryo engaged in process. The body structure is not only made but also maintained by ongoing processes—if they stop, the body disintegrates.
> (Gendlin, 2017, p.6)

The body as a homegrown environment has developed and is sustained by the living process, which again implies this environment in order to live.

This understanding paves the way to conceive meaning as an environment, inseparable from the embodied living process it has emerged from and together with. Meaning implies the structures of embodied lifeforms, as Wittgenstein already noticed, and vice versa. Lifeforms are transmitted by using language, and language is implicit in lifeforms. Gendlin adds the "intricacy" of the responsive, experiential dimensions involved (Gendlin, 1991, 1997).

Unforeseeable experiential and felt implications and relations are part of the "homegrown" environment which language brings along when used in situations. That is why one can go on and on spelling out what a meaningful word holds (Cavell, 1979, Schoeller, 2019).

Yet, why would it matter to conceive language in this way? If meaning is understood in disembodied terms such as representing or constructing things or states of affairs, then listening to the embodied response does not seem a meaningful thing to do. Why would you invest time, and face the vulnerable challenge of giving situated experience a chance to speak back to how it is formulated? Grasping meaning as an inseparable environment of our embodied being changes the picture. Experiential responsivity can thus be considered as the other side of the moon, so to say. Attended to, it grants potential spaces of deeper situated understanding. So, the answers to the above question are very practical. Understanding meaning as the environment of living processes allows to cultivate more usages of language. This opens performative possibilities that are not covered by speech act theory (Schoeller 2018); most importantly, it encourages a use of language that meaningfully exceeds habituated "language games." This is a term Wittgenstein coined for the everyday language use in which we are trained since earliest childhood. Understanding meaning as an environment fosters a usage that allows our ancient organisms, interacting with environment down to the cellular level, to come into, and widen the culturally constrained language games. Integrating the embodied responses more deliberately when using language is a way to reconnect verbal meaning to the vast implicit dimensions of its enacted and embodied roots. Angelica's process is a good example. Noticing the response of her pain and her heart during her explications, utterly changed her understanding of an entire situation. Her use of language enacted a connection by acknowledging an ignored embodied happening, which affected this very process, which in turn re-affected her use of language and thinking. Sequences such as Angelica's are not determinable only by logical or conceptual categories, or by the rules of the language game. This is a point that Gendlin has made since his early work (Gendlin, 1997). Practicing such responsive use of language opens an often strange, more-than-logical realm of meaning. Not only minding the mind and its logical and conceptual rules and inferences, but the body, makes language become more receptive for the body–environment interaction that always involves more than explicit positions, thoughts, and cultural settings.

I would like to claim, and someday be able to elaborate more fully, that using language in such way can be considered an ecological speech act.

According to Wittgenstein, the role of philosophy is to show us the way out of confusions created by a wrong use of language. This wrong use of language creates problems in which we get caught like a fly in the fly glass. The fly glass are cultural conditionings, today especially social media bubbles that algorithmically close down the possibilities to sense and think outside the respective box.

Understanding meaning as an embodied environment makes one see that coming out of cultural and conceptual restriction is not just a conceptual, analytical and linguistic affair. A sense-making process that proceeds by getting in touch very precisely with the experience involved in formulating, sensitizes thinkers where they jump to conclusions or actions that are short cuts in terms of the situated and experiential intricacy involved. This is a diving beneath the conceptual boxes in which we think. One can feel how one misses the point even though the logic is clear. There remains a pain or puzzlement, even though the grammar is right, the story seems interesting, and the facts make sense. On the other hand, one can sense how something clarifies even though the sentence may be strange. A thinking that leads beyond conceptual restrictions and habituated language barriers is often enacted in a kind of proprioceptive way. Gendlin calls this zigzagging (Gendlin, 2004b). By zigzagging from saying to sensing, and from sensing to saying, one enacts a path in which one re-iterates different attentive modes. By experiencing the impacts of concepts and thought-ways, their constrictions, the discomfort, the hurt, the excitements, and the confusions, somebody's explication leads out of the fly glass. This possibility is at the core of my concept of a "freedom to make sense."

Enacting a "freedom to make sense" in academia

Husserl's practice of "époche" – the suspension of a natural attitude to interpret experience – can be regarded as the starting point: to establish sophisticated methods of approaching daily experience in non-biased ways – not by disregarding the specificity of lived experience, but by getting in touch with it deeply.

Even though 4EA cognition, the embodiment of cognition, is increasingly acknowledged, higher education provides little means to enhance the skills to clarify experiential backgrounds in the context of research. For reasons that have long traditional roots, the experiential part of meaning is still labeled and treated as merely subjective. The traditional focus on objective knowledge does not convey a knowing of how to cultivate and clarify a situated felt sense of relevance of a research topic, a discomfort that feeds criticality, the experiential *more* that surrounds concepts that matter to someone. What is cut off in this way in an academic use of language reenters as anger, anxiety, distrust, and discouragement. Frequently, just mentioning a word, a phrase, a concept is like dropping a bomb or experiencing an earthquake in academic contexts. Cancel culture is the result. And there is no way to get out of this trouble as we seem stuck in language, even when addressing the problem! Yet, the problem is not language, but how we understand meaning, and how we create it.

Thinking about environmental issues, gender, neurodiversity, populist movements implicitly hold strong felt dimensions that inform and motivate the research. The backgrounds and entanglements which one brings along as a decisive part of one's interest and engagements are the soil from which grow perplexities and relevance. In a conventional academic research setting, there are no methods to clarify the experiential side of thinking.

Embodied Critical Thinking (ECT) (ect.hi.is, trainingect.com) is a research and training initiative that applies clear principles of reflexive care in order to clarify these situated knowing in the context of research (ect.hi.is). To come closely into contact with lived experience, we also practice and are being trained in Micro-phenomenology, a research tool that allows to bring to awareness the fine-grained characteristics and structures involved in any kind of experience. Together with Gendlin's methods of Focusing and Thinking-at-the-Edge, the methods we collect support the holding and "letting be" of experience (De Jaegher, 2021), and a process of carrying forward meaning beyond habitual usages, by an experimental use of language.

We witness the transformational shift and insights when the experienced dimension of the students and researchers thinking is granted space and clarification. This process has several kinds of effects: a specific driving force may become clearer, an honest realization of a blind spot or limitation, an intuition that permeates the entire research starts to make sense and encourages the student's own thinking. Also, tears in the research context have an important function, processing major, at times, devastating insights that encourage critical thinking (Schoeller & Thorgeirsdottir, 2019). If situated and experiential backgrounds of one's research interests, holding sorrow or joy, etc., can surface and be heard, reflection deepens and becomes courageous.

In academia, we normally skip the challenge to articulate the lenses through which we ourselves look. We skip the challenge for good reasons. Articulating the felt sense dimension of thinking still seems merely personal, subjective. But there is another reason: exploring the lenses through which we look is a complex affair. These lenses are networks of experiences, knowings, and constellations, insights we read into insights (Barad, 2007).

Only exploring one aspect of an experience therefore is as difficult as it is promising. It connects to so much more.

In the context of ECT, we create a methodological space and make time to notice how key concepts and theoretical frameworks resonate with an experiential and felt dimension of thinking. Even if an approach might seem conceptually sound, logical, and coherent, something relevant might be cut off, ignored, or diminished. Mostly, one does not even know what exactly is missing, yet topics tend to become scholarly in a safe, flat, and non-relevant way. Therefore, ECT provides spaces in which one can practice to stutter and stammer while formulating one's questions and intuition freshly in ways that touch the experiential background involved. If that happens, also abstract formulation does something that Gendlin describes as *taking along experience* (Gendlin, 2004a, p. 134). When this happens, conceptual implications and theoretical constructions change in ways one cannot foresee, creating some more freedom from approaches or limitations in which one was caught, without knowing.

For this reason, a "freedom to make sense" also seems connected to some kind of humility. Not in making oneself small, but in the releasing of control of an outcome. This might also lie at the heart of the challenge of such a freedom. Attending to the delicateness and responsiveness of embodied experience in the context of research, and philosophy, ventures beyond an intellectual tradition of power. Stressing language, knowledge, and mind as the differentiating factor from body, animals, and plants, this kind of tradition strove to set humans free from natural restrictions and vulnerabilities. We know today this was illusion.

References

Barad, K. (2007). *Meeting the Universe Halfway: Quantum Physics and the Entanglement of Matter and Meaning.* Duke University Press.

Bensley, R. & Ellsworth, T. (1992). Bulimic Learning: A Philosophical View of Teaching and Learning. *Journal of School Health* 62(8), pp. 386–387.

Böhme, H. & Böhme, G. (1985). *Das Andere der Vernunft. Zur Entwicklung von Rationalitätsstrukturen am Beispiel Kants.* Suhrkamp.

Casey, E. & Schoeller, D. (Eds) (2017). *Saying What We Mean: Implicit Precision and the Responsive Order; Selected Works by Eugene Gendlin.* Northwestern University Press.

Cavell, S. (1979). *The Claim of Reason: Wittgenstein, Skepticism, Morality, and Tragedy.* Clarendon Press.

De Jaegher, H. (2021). Loving and Knowing: Reflections for an Engaged Epistemology. *Phenomenology and the Cognitive Sciences* 20, pp. 847–870.

Dewey, J. (1984). Qualitative Thought. In E. Boydston (Ed.), *The Later Works, 1925–1953,* Vol. 5, pp. 243–262. Southern Illinois University Press.

Dewey, J. (2009). *Democracy and Education.* Wilder.

Frodeman, R. & Briggle, A. (2016). *Socrates Tenured. The Institutions of 21st Century Philosophy*. Rowman & Littlefield International.

Gendlin, E.T. (1963). Experiencing and the Nature of Concepts. In *The Christian Scholar* 46, Nr. 3, pp. 245–255.

Gendlin, E.T. (1971). Unpublished manuscript.

Gendlin, E.T. (1991). Thinking Beyond Patterns: Body, Language and Situations. In B. den Ouden & M. Moen (Eds.), *The Presence of Feeling in Thought*. Peter Lang, pp. 25–151.

Gendlin, E.T. (1993). Words Can Say How They Work. In R.P. Crease (Ed.), *Proceedings, Heidegger Conference*, pp. 29–35. State University of New York.

Gendlin, E.T. (1997). The Responsive Order: A New Empiricism. *Man and World* 30(3), pp. 383–411.

Gendlin, E.T. (2003). Beyond Postmodernism: From Concepts Through Experiencing. In Roger Frie (Ed.), *Understanding Experience: Psychotherapy and Postmodernism*. Routledge, pp. 100–115.

Gendlin, E.T. (2004a). Introduction to 'Thinking at the Edge'. *The Folio* 19(1), pp. 1–8.

Gendlin, E.T. (2004b). The New Phenomenology of Carrying Forward. *Continental Philosophy Review* 37(1), pp. 127–151.

Gendlin, E.T. (2018). *A Process Model*. Northwestern University Press.

Habermas, J. (2019). *Auch eine Geschichte der Philosophie*. Suhrkamp.

Hampe, M. (2018). *Die Dritte Aufklärung*. Nicolai Publishing.

Harraway, D. (1988). Situated Knowledges: The Science Question in Feminism and the Priviledge of Partial Perspective. *Feminist Studies* 14, pp. 575–599.

Hayes, S. (2016, 12 March). Sandy Hook. One Year Later. *YouTube*. https://www.youtube.com/watch?v=gwgyxw4apKM.

Heidegger, M. (1967). *Sein und Zeit*. Max Niemeyer.

James, W. (2022). *The Will to Believe*. Reclam.

Jung, M. (2014). *Gewöhnliche Erfahrung*. Mohr Siebeck.

Kordeš, U. & Demšar, E. (2018). Excavating Belief about Past Experience: Experiential Dynamics of the Reflective Act. *Constructivist Foundations* 12(2), pp. 210–229.

Kordeš, U. & Demšar, E. (2019). Towards the Epistemology of the Non-trivial: Research Characteristics Connecting Quantum Mechanics and First-Person Inquiry. *Foundations of Science* 26(12), pp. 1–27.

Merleau-Ponty, M. (1976). *Phénoménologie de la perception*. Gallimard.

Pelluchon, C. (2019). *Nourishment: A Philosophy of the Political Body*. Bloomsbury.

Petitmengin, C. (2007). Toward the Source of Thoughts: The Gestural and Transmodal Dimension of Lived Experience. *Journal of Consciousness Studies* 14(3), pp. 54–82.

Nussbaum, M. (2000). *Women and Human Development. The Capabilities Approach*. Cambridge University Press.

Schoeller, D. (2018). Tentative Sprechakte: zur erstaunlichen Entfaltbarkeit von Hintergründen beim Formulieren. *Deutsche Zeitschrift für Philosophie* 66(2), pp. 183–201.

Schoeller, D. (2019). *Close Talking. Erleben zur Sprache bringen*. De Gruyter.

Schoeller, D. (2020). Felt Sense – A Beautiful Yet Misleading Term. In Judy More & Nikos Kypriotakis (Eds.), *Senses of Focusing*. Eurasia Publications, pp. 203–225.

Schoeller, D. (2022). Thinking at the Edge in the Context of Embodied Critical Thinking. Giving Words to the Felt Dimension of Thinking. *Phenomenology and Cognitive Science* 22(4), pp. 289–311.

Schoeller, D. & Thorgeirsdottir, S. (2019). Embodied Critical Thinking: The Experiential Turn and Its Transformative Aspects. *Philosophia* 9(1), pp. 95–112.

Stanier, J. (2022). An Introduction to Engaged Phenomenology. *Journal of the British Society for Phenomenology* 53(3), pp. 226–242

Stern, D. (2010). *Forms of Vitality.* Oxford University Press.

Varela, F., Thompson, E. & Rosch, E. (1983). *The Embodied Mind.* MIT Press.

Chapter 9

Kangaroo know-how

Animal practices from the perspective of implying

Greg Walkerden

Gendlin's (2018) *A Process Model*, one of his two main texts in the field he calls the Philosophy of the Implicit (Gendlin, 2013), explores how a process-first ontological schema can assist with understanding lived experience. The question this work emerges from is: how can understanding be *felt* (Gendlin, 2018, p. 18)? His first major philosophy of the implicit text, *Experiencing and the Creation of Meaning* (Gendlin, 1997a), and his extensive work on the practice he called Focusing (Gendlin, 2003) that is derived from it, demonstrated at length that this is so. *Felt* understanding can provide holistic, practical insight. But terms like body, meaning, and living need to be understood in non-standard ways for these observations not to be paradoxical.

A familiar example of the powers he is pointing to is the discomforts we feel, when we are editing a text, when we encounter a phrase or a passage that we know – sense – needs to change. As we sit with the discomfort, we may, for instance, recognize that there are uncomfortable implications for some relationships, that what we have written is confused, that we don't yet know *what* we actually want to say in this place, and potentially much more... On some of these occasions, a better articulation – an articulation that feels more comfortable, that feels like it fits – comes quickly. On others, ruminating ... perhaps leaving aside and returning to ... is needed. Gendlin's sensitivity to these microprocesses led to a practice of heeding this felt layer of understanding in a sustained, holistic, creative way. For many people, this comes as a large expansion of their thinking skills (Gendlin, 2003; Hendricks, 2001). Art practices often involve sustained felt sensing (Gendlin, 1997a), but artists may well not apply these skills in a general way, to situations of all kinds. For many others, the possibility of such sustained exploration of *felt* understanding is counter-intuitive: working with familiar, articulated content can seem to be the heart of thinking. Gendlin names this process 'thinking with the implicit' (Gendlin, 2018 p. 198), as central to it is allowing words to come that explicate felt understandings in which many experiences and understandings cross in an implicit way.

In ordinary usage, the phrase 'felt understanding' (Gendlin, 1991, p. 30) is paradoxical. Understanding is of the mind; a body is a physical reality.

DOI: 10.4324/9781003296706-10

From a commonplace, unself-conscious, tacit mind/body dualism, tissues are not a site where meaning is. Much disciplined philosophical understanding also orients from here.

To subvert these paradoxes, Gendlin takes a radical, simple approach: he simply starts from our lived experience and builds concepts that explicate what we find as we explore it.

> We *start from* how we know (feel, are .....) our own more complex body. From the start, let us develop concepts of "body" and "environment" that can apply also to our own bodies. [...] We can speak from living, and we can make rudimentary concepts from speaking-from, and especially from focusing and from the process of explication. Since these are possible in reality, they can lead us to an alternative set of "basic" concepts of a "reality" in which we [living bodies experiencing meaning] would not seem impossible.
>
> (Gendlin, 2018, p.17)

First person human experiencing is his starting point, and from this, in *A Process Model*, he builds a model of being alive, such that animal behavior is an elaboration of tissue process (Gendlin, 2018, p. 44), symbols and 'protolanguage' are an elaboration of animal behavior, and 'thinking with the implicit' is an elaboration of protolanguage (Gendlin, 2018, pp. viii-x; see Walkerden, 2004). His elaboration of his conceptual model echoes evolutionary history.

Gendlin explores animal behavior as a phenomenological philosopher, and as a bodily presence explicating his own experiencing. He embraces the possibility of having the interpretive power of his conceptual schema for understanding animal behavior tested:

> One can certainly question and reject these concepts, and better ones will surely be devised. We need not feel sure of our new concepts, but we can be sure that some concepts are needed to perform *the functions* which our concepts perform.
>
> (Gendlin, 2018, p. 93)

> These concepts are the first of their kind; they are not likely to be perfect or the best. By using them, better ones will develop.
>
> (Gendlin, 2018, p. 113)

My explorations of kangaroo know-how, and animal practices generally, take up this challenge. In the argument that follows I show:

1   That the perspective of implying provides tools for thick description (Geertz, 2008) of animals' forms of life, which natural history writing is

able to do, but which the kinds of quantitative investigation that dominate research into animal behavior are not able to.

2 That models of animal behavior built around the concept of implying can make explicit underlying regularities in animal living in a way that natural history handles more awkwardly. In natural history, narratives *point toward* patterns in animal experiencing through instances; Gendlin's concepts enable systematic delineation of underlying patterns and variations to them.

3 That standard means of researching animal behavior systematically exclude recognition of implying, which is very striking as, as I will show echoing Gendlin, implying is constitutive of being alive. Standard methods are therefore strongly biased against looking at animal behavior from the animal's point of view.

4 That there is pervasive complexity in animals' lives that standard observation protocols, which focus on discrete behaviors, systematically obscure. Often what an animal is doing can fruitfully be understood as doing many things at once.

5 That using Gendlin's concepts to explicate something of kangaroo practices brings out areas where elaboration, and perhaps revision, of his schema is needed, notably around reproduction and more generally around otherness. Reproduction has patterns in it that are not covered in *A Process Model*, and how what is *not* implied arises is arbitrary – he simply assumes that this occurs.

My use of kangaroos – in fact a particular species, the Eastern Grey Kangaroo (*Macropus giganteus*), and a particular mob (at 'Wallaby Creek', Jarman et al., 1987), and within that locale a few focal individuals (Aldenhoven & Carruthers, 1992) – is a mixture of pragmatic considerations and their usefulness as instances. First and foremost, to explore the usefulness of Gendlin's conceptual schema for behavior, I needed a rich account of the forms of life of some animals. The testing process involves looking at some animals' behavior through his lens to see what it brings out, and looking at what his lens seems to struggle with to identify places where his schema needs further work. For this dialogue to be rich, a rich account of some animals' forms of life is needed. As I indicated above, and will show below, a great deal of research in animal behavior is unable to provide such rich descriptions. Natural history reporting, particularly when speaking from long-term observation, is a place where such narratives *can* be found, and the documentary used here – *Kangaroos: Faces in the Mob* (Aldenhoven & Carruthers, 1992) – is a particularly strong example. The documentary is grounded in a long-term research project that was led by Peter Jarman (University of New England, Australia) looking at the lives and dynamics of a population of kangaroos – see the series of ten papers, titled 'Macropod Studies at Wallaby Creek I–X', (Jarman et al., 1987; Payne & Jarman, 1999). Jarman and a number of his colleagues were scientific advisers for the documentary. The documentary follows the behavior of six individual kangaroos over a year (two females, their two joeys, and two males). It provides, so to speak, biographical accounts and stories from kangaroo practice. The discussions below demonstrate that its narratives are quite rich enough to support an exploration of how, in an initial way, as a proof of concept, the perspective of implying can serve as a lens for understanding animals' forms of life.

Secondly, and rather sadly, kangaroos, and especially Eastern Grey Kangaroos, are a useful illustration of the ethical incoherence of modern industrial societies' relations to animals. In these societies, we relate to animals as wild animals, not so closely connected with us, though deeply affected by what we do; as livestock, whom most of us are superficially aware of, but principally relate to as flesh we eat or sources of fibers; and as pets, who are perhaps our companions, or at any rate are sources of pleasure close to hand. We may want wild animals to have wild lives, taking for granted that they have intrinsic value. Livestock we may value only instrumentally. Pets we often relate to from an inarticulate fusion of intrinsic and instrumental value.

Kangaroos appear in these relations in multiple guises. Some kangaroo joeys (dependent young), whose mothers have died, are cared for meticulously and released back to the wild. Some kangaroos are threatened species, and plans are in place to support their ongoing survival and growth in numbers. Others are hunted; and of those some are sold for meat. Kangaroo farming has been considered for many years (Lunney, 2010); however, demand for kangaroo meat is met by hunting wild kangaroos, so farming has not been taken up in practice. Where kangaroos on farms compete with cattle and sheep for pasture, they may well be hunted, however. A joey that has been meticulously cared for may be shot a few years later as it competes with livestock, and its meat may be eaten in a city restaurant.

Playing into this rather incoherent care-and-lack-of-care is our lack of appreciation of kangaroos' lived experience. 'How are *we* experienced by kangaroos?' is a question that is unasked. This incoherence contrasts markedly with the understanding and respect with which hunter gatherer communities relate to the animals they interact with (Berkes & Folke, 2002; Unaipon, 2006 p. 60ff.). By supporting efforts to place ourselves in animals' shoes, Gendlin's philosophy of the implicit supports challenges to this ethical incoherence and supports efforts to shape our relations to animals more considerately, e.g. improving conservation planning.

Placing 'implying' at the center of understanding being alive

Before turning to implying as we find it in the lives of other animals, I will show how it is in play in our experiencing, so that the job that Gendlin's concept of implying is doing is clearer. Implying, as Gendlin uses the term, points directly to first person experiencing, so one needs to understand it *from* and *in* one's own first person experience to understand the concept clearly. Writing is a practice we are each familiar with, so I am using it as an example. I invite you to explore how the following explication fits your own experience of writing.

When, as when we are drafting or editing, we *feel* that a sentence we have written needs to change, we 'imply' a change. A great deal crosses in this feeling a change is needed: what the topic needs here, how we are wanting to affect our readers, our sense of what is likely to make sense (and not make sense) to a reader at this point in the text, matters of tone, of argumentation. What the change in the text will be is not yet resolved. We find ourselves waiting for words to *come* that, when they have come, we will say *fit* our *felt* understanding of what is needed. Fit, though, is recognized looking backwards. From the felt need we cannot say, in advance, what words will work. They have to come. When words that fit *do* come, we *feel* the fit. Discomfort has segued into comfort. The coming of the discomfort helped; the easing we experience, as words that fit come, marks our writing process carrying forward further.

We can see in this example four pivotal characteristics of what Gendlin is pointing to with the term 'implying':

1 a forward orienting: living has integral to it an implying happenings that will help, that work, a carrying forward; e.g. implying the coming of some words that work better here, and implying the differences such better words may make (Gendlin, 2018, p. 47);
2 a great deal that is relevant here is crossing in this implying ... the complexity vastly exceeds what we can lay out analytically, with clarity and precision; and these relevances function together, shaping the forming of a specific, particular discomfort (Gendlin, 2018, p. 41);
3 the forward orienting involves an openness: our implying makes quite precise demands of what is to come – it has to fit *all this* (*our* situation, had together in some holistic way) – but this demanding does not specify in advance, or in particular, specifically what must occur: rather, fitting is recognized *as* the words are coming – as we are receiving them – and as we are looking back, sitting with, savoring, the revised text (Gendlin, 2018, pp. 52–53); and
4 when something comes that *does* fit, we feel carried forward: our process (here, as writer) is moving on to what is next, rather than continuing to iterate with a sense that something that is not here is needed (Gendlin, 2018, p. 46).

By placing implying in this sense – forwardly oriented, richly integrating what is at stake for us in our situations, being inherently open (not needing a *specific* thing, selected in advance, to happen), and being able to be carried forward by what actually occurs – Gendlin makes our first person experience of feeling and being alive the heart of his model.

The openness of implying (Gendlin, 2018, p. 53) needs closer consideration. When we are observing others, it is often not obvious. Commonly what occurs that carries a living process forward is what we expected – the grass nourishes the kangaroo, the words that are said fit the situation. However, if we shift from observing others to noticing our own experiencing, the openness is hard to miss. Time as we experience it has a fundamental asymmetry: looking back what has happened has a solid fixed quality, looking forward has an openness. What will my next sentence be? Until you read it, you won't know. But you *imply* a sentence that will fit the evolving argument – and if for you my next sentence does not seem to do that, it will jar, it will not be carrying you forward as reader; and you may pause, puzzled.

The great deal that is relevant, crossing in implying, is a place of particular complexity. We can *see* that our implying is finely tuned and richly sensitized to our circumstances in what it demands. Our felt sense of what is needed is a sensitivity-to-fit that holds at once many, many considerations in place *together*, as one whole. *A Process Model* provides considerable explication of this process. We imply words that fit, not knowing in advance what they will be, but having here a strong sense of *relevance*. Gendlin (2018, pp. 24, 41) coins the terms 'interaffecting' and 'everything-by-everything (eveving)' to point to the complexity of this crossing of what is relevant. Eveving speaks to the breadth of implying: everything experienced as *relevant* is involved in the crossing. Interaffecting points to the fact that these relevances do not function as a set of *separate* considerations; rather, the implying is of them already crossing with each other. The words that come when we are speaking don't involve a process of all the considerations that are relevant (political, analytical, evidentiary, emotional, history together, ...) affecting each other, then those effects on each other feeding back, then after the feedbacks have impacted, a new set of reverberations occurring, and on and on ... Rather, words that fit (as well as they do) come. Interaffecting helps define what implying is: relevances crossing in the forming of what occurs (Gendlin, 2018, p. 42).

If though we think *from* our own first person experience, e.g. our implying a *different* phrase that fits better as we are editing a text, the *need* for these concepts is clear. Considerations that are relevant function together when we feel the need for a better phrase – so we need a concept like interaffecting – and there may be a great many relevant considerations in play in our feeling for what fits – so we need a concept like eveving. As Gendlin points out at various places (e.g. Gendlin, 2018, p. 93), one *could* use different concepts here, but *some* concepts that are doing the jobs that interaffecting and eveving are doing will be needed. "[Living] moves from one differentiated whole of multiple aspects to another [...; we need] concepts for the process in which a newly differentiated multiplicity forms" (Gendlin, 2018, p. 40).

The picture of living process that is emerging here is very different from what we conventionally assume. Gendlin is following the intuition that process first descriptions – models in which processes are fundamental and objects are derived – are a better starting point for describing experiencing and living more broadly. As he put it in *Experiencing and the Creation of Meaning*, originally published in 1962, when you look at experiencing:

> you will always find a subtle, richly complex maze of many many meanings, perceptions, interpretations, past, present, and future concerns [...] *Content categories would seem to be ineffectual, if the phenomena are more basically ordered by a process in which contents are at most momentary, and can be endlessly differentiated by the symbols and events that occur.* We will require 'process' categories that attempt to distinguish, not contents, but different modes or dimensions of process. [...] We will have to devise categories for a felt, preconceptual process that we can only momentarily divide into contents.
>
> (Gendlin, 1997a, p. 32–33)

Implying, eveving, interaffecting, and carrying forward are examples of such process categories. For our purposes, the complexity of implying is the key thing to appreciate; our open sense of what is forward is attuned and flexible in ways that can't be characterized by dissecting it into interacting parts or saying it is of *particular* possible occurrences. Increasing complexity enables *more* creativity (Gendlin, 2018, p. 54).

Implying, as Gendlin uses the term, is wider than simply this open, forward orientation. Breathing is drawing in (a bodily side) and a being drawn in (an environmental side) – drawing in and being drawn in imply each other. They are the one process; we can differentiate the sides, but the process is primary. Looking *from* the process of living, body and environment fall out *provisionally* as separate. "Body and environment are one, but of course only in certain respects", Gendlin says, at the start of *A Process Model* (Gendlin, 2018, p.4). Living is occurring-into-implying carrying forward.

In this schema:

> Implying implies something so intricate that only a very special occurring "changes" it as it implies itself changed. Anything else may disrupt the body or leave the implying unchanged – still implying as before. For example, while the animal is hungry something other than food happens. Then the implying of feeding continues unchanged. Or, a predator may chase it so that running may come to be implied. Or, the animal may be killed. Since there is always implying, all occurring happens

"into implying," but not always as the implying implies. We can already say that certain distinctions are coming here. Implying implies an occurring that will change it so that it no longer implies as it did, but not because it was disrupted, rather because what occurs relates to the implying in a certain (not fully predetermined) way.

(Gendlin, 2018, pp. 12–13)

Being carried forward in certain respects, and not in others, is the basis on which differentiations in implying, and differentiations into subprocesses, arise. Implying, as a whole, is not made from parts of implying: differentiations are (in Gendlin's schema) always within and from a one whole implying that is the heart of being a living presence. Occurring-into-implying carrying forward is a description of living process from the process's perspective. Events occurring into openness; and the occurring-into-openness continuing on or, in the limit, dying. This is us – me (i.e. each of us) – living on, or not. I am the changing of implying carrying forward.

The implying side of occurring-into-implying carrying forward holds the presence of first person experiencing, and the occurring side holds the presence of an environment. The schema privileges neither, ontologically, by taking the *process* of living carrying forward as fundamental. In developing his Philosophy of the Implicit, Gendlin has focused on experiencing (Gendlin, 1997a) and implying (Gendlin, 2018). Letting *any* term that names an aspect of being-in be a root concept in a model would lead to a process first schema: presence, place, here, now, ... Experiencing foregrounds taking in, implying foregrounds orienting toward.

A Process Model demonstrates that basic concepts for describing animal and human forms of life can be built from a root conception of living as occurring-into-implying carrying forward. This shift in ontological intuitions is not offered as *the* way of describing this phenomenon; Gendlin's epistemological intuitions are pragmatist: we use models when they are helpful (Gendlin, 2018, p.253ff.; Schoeller & Dunaetz, 2018). *A Process Model* is 'a' model: for use alongside other models (Gendlin, 2018, p. 257); for use as a starting point to be improved upon (Gendlin, 2018, p. 113). The heart of its distinctive contributions is that its crux is first person experiencing. It speaks from and elucidates how being here feels and is for each of us personally; from our interiority, so to speak. Many alternative models tacitly elide first person experiencing from reality.

Know-how from the perspective of implying

Looking closely at animal know-how gives us an opportunity to explore the utility of Gendlin's schema – the interlocking terms it provides – as a platform for ethological enquiry, exploring its contributions to "find[ing] nonanthropomorphic terminology that reflects meaningful levels of congruence between human and animal behavior" (Asquith, 2011, p. 239).

In Gendlin's schema, the prototypical form of know-how is a process resuming when an absence ends. A metabolic process may pause when nutrients are absent, and resume when they are present. The shift in the process is dramatic as the occurring-in shifts: a (strand of) implying that was paused, being 'carried' (held) by the living process that is ongoing, changes markedly with the occurring of nutrients into implying metabolizing. Metabolizing resumes. He posits this as the roots of recognizing (Gendlin, 2018, p. 15). "[T]he body 'implies' the object by implying the process which the object resumes" (Gendlin, 2018, p. 19). When the nutrients are present, they are not being recognized, they are a taken-for-granted environ. When they are absent, they are not known either, though somesuch that will carry the implying-a-metabolizable-input forward is implied. The implying/occurring-in relation is not representational – what is implied is *whatsoever* will carry the subprocess forward – but being resumed is a prototype of recognition.

There is in this schema nothing of feeling or perceiving; simply a large process shift when somesuch occurs in. When something that carries forward the implying continues to *not* occur, something decidedly repetitive is occurring. A strand of the life process – a paused subprocess – is repeating with fine variations, carried by the living that *is* ongoing. Gendlin's intuition here is that an iterating openness (poised-to-encounter-ness) can become a medium against which something can stand out, as a figure against a quasi-stable background.

In Gendlin's schema, behavior develops from these underpinnings when something happens that is helpful – something occurs that carries the implying forward in a new way – and what Gendlin calls the 'open cycle' (the reiterating being-poised) registers both the body side and the environment side of the ongoing process (Gendlin, 2018, pp. 86–87). Initially what has occurred is unexpected, but because the shift is helpful, its occurring comes to be implied. Schematically, registering the shifting body is feeling, and registering the changing environment is perceiving. The carrying forward in a new way, the bodily shifting, and the environmental shifts are all thus facets of the one new process, and, because the living process comes to imply its own shifting, as registered in feeling and perceiving, a new kind of carrying forward can come to be implied. In such a process, "[t]he body changes itself and moves itself through these changes" (Gendlin, 2018, p. 88). A new kind of feedback loop emerges. Living process finds a way to imply changing itself. This is the core of his schema for behaving.

There are a few points to underline here. Firstly, behaviors such as foraging, fleeing predators, and staying with one's group are all understood as elaborations – fruitful detours – on a root implying of tissue process carrying forward: on implying continuing being alive. In animals, such as kangaroos, a hunger-ingesting-metabolizing-hunger loop has elaborated to include a wider foraging for food loop, for example. Behaving comes as an elaboration of tissue process. Tissue process becomes more complex, involving a new kind of carrying forward (cf. Walkerden, 2004). Secondly, perceiving, feeling, and behaving are not separate processes that somehow get added together, constructing a form of life. Rather, because body-environment is one process carrying forward, and a capacity for registering occurs, they are internally arising together, as facets of the one process. Gendlin calls feeling here 'feeling-in-behavior' and perceiving 'perceiving-in-behavior' (Gendlin, 2018, p. 91) to underline that we are not talking here about feelings or perceivings apart from an ongoing behaving. Thirdly, the organism (living process) comes to imply its own bodily shifting, and it registers its own bodily shifting occurring in a way that carries forward this implying, and this is the core schema of 'sentience' of 'consciousness' as 'self-registry'. Living process comes to experience itself.

From here, in Gendlin's schema, a kind of experienced 'space' emerges for the first time. For the animal, this is not the space we as observers see it acting within, in which our objects, interests and intentions are tacitly salient. It is feeling-and-perceiving the openness-relevances of implying:

> Behavior space is *had space*, that is to say felt and perceived space. It is not the external observer's space within which an organism might be viewed. Rather, it is a process's own space, the body-process's own implying of behavior sequences. [...]
>
> As the doubled bodily-behavioral implying is carried forward, the organism feels and perceives the space (the mesh of the implicit sequences). Any occurring now *goes on in* (is a carrying forward of) that space (that context of other sequences).
>
> We say that behavior space consists of "behavior possibilities," but we must keep in mind that only the occurring one "was" really possible. It is not as if any of the implicit ones could have formed just as well. The one that occurred was focaled in eveing with the actual en[vironment].
> (Gendlin, 2018, p. 98)

Behavior space *is* the mesh of ways of behaving that are implicit in the behaving that is actually occurring, a having of possibly relevant ways of moving-feeling-perceiving. The animal lives in a field of possible ways of moving that keeps shifting as the animal behaves and as circumstances change (cf. Gendlin, 2018, p. 112). From this schema we can define – in a Gendlinian way – terms to help with linking the philosophy of the implicit to research into animal behavior:

- *Know-how*: The mesh of the implicit sequences that the animal orients from, i.e. the field of 'behavior possibilities' eveing in its implying is its *knowing-how* to behave. In this schema, know-how is not internal contents that map to external situations, as a tacitly dualistic, things-first schema would have it. Know-how is implying relevantly and helpfully in relation to what may occur. The more relevant experience that is eveing in the implying, the more refined is the knowing-how (cf. Gendlin, 2018, p. 54).

• *Practice*: Cycles are fundamental to living process in this schema. Hunger implies foraging, feeding, and getting hungry again (Gendlin, 2018, p. 9). Cycles involve a kind of repetition. An animal practice is a family of ways of behaving to carry forward in resonant circumstances to arrive at resonant closures (e.g. satiation). Know-how guides practicing, and practicing develops know-how.

• *Tradition*: Social learning is a feature of some animals' lives (Thornton & Raihani, 2008; cf. Gendlin, 2018, p. 110). Some know-how is passed on from parents to children, and some is shared more widely in networks (Avital & Jablonka, 2000). Behavior space is 'inherited', Gendlin notes (Gendlin, 2018, p. 103). Social learning is a behavioral inheritance system (Jablonka & Lamb, 2014). What is passed down through this inheritance system is animal traditions (Avital & Jablonka, 2000): implied ways of carrying forward.

When using *A Process Model*'s schema to help make sense of animal behavior, the terms behavior, know-how, practice, and tradition each need to be understood as instancing occurring-into-implying carrying forward. Practices are ways of carrying occurring-into-implying forward that we use and reuse. Know-how points to the eveing aspect of this implying. Practice traditions pass on useful know-how.

A hermeneutic enquiry

Exploring the utility of Gendlin's 'occurring-into-implying' concepts and framework for describing kangaroo know-how, and animal practices generally, is a hermeneutic project. We are trying out an approach to interpretation, refining the approach based on the results we get, and trying it out again.

The trying and refining is enabled by following hermeneutic circles of which two are paradigmatic, and used here:

1 starting from "an unfocused 'feel' that questions the adequacy of the received interpretation" then "more explicit questioning" then "[a]s answers are received to initial questions, these questions are often modified and sharpened to produce a new series of questions better attuned to the [...] subject" (Polkinghorne, 2000, p. 472, on Gadamer); and

2 moving from a whole to its parts, from the parts to the whole, back and forth, heeding each on its own terms and each in relation to the other resolution(s) (Crotty, 2003, p. 92).

Gendlin emphasizes a third hermeneutic circle: going back and forth between felt understanding and words coming from it, letting each evolve (Gendlin, 2003, p. 44). These three circles are not either/ors, they are embedded in each other. Gendlin (1997b, s. IV) points out that the implicit has obvious roles in the classic whole-part-whole hermeneutic circle. His practice for thinking with the implicit, Focusing, scaffolds the to and fro of both the above circles; for example:

- "Let yourself feel the unclear sense of *all of that*" (Gendlin, 2003, p. 44).
- "Let a word, a phrase, or an image come up from the [unclear] felt sense itself" (Gendlin, 2003, p. 44).
- "[W]hat does this whole thing feel like?" (Gendlin 2003, p. 54).
- "What are the two or three things about [this issue] that trouble me the most?" (Gendlin, 2003, p. 105).

Focusing emphasizes the somatic ground of hermeneutic thinking: easing marks one's way forward (Gendlin, 2003, p. 39). The hermeneutic circles highlighted above offer scaffolds for deepening insight into particular topics.

My underlying epistemological assumptions are not realist – a true idea must copy its reality – rather, after William James (1991), they are pragmatist – truth is understood as processual, evident in helpfulness. These epistemological roots give the hermeneutic expectation of continuing revision a central place. Realist epistemological intuitions make stronger assumptions about the relations between what we say and what is: they imply a stronger homology. Realist epistemologies lead one to expect the order of the real and the order of logic to mirror each other in some way (cf. Rorty, 1980); the similarity is actual. James's pragmatist intuitions are pluralist: they leave this relation open. One appreciates the practical power of conceptual schemas without making the further step of (at least tacitly) anticipating closure.

The main elements of my methodology are as follows.

Working from natural history reporting

The challenges in describing kangaroo practices, and the know-how they involve, have much in common with the challenges of describing human practices. Practitioners engage with situations holistically – necessarily, because everything that is in play in a situation *may* be relevant to getting the practical benefits one implies. Brunner draws the following contrast:

> The practitioner needs to construct a detailed map of the particular context comprehensive enough to guide action in the context – a theory

for n = 1. Conversely, the reductionist must abstract relatively few observations from many contexts to test a general hypothesis or theory.
(Brunner, 2006, p. 152)

In these terms, kangaroos are practitioners: *their* stance is toward the whole of their circumstances, together, as they encounter them. Natural history research – particularly research that focuses closely on the lives of individual animals – shares these interests. It asks about situations and trajectories as wholes and may ask about lives as wholes.

Most of the research that is published on kangaroos measures a few variables across the lives of many animals. Such research is obviously very helpful for discussing particular aspects of kangaroos' forms of life, but even added together is strikingly inadequate for characterizing kangaroo practices from a kangaroo's standpoint. Firstly, mainstream quantitative research methods provide findings that apply statistically to categories of kangaroo, not to specific, individual kangaroos as such. Secondly, they provide findings about a few elements of their forms of life, not about the shapes of these lives as wholes, and not, in particular, about the kinds of crossing of large numbers of considerations that is at the heart of understanding implying. Such quantitative research *compliments* enquiry into individual kangaroos' forms of life, but is no substitute for it.

Where one's research questions are about the shapes of practices and forms of life, quite different research methods are needed: animals need to be approached holistically, in ways that let these shapes come into view. Natural history approaches are a far better fit. The primary data set used in *this* exploration of kangaroo know-how is the documentary film *Kangaroos – Faces in the mob* (Aldenhoven & Carruthers, 1992), because, as I indicated above, it follows closely the lives of a small number of kangaroos, pays close attention to some important kangaroo practices, notably parenting, is grounded in long-term observation of a mob of kangaroos, and is supported by disciplined scientific research.

Modeling (something of) two kangaroos' sensibilities

A 'sensibility' (a term being used here in a somewhat specialized sense) is a way of representing implying, in a way that is relevant to describing practicing – and more generally living – from a first person standpoint. Using it as a central concept in describing kangaroo know-how from the perspective of implying is an instance of taking something from practice theory developed for understanding human practices (Walkerden, 2009, 2010, 2019) and experimenting with using it to describe animal practices.

A sensibility, as the term is used here, is an organism's sensitivity to what may occur and what it may be helpful to do. Describing a sensibility is pointing to what is crossing in the implying, the eveving, when the sensibility is in play *here*, and what *may* be crossing in the implying, eveving, *when* circumstances make such knowing-how relevant.

The logic of – the fundamental patterns in – implying differ markedly from those we conventionally use for describing human practices: repertoires of procedures, procedures that involve steps and decision points, etc. There are two main points of contrast:

1   repertoires and procedures have an exclusive-OR at their core: one is doing A OR B: selecting from the repertoire, doing this step not that step;
2   the patterns they offer are closed: as one is doing A, detail will need to be filled out – it will need to be instantiated so local fitting to circumstances may occur – but all that local detail will be instancing A: the field of options the practitioner is being invited to use is, at some relevant fundamental level, defined by the repertoire and decision tree.

In teaching people new practices, these simplifications are useful heuristics. However, if used to understand know-how from the perspective of implying, they deform it profoundly, because acting from implying involves neither of these constraints.

Implying, as we emphasized above, involves a very, very rich crossing of relevant considerations. What is being experienced as *relevant* is in play in this crossing. Secondly, implying has a fundamental openness: *implying* is not of a specific, concrete occurring, although it may be carried forward by such. To portray sensibilities in diagrams, therefore, a distinctive grammar that points to the unconventional orderliness of practice know-how is needed. The grammar I use in sensibility models (*sensu* Walkerden, 2009, 2010, 2019) is designed to do this. Its two key terms are 'perhaps finding' and 'perhaps implying':

•   'Perhaps finding' points to what may be occurring that a process may reorient from. In practical terms, in a sensibility model a 'perhaps finding' node is used to mark something noteworthy that will help one understand where the practitioner – here the animal – is coming from.
•   'Perhaps implying' is used – rather than say 'perhaps doing' – because what a sensibility model is depicting (pointing to) is the *implying* an animal is coming from. In any actual doing, *many* of the nodes differentiated in a sensibility model, and much else that is unspecified, may be in play crossing in the implying that is shaping the behaving that happens. What is implied is not *defined* by what the nodes say. Rather the nodes suggest or indicate the implying that is in play by pointing to kinds of occurring that may carry such implying forward.

'Perhaps' has a central role because it points very directly to the practitioner's – here the animal's – first person experience. It invites one to ask: what *is* in play here shaping the behaving? 'Perhaps' invites testing possibilities through close observation, close engagement, and careful reflection.

A sensibility model is not designed to be read procedurally, although occasionally procedural readings of parts of them are illuminating. The core way of reading it is to understand that it is a model of – a scaffold that points to – a *whole* implying that the animal (person...) may be living from. So one reads it looking for what nodes and strands *may* be in play in a particular passage of behaving. Many nodes, perhaps all, may be in play at once. The differentiations marked out with words in nodes and arrows are provisional. The reality that the diagram is pointing to is whole and crossed and open in ways that elude – both by far exceeding, and by being open in unspecifiable ways – what one can actually convey explicitly in a diagram and its accompanying explications.

When a sensibility model is portraying the openness-relevances of implying that an animal is or may be feeling and perceiving it is a model of behavior space. It is a model of the mesh of implicit sequences, had as a whole, by the behaving animal as it behaves, that it behaves within. In this enquiry, we use a sensibility model of (something of) a kangaroo's behavior space as a basis for discussing kangaroo practices as kangaroos live them – exploring kangaroo know-how from a first person standpoint.

Reflecting on results, furthering understanding

This hermeneutic enquiry has three main movements:

1   Brokering an encounter between the sensibility model conventions, as a way of representing animal practices understood from implying, with the natural history reporting provided in *Faces in the Mob*.
2   Reflecting on this encounter, bringing Gendlin's understanding of implying in more deeply; this section focuses on 'behavior space' (a core concept of Gendlin's) and interrupts, surprises, and adaptation.
3   Stepping back further and considering some of the limitations of Gendlin's approach, and what they imply for further work to extend his model, and the potential for combining Gendlin's phenomenologically astute lens with other lenses to deepen understanding of animal practices.

Both paradigmatic hermeneutic circles have shaped each of these three movements: spiraling from question to answer to refined question to refined answer to...; and moving back and forth between wholes and parts.

I am laying out the hermeneutic trajectory of this enquiry in some detail so that others interested in disciplined thick description of animals' practices, and their forms of life, can use my approach as a reference point, as they design their own enquiries.

A first hermeneutic movement: Embracing a natural history approach

Figure 9.1 provides a sketch of two female kangaroos' implying. Although it conveys the major behavioral domains, it barely hints at the richness of kangaroo implying: many terms, e.g. 'eating grass, etc.' (node 16), are capable of a great deal of explication. It is based on close observation of two female kangaroos named in this long-term field study 'Eucalypt' and 'Columbine' (Aldenhoven & Carruthers, 1992). The differentiations between them that are annotated in the model (Figure 9.1, nodes 20–25), that we will return to, are aspects of parenting.

Implying is wider than behaving. All behaving involves underpinning tissue process, but much tissue process is only evident in behaving through the absence of difficulties – digestion and immune responses are implicit in behaving not being disrupted, for instance. In Figure 9.1, the focus is on behaving: on what does the animal do that we observe, rather than on physiology.

How does modeling a kangaroo's form of life from the perspective of implying help with understanding animal behavior?

The breadth of kangaroos' know-how

Documenting kangaroos' forms of life with a sensibility model is a reminder of the breadth of a kangaroo's know-how. In Figure 9.1, feeding, medicating, mating, parenting, and avoiding predators (nodes 1–14) are all foregrounded together. Because quantification has such a central role in kangaroo research, and because that implies methods that examine a subset of phenomena over many animals – e.g. Austin & Ramp (2019), Balland et al. (2020), Plaisir et al. (2022) – the overall shape of kangaroos' forms of life easily drops into the background.

Nodes 1–14 are all at a very high level; a great deal of fine-grained know-how is just hinted at. However, reading Figure 9.1 as a model of *implying*, rather than as a model of a family of separate practices, points toward a related important truth: that *all* these sensitivities and forms of behavior may be in play together. Conventionally, field protocols direct observers to recording a set of separate behaviors (Ryan, 2018). But looking at kangaroo know-how through a sensibility lens underlines that we are *not* looking at radically separate competencies.

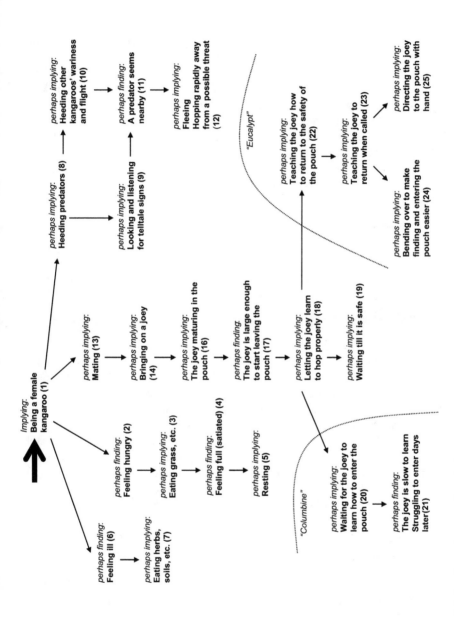

Figure 9.1 Implying being a female kangaroo.

The ways kangaroos are poised to handle surprises reveal a readiness that it is easy to underemphasize, observing. A female kangaroo may be being sensitive, at one and the same time, to the behavior of its joey, the availability of food, the behavior of the mob [its current group of kangaroos], and the (absence of) sounds of predators. In conventional field observations this multiplicity is easily obscured. A sensibility lens makes it much easier to see that kangaroos' forms of life involve many crossed practices, for example, feeding-parenting-predator-heeding is all the one practice for a female kangaroo with a joey out of the pouch. Behaving, like human action, is usually understood as doing one thing at a time in a useful sequence – talk of procedures, repertoires, and decision trees all make this assumption, for instance. The perspective of implying brings out how radical a simplification this assumption is. The complexity we encounter in the field is easier to see if an orientation toward implying is guiding our observing.

Parenting practices: Explicating intricacies

An emphasis on implying is also well suited to explicating particularities of animal behavior, bringing out individual differences in practices. Nodes 13–18 (Figure 9.2) lay out a common thread of parenting, while nodes 20 and 21 (Columbine), and 22–25 (Eucalypt) convey significant differences in two kangaroos' parenting practice.

Letting a joey leave the pouch, providing it with opportunities to learn to hop, forage, stay with the mob, come to know its local area, recognize and escape predators, etc., is basic to parenting a joey. One practice that governs this is 'Waiting till it is safe' (node 19), which can be understood as a crossing of two main practices: (i) holding the pouch pulled tight so that the joey cannot leave, and (ii) checking for dangers (nodes 8–10). Both Columbine and Eucalypt share this practice.

A place where the two kangaroos differ is around how they approach their joey returning to their pouch (Aldenhoven & Carruthers, 1992). Eucalypt adopts a low posture, leaning forward to make the entry to her pouch more accessible, and provides guidance with her forearm, to help her joey move toward the entry (nodes 22–25). Columbine, by contrast, stands erect – no stooped posture – and provides no guiding hand. Columbine's joey learns more slowly and takes longer to return to the pouch. When Columbine's joey approaches his mother from the rear, for example, and attempts to get into her forward-opening pouch, he fails to do so and attempts again and again (nodes 20 and 21). Only when he realizes he should go to where her hands are, and turn to face her, does his implying carry forward, he enters the pouch (Aldenhoven & Carruthers, 1992). Evidently if a dingo (native dog, top predator) approaches, Columbine's joey is at greater risk. If we look at this process from the standpoint of Columbine's joey, we have an instance of implying *not* being carried forward for some time,

Figure 9.2 Letting a joey leave the pouch and teaching it to return there for safety. (a) Pouch pulled tight (Eucalypt). (b) Checking whether it's safe (Eucalypt). (c) Joey can't find pouch, no guiding hand, no stooped posture (Columbine). (d) Stopped posture, guiding hand (Eucalypt).
Source: Aldenhoven & Carruthers (1992).

and his implying iterating, as repetitious but generally unhelpful occurring continues.

Focusing on the richness of individual animals' implying carrying forward in their circumstances provides a way of bringing resonances and contrasts in animal practices into focus (nodes 13–25).

There are other differences in parenting that could be included in a more elaborated version of this sensibility model that are worth remarking on (Aldenhoven & Carruthers, 1992). Columbine lets her joey wander off while she is feeding. Eucalypt uses soft calls to keep her joey from straying. Eucalypt has her joey practicing 'come when called' a lot. Columbine practices 'come when called' less. Columbine is an older female; all her previous eight joeys have died. Eucalypt is a younger female, who has already raised two joeys successfully. Eucalypt learned her parenting skills from her mother, who in turn learned them from Eucalypt's grandmother. Her grandmother's descendants are the largest group in the valley.

The contrasts between Eucalypt's and Columbine's parenting under-line the importance of animal traditions (Avital & Jablonka, 2000), and thence the importance of ways of documenting animal know-how. The per-spective of implying and sensibility models as a means of describing imply-ing are a resource that can support explication of animal cultures.

Quantitative research and thin description

Comparing this natural history-based sensibility model (Figure 9.1) with findings about kangaroos published in the research literature illuminates some of the contributions that orienting from implying can make to an understanding of animal behavior. Nodes 1–17, which draw out some threads of foraging, mating, and predation, overlap extensively with the research literature. (Indeed, the strands of nodes are so succinct that they do little more than identify topics taken up in the research literature.) Nodes 18–25, on the other hand, which explicate some of the intricacies of kangaroo parenting, bring out features of parenting that are invisible in the research literature.

The research literature provides a broad outline of the forms of life of Eastern Grey Kangaroos, including their practices. Regarding parenting, for example, it is well documented that kangaroo mothers nurse their "young for at least 18 months after birth, with weaning occurring about 8 months after the offspring has permanently left the pouch" (King & Goldizen, 2016, p. 60). In the first phase of their development, after birth, joeys are confined to the pouch and are suckling. The second phase of a young kangaroo's development (the pouch-infant phase) dates from when they are first allowed out of the pouch to when they are no longer allowed to climb back into the pouch. This is followed by the young-at-foot phase, where they are still suck-ling but are permanently out of the pouch.

Taking the young-at-foot phase as an example, some of the notable find-ings reported in the literature include:

- Young-at-foot are the group of kangaroos with highest mortality in a mob (Clarke et al., 1995).
- Young-at-foot were more often found at safer sites: where human pres-ence reduced human and other predator hunting (Austin & Ramp, 2019). Austin and Ramp (2019) note that this could be simply because they survive better there; however, evidence of kangaroo mothers tak-ing young to safer locations makes it much more likely this is a result of awareness and caution regarding predators.
- "[F]emales with accompanying young-at-foot are the most solitary, [...] and the most vigilant" group of kangaroos (Clarke et al., 1995, p. 527; cf. Banks, 2001). This is understood to be protective for young and mother.

- When predators are feared, females with young-at-foot flee farther than females with no pouch young (Jarman & Wright, 1993, p. 837).
- Young kangaroos and their mothers call to each other to identify and locate each other (Baker & Croft, 1993).

Concatenating findings reported in the research literature creates the impression that the literature, taken as a whole, describes parenting relatively richly. *Juxtaposed* we get a sense of how these findings hang together, in a form of life. However, tacitly, here, as readers, we are doing something similar to ruminating on a sensibility model: allowing a sense of the *whole* of these kangaroos' way of parenting to form. The reality of most of this writing – considered as individual texts – is that just as concrete human beings are missing from the pages of much psychological research, so too concrete animals are missing from the pages of much kangaroo research:

> Basically, the standard [psychological] experimental report is empty of humans. The authors discuss the effects of variables on other variables [...]. No actual participant is introduced to the reader; rather, the aggregate scores representing the tested variables are what seem to be real. In consequence, experimental reports can be example-free, human-free zones. [...] Example-free psychology [is] impoverished psychology, disconnected from the lives of those who were being studied.
>
> (Billig, 2019, p. 4)

In a similar way, most of the research literature does not take us into the intricacy of kangaroo lives, in the way that a documentary like *Faces in the Mob* does. It, too, is example-free.

In Eastern Grey Kangaroo research, Robyn Stuart-Dick's work is the research that diverges most from this pattern. Stuart-Dick was one of the scientific advisers to *Faces in the Mob*. Her PhD thesis (Stuart-Dick, 1987), *Parental investment and rearing schedules in the Eastern Grey Kangaroo*, is the richest account of parenting in this species. Her field work was extensive. It involved approximately 360 days in the field, over a period of three years, averaging ten days per month, visiting every month. Field work was conducted from dawn to dusk, and each month seven to twelve mother-young pairs were chosen as focal dyads. A further year's data collected by other researchers was included in her analyses (Stuart-Dick, 1987). This level of extensive, close engagement – which is resonant of leading primatologists and ethnographers (cf. Asquith, 2011) – *does* enable very nuanced understanding. By way of illustration, she writes,

> the [pouch-infant phase] young played as much as many eutherian young. It's behaviour when out of the pouch was more randomly

structured than the mother's behaviour and comprised a wide variety of activity states defined as 'play'. A pouch-infant was strongly oriented toward the pouch and readily re-entered whenever the mother signalled. One third to one half of its time out of the pouch was spent with its head in the pouch (suckling?). The mother of a pouch-infant significantly altered her behaviour when the young was out of the pouch. She surveyed more frequently and rested less than usual: also her behaviour became less structured. However, the mother appeared proximately at least, in control of the times and durations of her infant's exit from the pouch. Infants were allowed out of the pouch less than one third of the daylight hours.

(Stuart-Dick 1987, p. iv-v)

Even so, in her thesis, the individual, concrete animals – their lives, their stories, themselves as individuals – do not appear explicitly.

Standard research questions and methods in mammalogy do not aspire to the kind of thick description natural history can provide. Indeed they eschew it. Ryan's (2018) *Mammalogy Techniques Lab Manual*, for example, contains the following injunctions:

The first step in studying the behavior of a species is to construct an ethogram. In its simplest form, an ethogram is a catalog of an animal's behaviors [...] Constructing ethograms requires careful observations of and notes on each behavior. The result is a complete list of behaviors with a definition of each. *Ideally, each behavior should be unambiguous; it should not be possible to assign a new observation to more than one category in your ethogram.*

(Ryan, 2018, p. 327; emphasis added)

Complexly crossing practicing is excluded from observation by design.

Among the most important decisions is how many individuals to observe (i.e., to have a large enough sample size for statistical tests). It may be much easier to observe many behaviors in one individual, but this practice leads to pseudo-replication (treating the data as independent observations when they are in fact interdependent). Observations need to be independent events. If you measure the same behavior multiple times in the same individual, the behaviors are not independent events (i.e., not true replicates). At times, your study design may require you to take repeated measures on the same animal (e.g., behaviors before and after an environmental disturbance). *In general, though, the best way to characterize an animal's natural behavior is to watch as many different individuals as possible and then summarize their "average" behavior.*

(Ryan, 2018, p. 327; emphasis added)

This stricture will obscure individual differences in animals' practicing; it excludes careful exploration of 'first person standpoints' (the particularity of individual animals' occurring-into-implying carrying forward) by design.

> The second method for analyzing behavior patterns is to derive a transition matrix. A transition matrix expresses the probability that one behavior is followed by another. For example, we might expect that digging a hole has a 0.85 probability (85% of the time) of being followed by burying an acorn, but digging a hole has only a 0.15 probability of being followed by chasing another squirrel. *By linking "chains" of behaviors, a transition matrix is a technique for looking at relationships between different behaviors.* Creating a transition matrix requires knowing the sequence in which each behavior was performed.
>
> (Ryan, 2018, p. 335; emphasis added)

Behaviors are atomized by design and then recombined as statistical relations. The orderliness of implying is deliberately designed out.

Ryan (2018, p.329) comments: "One of the hardest lessons to learn when studying animal behavior is to avoid projection (of either adaptive function or anthropomorphism)". What this misses is that the 'observational protocols' and 'statistical analyses' are profoundly human artifacts. An understanding arrived at in this way *is* radically anthropomorphic, just in a different way:

> [W]herever science is concerned with measurement, the particular aspect of nature involved has first to be prepared quantitatively. This entails dividing it into a set of homogeneous parts that are intellectually superimposed on nature like a grid or scaffolding. Nature is then seen in the perspective of the framework, which is not part of nature at all, but is really an intellectual rearrangement of nature that reduces it to the purely quantitative – i.e., to parts which are external to one another. [...] It is a form of thought entirely appropriate to the inanimate world, but quite inadequate for apprehending life.
>
> (Bortoft, 1996, loc. 2799)

Primatologists have demonstrated that the kind of sustained field work that Robyn Stuart-Dick's research illustrates is a different kind of remedy for the challenges of anthropomorphism:

> Primatologists who have gotten to know their animal subjects over many years can predict behavior in some situations, as much as anyone can predict another's behavior, and can respond appropriately in "baboon" or "gorilla" terms to incidents in which the animals have involved them. Other primate species' abilities to learn, invent, have a social memory and strategize should not need to be defended just because humans also do them. At the same time, in providing us with such a full picture of

their lives, we have enough of a context to understand the concepts in "baboon terms," for instance, without fear of naive anthropomorphism.

(Asquith, 2011, pp. 241–242)

Fundamentally what is at stake here is having astute questions explored with appropriate methods. The questions and methods used in the Eastern Grey Kangaroo research literature can illuminate general features of kangaroos' lives because the research focus is categories of animal. However, even there, the combination of observational protocols and statistical methods mean that when one is investigating more complex phenomena in which many considerations cross, shaping behavior, what is occurring is very hard to discern. The number of possible interactions between the putatively separate factors increases exponentially as the number of 'factors' increases arithmetically. What this means is that unless a relationship is pervasive, it cannot be discerned. One of the side effects of this is that many research articles reintroduce some of these quantitatively excluded considerations (matters not measured) in the form of suggestions about what *might* explain, account for, various of the quantitative data they report. It is not uncommon for an article to be definite quantification positioned in a sea of interpretive uncertainty; descriptive statistics as synthesized observation offering only slight leverage on wider questions about animals' lives.

Evidently, as the work cited above shows, traditional quantitatively oriented observation and analysis of kangaroo behavior has useful contributions to make. However, a documentary like *Faces in the Mob* shows that much that is precious is largely missing from this literature. If we want to move imaginatively and in a disciplined way in the direction of understanding kangaroos' experience, then we have a different kind of question and need different methods.

Simply doing more natural history research is one possibility. However, the perspective of implying brings a kind of orderliness to understanding first person experiencing – an organizing principle – that is absent from, or only tacit in, narratives. A sensibility model points toward an underlying pattern in living, and seeing these patterns is empowering for interpreting and understanding. Of course Figure 9.1 is just a proof of concept. (For a much more developed example, looking at ecosystem management practice, see Walkerden (2019)). But it points to the potential for a more disciplined grasp of kangaroo living, from the perspective of implying.

A second hermeneutic movement: Improving interpretations

The first hermeneutic movement (Figure 9.1) combined a grammar and logic derived from Gendlin's account of implying (Walkerden, 2009, 2019) with observations and a vocabulary derived from a natural history project (which was embedded in a long-term study of a mob of kangaroos), and an exploration of how that crossing contrasts with mainstream kangaroo research practice. This second movement is devoted to sharpening questions and improving interpretations, in the process identifying ways in which consideration of implying can be better used in interpreting and understanding animal practices.

Behavior space

A sensibility model (e.g. Figure 9.1) is a model of the sensitivities to what may be occurring (perhaps finding) and what it may make sense to do (perhaps implying), laid out in a way that respects key features of what we observe in implying, notably: (i) that a great many considerations may cross in what actually happens ('doing one thing at a time' is an unhelpful simplification if one is trying to understand a form of life holistically), and (ii) that there is an inherent openness in living forward, such that what occurs (how the animal behaves) is fresh, specific to its particular circumstances, and may be quite novel. Figure 9.1 can thus be read as a model of what Gendlin calls behavior space: a description of the behavior-feeling-perceiving paths (subsidiary implyings) that an animal is living in and from.

A qualification is important. Figure 9.1 describes behavior space at a very general level: the main relevances for behaving for a female kangaroo are conveyed. There is a great deal more that can be differentiated when one looks in a fine-grained way at what is relevant when behaving. For example, one passage of behaving documented in *Faces in the Mob* (Aldenhoven & Carruthers, 1992) is of

- males gathering near a female approaching estrus,
- the female kangaroo in estrus mating with the dominant male kangaroo,
- their coupling being interrupted by the close approach of another male which the dominant male chases away,
- other subordinate males approaching her to mate while the dominant male is absent,
- the female bounding away until she arrives at the hollowed base of a fallen tree which she can retreat into to stop mating happening if a subordinate male attempts this, or if mating with the dominant male is interrupted again,
- the dominant male catching up with her at this place, and
- mating resuming.

As the animal behaves, what is focal for the animal shifts. Hopping down the path the female in estrus is carried forward by the changing environment (cf. Gendlin, 2018, p. 112), and the relocating comes to an end as the female finds herself at the patch of ground adjacent to the hollowed out tree trunk: what is focal shifts from implying-moving to implying-mating. The behavior space presence of retreating to this location might be schematized as something like moving-to-feel-surer-of-copulating-with-the-dominant-male, or perhaps moving-to-have-shelter-ready-to-hand, or perhaps bringing-about-being-able-to-shelter-if-interrupted. How these phrases point in somewhat different ways to implying invites further enquiry. This 'implying available shelter' is crossing with, and carrying forward, implying mating with the dominant male. Implying mating with the dominant male is being carried forward by bounding away *from* the subordinate males *to* this place with refuge to hand, *while* giving the dominant male time to rejoin.

In Gendlin's (2018) understanding, animals do not know places like the valley and ridges where this mob of kangaroos live as an empty space, in the way that we do (an experience that has very sophisticated cultural achievements embedded in it). Rather, their experience is of a manifold of crossing affordances. Looking on, *we* see the kangaroos making use of, so seeming to differentiate, and find salient, tracks, shortcuts, fence crossings, locations of good water, safe places to rest, shady areas, special resources like the hollowed base of the fallen tree that can be used as a refuge (Aldenhoven & Carruthers, 1992). They know these opportunities and resources in an in-behaving way. How, though, does *their* way of experiencing these different potentials differ from ours and express kangaroo-being? These are questions that invite both further close observation and sensitive hermeneutic reflection. Such enquiry has a central place in research into animal practices *as* ways their implying behaving carries forward.

In the broad, behavior space encompasses a vast crossing of behaving possibilities with at least background relevance; usually a few of these are prominent in a particular passage of behaving. How the animal behaves specifically is a crossing attuned in some way to the situation. Behaving is not choice, in the sense of deliberate selection of an option. How the animal behaves forms in the occurring-into-implying. The behaving that comes is what specifically the implying (the animal's aliveness) implies being carried forward by *crossing with* occurring-in. What *can* occur occurs. The behaving that happens is as much carrying forward of the implying as proves possible in the circumstances. There is a precision here that Gendlin's term interaffecting points to. As the female kangaroo is bounding along the path to the safer place to copulate, she bounds over logs, moves round trees, adjusts stride length to the surfaces she is encountering, keeps implying future copulating, keeps alert for predators, etc. Her movements are not the result of a calculative process that takes all these, considered separately, into account. Rather, each bound instances a crossing: 'occurring-into-implying'. In this crossing, what participates is each consideration already affecting and affected by each other, as far as they may. What occurs is an evolving crossing.

Perhaps finding: Interrupts, surprises, and adaptation

In behavior space, the phrase 'perhaps finding' points toward what Gendlin calls registering something that is occurring – the feeling-in-behavior, such as feeling hungry (node 2), or perceiving-in-behavior, such as heeding predators (node 8). Finding is a more general term than registering, however. It links to implying: whatever may 'occur in' that may catalyze a shift in implying can be annotated (i.e. be made explicit with a node in a sensibility model) as 'perhaps finding...' The warrant for singling out some (aspect of a) circumstance is simply that remarking on it helps with understanding what is going on, understanding where the organism is coming from. 'Perhaps finding' nodes highlight places from which behaving, or living forward generally, may reorient.

The places from which life processes reorient range from being quite unfamiliar (perhaps vehicles on a country road) to being expected (e.g. predators hunting adult kangaroos or joeys) to being relied on (e.g. feeling satiated). Once a 'not being carried forward' has been experienced, it may come to be implied. Animals come to imply many shifts in circumstances, e.g. being interrupted by a predator, and imply ways of carrying forward from there (e.g. nodes 8–12). This is adaptation, from the perspective of implying.

The focus of much of Figure 9.1 is such implied findings. Much of Figure 9.1 could be seen as an explication of a female kangaroo's 'core competencies'. The kangaroo populations whose behavior *Faces in the Mob* documented lived on a cattle farm, so their circumstances were fairly close to pre-European kangaroo experience in that location. The openness of implying is important for appreciating this. Cattle, not being predators, don't disrupt kangaroo forms of life greatly (cf. Payne & Jarman, 1999). The kangaroo's behavior space can include cattle occurring-in (e.g. approaching where the kangaroos are feeding, or being encountered in a usual feeding spot) carrying forward a general implying sharing the landscape with other herbivores. Pre-European settlement kangaroos implied encountering wombats while grazing. Encountering cattle has similarities. Similarly, modern hunters (e.g. shooting at night with torches and guns) overlap substantially with a pre-European implying being hunted by people – it is a shift from being hunted with spears, but the pre-European implying provides a ground from which a distinctive pattern of evasion can form. How evading daylight hunting with spears, daylight hunting with guns, and nighttime hunting with guns and torches are related to each other, from a kangaroo's perspective, takes us into an exploration of how animal practices evolve. Close understanding of these aspects of kangaroo behavior needs more fieldwork.

Such behavioral shifts as circumstances change do not need preparation. "When there is a change in the body or in the environment, the usual process of a living thing immediately has a new organization" (Gendlin, 2018, p. 76). For example,

> [S]ay a walking animal falls into the water. Walking in water immediately assumes an unusual form since the movements do not encounter ground-resistance. So there is also no foot pressure. The movements will *therefore* be much wider. We call it "thrashing." [...] Thrashing is a

new sequence. It is certainly not unorganized. It has the organization of walking but in water. The movements are *immediately* wider because there is less resistance from the water. [...] We could phrase it this way: when the implied further walking "bites into" the changed en[vironment], neither walking nor chaos results. Rather, a new organization results. Or, to use our more careful terms, when the en is different, *what occurs into the (unchanged) implying* is different. It is still an occurring into the implying. A process is more than just the explicit arrangement of explicit parts, that an observer sees. When the usually observed process cannot happen, a different but orderly process can newly form. [...] In our simple example we can see how implied walking plus water makes thrashing. [...] *The implied walking participates in the formation of thrashing, yet the walking does not occur.* [...] If either the body or the environment changes, the process will go on differently.

(Gendlin, 2018, p. 75)

Thrashing may or may not carry the animal forward: the animal may drown, or the process may serve well enough and the animal may reach safety. When it serves well enough, the experience of having made its way to safety plays into a future experience of falling into water: its future implying is richer, and its practice gets refined. We can see from this example that adaptive capacity cannot be grasped by simply looking at the animal's observed past behaviors, body structure, and the physical changes of the environment. One has to understand how the implying is in play in the shaping of what occurs.

It is important to stress that it is not differences that are salient to us, as observers, that matter here – our experience of wombat vs cow, bullet vs spear, etc. Differentiations that are relevant are those that affect the kangaroo's implying carrying forward. In a sensibility model such as Figure 9.1, differentiations *are* differentiations because they are relevant to implying carrying forward or not. The significance of this shift in point of view is explored at length by Bourdieu in an analogous context in his comparison of what is salient for practitioners versus what stands out when looking from a 'scholastic' point of view (Bourdieu, 1990). What scholarly onlookers and embedded practitioners experience as relevant differs greatly in systematic ways. (Cf. also Bourdieu & Wacquant, 1992; Bourdieu, 2004.)

When something new, like thrashing, occurs, if it is helpful – if it carries forward the organism's whole implying in some way – it has evolutionary significance. The neo-Darwinian synthesis foregrounds just one inheritance system, but evolution has *four* inheritance systems crossing: genetic, epigenetic, behavioral, and symbolic (Jablonka & Lamb, 2014). Three of these four have Lamarckian characteristics. New practices and new versions of practices may be passed on through social learning, and if they are not, they may still influence what is passed on in each of the four inheritance systems, simply by influencing which organisms stay alive to participate in passing variations on.

Reflecting on Gendlin's schema

We can see from the above two hermeneutic movements that the perspective of implying provides a way that the lived experience, and more generally the form of life, of an animal can be explicated. Reflecting deeply on implying – on where an animal is coming from – raises new questions about how animals may be understood, and suggests new possibilities.

I hope the above explications demonstrate that implying is a lens with potential, when one's goal is to look at situations from a kangaroo's point of view, as one does when considering cumulative impacts on populations, or designing threatened species conservation plans, for instance. Its strengths include: it encourages a *holistic* appreciation of circumstances from the animals' perspectives, and it creates new opportunities for thinking about how novel situations are being experienced, and are (or are not) being adapted to.

I want to turn now to turn two major limitations of Gendlin's schema, which point toward opportunities for developing it further, and for using it in conjunction with other lenses.

Reproduction from the perspective of implying

Reproduction (nodes 13 and 14) is a central presence in a female kangaroo's implying (Figure 9.1). It naturally has, tacitly, a central place in Gendlin's understanding of animals' forms of life:

> The main "environment" of any animal is its species members, other animals like it. [...] By far the greater proportion of animal activity is with and towards them. The mother for the infant, female and male for each other, the group for the individual, these are crucial environments. We must not take the physical environment as our basic model of environment[.]
>
> (Gendlin, 2018, p. 7)

What is striking about *A Process Model*, then, is the paradoxes that reproduction creates for its basic schema. Asexual reproduction is one living process spawning many other living processes that carry the parent's living forward. Sexual reproduction has this one-to-many pattern present in it in the production of sperms and eggs, and then a 'two processes becoming one' process in fertilization creating a new viable organism. *A Process Model* does not engage with what is going on in these one-giving-rise-to-many and two-becoming-one processes.

The organizing logic of *A Process Model*, as it relates to creating concepts with which to understand the evolution of forms of life, is of one living process carrying forward, becoming progressively more differentiated and complex, as implying finds new ways to carry forward (Walkerden, 2004).

The major shifts are the emergence of behavior (tissues come to move and imply their own moving), symbolic understanding (gestures and protolanguage which are *about* situations), and direct referencing (where one thinks directly with the implicit, rendered as felt understanding). These shifts are all described as elaborations of 'the body's implying', as *'one* implying' carrying forward. Explaining what he means by implying and carrying forward, Gendlin provides large numbers of examples which are of a *single, individual* organism's process (the quotation above is an example). Am I, living forward, writing this, *one* implying, while you, living forward, reading this, are another *one* implying? If we answer yes to this, then Gendlin's process first ontology needs new concepts to describe ways occurring-into-implying can carry forward that follow patterns very different from the patterns he has explored in *A Process Model.*

In many respects, as writ, the core concepts of *A Process Model* are better positioned to describe developmental processes than evolutionary processes. However, as reproduction and *a fortiori* evolution clearly need these two new patterns – one-giving-rise-to-many and two-becoming-one – the direction in which the model needs to be elaborated is clear. [Such elaborations *could* be embedded in a monist ontology in which all existence ('the Big Bang'), and all life on earth ('the origin of life'), are understood as (in some meta-sense) one process carrying forward. Such elaborations would be consistent with mystical intuitions; cf. Walkerden (2021).] 'Otherness' needs to be understood more deeply.

First person phenomena and their contexts: Pluralistic interpretation

A Process Model only describes living process: bodily implying carrying forward (or not). So, another lens is needed for looking at non-living process. One possibility would be to schematize physico-chemical processes as, or as involving, some kind of proto-aliveness. However, it is equally natural, from a Gendlinian perspective, to use another kind of model for this purpose.

A second, related, limitation is that, in focusing on implying carrying forward, Gendlin has not built a model in which *not* carrying forward is *derived.* Rather, initially, this simply happens – it occurs, in an unmotivated way. Only subsequently may some kinds of not carrying forward come to be implied. We can see how not carrying forward does not arise from the implying side of living process in his discussion of relevance:

> Events that "were" in no way implied and do not carry forward can impinge on the body. As we will see, even such events happen into the ongoing relevanting, sometimes with a new but highly organized result. But irrelevant events are not produced by the body. Even with all your human capacities you are unable to think of something that is in every way irrelevant. Right now something irrelevant would be a relevant

example in this discussion. But at other times when you think of something irrelevant you can usually trace how it came – quite relevantly – in that situation.

(Gendlin, 2018, p. 48)

If what occurs is "in no way implied", then, in Gendlin's schema, it has an arbitrary outsideness: here it "impinge[s]". He uses resonant language at many points. "[A] different tree is about to *crash and hit* the beaver – the observer may see that it is about to happen", but from the standpoint of the beaver's life process this is "*arbitrary*", an "*intrusion*" (Gendlin, 2018, pp. 6–7, emphasis added). A spider is taken off its web – again this is just assumed: *how* such a thing might come about is unexplained (Gendlin, 2018, p. 10).

Gendlin provides a warrant, of sorts, for these arbitrary elements of his examples by giving "the spectator's environment" a foundational role in his ontology – it is "en#1" alongside the "en#2" of the environment in play in living process (e.g. the air coming into breathing lungs) and "en#3" (the environment organized by a life process for going on in, but not actually *in* occurring-into-implying at the moment, e.g. the nest a bird is away from). This just relocates the arbitrariness. "En#1" is a way of *assuming* an outside, a relevant otherness, without explaining how such is possible, how such might arise. Of course we cannot, and would not want to, ignore the great amount that is involved in an animal's living process, or in particular it's experience, that *we*, as observers (and indeed as ecologists or ethologists or environmental managers), are aware of. But "the spectator's environment" has no place in the explication of living as occurring-into-implying carrying forward. The latter is radically focused on first person process and (often) experience. Although he introduces the term "en#1" at the start of *A Process Model*, he subsequently uses it very rarely in the text (although he often relies on knowledge *we* have as observers, as we have done in our explication of kangaroo know-how).

In not having concepts to account for physico-chemical processes, not having ways of showing how reproducing occurs and populations persist and grow, and not having a way of deriving an organism *not* carrying forward, Gendlin's schema is bumping up against the problem of understanding otherness *from* a model that is built from its root concepts for describing first person process and experience. How then should we work with and around these gaps in his model, in exploring animal practices from the perspective of implying?

Bourdieu's framework for sociological research provides a viable, attractive model (Bourdieu & Wacquant, 1992). Bourdieu embraces using two complimentary lenses:

> Bourdieu turns [...] seemingly antagonistic paradigms into *moments* of a form of analysis designed to recapture the intrinsically double reality of the social world. The resulting *social praxeology* weaves together

a "structuralist" and a "constructivist" approach. First we push aside mundane representations to construct the objective structures (spaces of *positions*), the distribution of socially efficient resources that define the external constraints bearing on interactions and representations. Second, we reintroduce the immediate, lived experience of agents in order to explicate the categories of perception and appreciation (*dispositions*) that structure their action from the inside. [... Recognising that] the viewpoints of agents will vary systematically with the point they occupy in objective social space.

(Wacquant, 1992, p. 11)

Analogously, we can embrace, say, socio-ecological systems analysis (Walters, 2001; Walkerden, 2006) to provide an analysis from 'outside' the lived experience (or lived presence) of the organism that is capable of bringing together the physico-chemical, the biological, and the socio-economic, *and* an analysis from the 'inside', from the standpoint of implying that brings into focus what living is, had from *being* a living being. We do not have to privilege the outsider's standpoint, as Bourdieu does valorizing it as 'objective'. We can simply embrace hermeneutic pluralism. When developing threatened species conservation plans, for instance, we can move back and forth between socio-ecological systems analysis and looking from a phenomenological perspective at how the system dynamics land for the organism. Similarly, when designing a farming system, one can move back and forth between looking at it as a physical and financial system, and considering how the farming system works for – will be experienced by – the livestock, in the way that Temple Grandin commends and her practice illustrates (Grandin & Johnson, 2005). In any context where we are looking at shaping how we are interacting with non-human beings, we can combine our usual distanced, outsider-oriented modes of analysis *with* an exploration of how what we are proposing is likely to sit for the animals by considering our proposals from the perspective of their implying.

Each lens reveals phenomena that the other elides. The implying lens speaks powerfully to how a conservation plan is likely to be experienced by a group of kangaroos – what it integrates to, from their perspectives. The socio-ecological systems analysis lens speaks powerfully to understanding drivers of changes in kangaroo distribution and abundance, and to identifying policy and management interventions that may help the kangaroos thrive. Suppose a housing development is proposed that will impact kangaroo habitat. For the kangaroos, the housing development occurs into the kangaroos, as implyings, when work starts on it. In a kangaroo occurring-into-implying lens, the housing development is only revealed in the ways it is directly experienceable. Food availability and predation risks (cats, dogs, foxes...) may change, for example. The kangaroos, as implyings, may iterate and carry forward – perhaps with novel responses to novel circumstances. The *holistic* impact of the new development, and the potential adaptive openness of kangaroo living, only become visible if we look from the perspective of implying. Changes happening *outside* the lifeworld of the kangaroo – for example, in policy, design, flows of finance and materials, etc. – do not register in explorations of kangaroos *as* occurring-into-implying carrying forward; they *are* foregrounded in socio-ecological systems analysis.

Both lenses foreground real phenomena, and they complement each other. To embrace such a dialectical analytical strategy is consistent with Gendlin's epistemological intuitions:

> Having pursued some line of thought along the lines of a consistent and powerful model, having noted what this power just now gives one, why would one be unable to employ, moments later, a different model to see what that would lead to? To do this doesn't contradict the consistency of models, on the contrary it is possible only because consistent models do have powerful results and different models have different results.
>
> (Gendlin, 2018, p. 257)

Gendlin's intuitions here are pragmatist: we use multiple models – and move beyond them to fresh concept formation – as and when we find this helpful.

Conclusion

A Process Model demonstrates that it is possible to derive behaving, motivation, perception, consciousness, etc. from a rudimentary conception of living as a process of occurring-into-implying carrying forward. Its schema of interlocking terms provides an alternative to simply appropriating key terms used to describe human experiencing to describe animal experience in ways that leave the slippage from one context (human) to another (animal) unclear; it supports research efforts that focus on getting to know particular animals well (Asquith, 2011).

Understanding the lives of actual animals is necessarily a hermeneutic process. We follow hermeneutic circles from questions to answers to revised questions to improved answers and on, and from parts to wholes and back. Researching implying, we can build models of the sensitivities that are in play together – the sensibilities – that shape, underpin, kangaroo living. Sensibility models support disciplined thick description of animals' practices and their forms of life. Looking, for example, at passages of kangaroo mothers' living reveals their concurrent, crossed sensitivity to grass and other food, to their joey's behavior, to predators, to what other members of their mob are doing. Standard animal research methods make this kind of complexity invisible. Both protocols for observation, and the challenges of quantifying what is occurring here, wholly or largely elide it. A focus on implying directs attention to the intricacies of individual animals' practices. The differences in parenting skills between Columbine and Eucalypt are a striking example of the importance of behavioral traditions in animal species with social learning inheritance systems. Standard animal behavior research methods, with their emphases on categories of animals and quantification, obscure these kinds of intricacy. Looking at animal lives from the perspective of implying offers new ways of approaching animals' lives holistically, inviting new kinds of research question. The hermeneutic approach used here illustrates some methodological possibilities.

A model of a sensibility, as utilized here, is a model of behavior space, a model of practices, a model of know-how, as had from being alive, being present. Looking from implying supports systematic delineation of underlying patterns and variations in animal behavior. It helps specifically with looking at animal behavior from the animal's standpoint: with understanding where animals are coming from, as they behave. For ethologists, explicitly modeling animals' know-how is a way of deepening understanding of their forms of life. For conservation biologists, it is a way to bring behavioral implications of conservation strategies into focus. More fundamentally, a lack of sensitivity to other beings' wellbeing grounds the relative indifference with which their flourishing has been treated as human communities have expanded and developed. By providing more astute ways to place ourselves in non-human beings' shoes, the Philosophy of the Implicit makes a contribution to addressing, to reducing, a major Western cultural blind spot.

References

Aldenhoven, J., & Carruthers, G. (1992). *Kangaroos – Faces in the Mob.* Documentary Film. Green Cape Wildlife Films. Scientific Advisers: Peter Jarman, Robyn Stuart-Dick, Linda Walker & Susan Wright – University of New England. Released in the US by National Geographic as *Valley of the Kangaroos.*

Asquith, P. J. (2011). Of Bonds and Boundaries: What is the Modern Role of Anthropomorphism in Primatological Studies? *American Journal of Primatology*, 73, 238–244.

Austin, C. A., & Ramp, D. (2019). Behavioural Plasticity by Eastern Grey Kangaroos in Response to Human Behaviour. *Animals*, 9, 244.

Avital, E., & Jablonka, E. (2000). *Animal Traditions: Behavioural Inheritance in Evolution.* Cambridge University Press.

Baker, M. W. D., & Croft, D. B. (1993). Vocal Communication Between the Mother and Young of the Eastern Gray Kangaroo, Macropus-Giganteus, and the Red Kangaroo, M-Rufus (Marsupialia, Macropodidae). *Australian Journal of Zoology*, 41(3), 257–272.

Balland, J., Herbert, C. A., Welbergen, J. A., & Martin, J. M. (2020). Habitat Selection in a Peri-Urban Area by a Large Mammal Indicates a Low Potential for Human–Wildlife Conflict. *Wildlife Research*, 47, 381–390.

Banks, P. B. (2001). Predation-Sensitive Grouping and Habitat Use by Eastern Grey Kangaroos: a Field Experiment. *Animal Behaviour*, 61, 1013–1021.

Berkes, F. & Folke, C. (2002). Back to the Future: Ecosystem Dynamics and Local Knowledge. In L. H. Gunderson & C. S. Holling (Eds.), *Panarchy: Understanding Transformations in Human and Natural Systems* (pp. 121–146). Island Press.

Billig, M. (2019). *More Examples, Less Theory*. Cambridge University Press.

Bortoft, H. (1996). *The Wholeness of Nature: Goethe's Way toward a Science of Conscious Participation in Nature*. Lindisfarne Books.

Bourdieu, P. (1990). The Scholastic Point of View. *Cultural Anthropology*, 5(4), 380–391.

Bourdieu, P. (2004). *Science of Science and Reflexivity*. Polity Press.

Bourdieu, P., & Wacquant, L. J. D. (1992). *An Invitation to Reflexive Sociology*. Polity Press.

Brunner, R. (2006). A Paradigm for Practice. *Policy Sciences* 39(2), 135–167.

Clarke, J. L., Jones, M. E., & Jarman, P. J. (1995). Diurnal and Nocturnal Grouping and Foraging Behaviours of Free-ranging Eastern Grey Kangaroos. *Australian Journal of Zoology*, 43, 519–529.

Crotty, M. (2003). *The Foundations of Social Research: Meaning and Perspective in the Research Process*. Sage.

Geertz, C. (2008). Thick Description: Toward an Interpretive Theory of Culture. In T. S. Oakes & P. L. Price (Eds.), *The Cultural Geography Reader* (pp. 41–51). Routledge.

Gendlin, E. (1991). Thinking Beyond Patterns: Body, Language and Situations. In B. den Ouden and M. Moen (Eds.), *The Presence of Feeling in Thought* (pp. 25–151). Peter Lang.

Gendlin, E. T. (1997a). *Experiencing and the Creation of Meaning: A Philosophical and Psychological Approach to the Subjective*. Northwestern University Press.

Gendlin, E. T. (1997b). The Responsive Order: A New Empiricism. *Man and World*, 30(3), 383–411

Gendlin, E. T. (2003). *Focusing*. Random House.

Gendlin, E.T. (2013). Implicit Precision. In Z. Radman (Ed.), *Knowing Without Thinking* (pp. 141–166). Palgrave Macmillan.

Gendlin, E. T. (2018). *A Process Model*. Northwestern University Press.

Grandin, T., & Johnson, C. (2005). *Animals in Translation: Using the Mysteries of Autism to Decode Animal Behaviour*. Bloomsbury Publishing.

Hendricks, M. (2001). Focusing-Oriented/Experiential Psychotherapy. In D. Cain and J. Seeman (Eds.), *Humanistic Psychotherapy: Handbook of Research and Practice* (pp. 221–251). American Psychological Association.

Jablonka, E., & Lamb, M. J. (2014). *Evolution in Four Dimensions: Genetic, Epigenetic, Behavioral, and Symbolic Variation in the History of Life*. MIT Press.

James, W. (1991). *Pragmatism: A New Name for Some Old Ways of Thinking*. Prometheus Books.

Jarman, P. J., Johnson A, C. N., Southwell C. J., & R. Stuart-Dick, R. (1987). Macropod Studies at Wallaby Creek I: The Area and Animals. *Australian Wildlife Research*, 14, 1–14.

Jarman, P. J. & Wright, S. M. (1993). Macropod Studies at Wallaby Creek. IX. Exposure and Responses of Eastern Grey Kangaroos to Dingoes. *Wildlife Research*, 20, 833–843.

King, W. J., & Goldizen, A. W. (2016). Few Sex Effects in the Ontogeny of Mother-Offspring Relationships in Eastern Grey Kangaroos. *Animal Behaviour*, 113, 59–67.

Lunney, D. (2010). A History of the Debate (1948–2009) on the Commercial Harvesting of Kangaroos, with Particular Reference to New South Wales and the Role of Gordon Grigg. *Australian Zoologist*, 35(2), 383–430.

Payne, A. L., & Jarman, P. J. (1999). Macropod Studies at Wallaby Creek X: Responses of Eastern Grey Kangaroos to Cattle. *Wildlife Research*, 26, 215–225.

Plaisir, C-A, King, W. J., Forsyth, D. M., & Festa-Bianchet, M. (2022). Effects of Rainfall, Forage Biomass, and Population Density, on Survival and Growth of Juvenile Kangaroos. *Journal of Mammalogy*, 103(3), 491–502.

Polkinghorne, D. E. (2000). Psychological Inquiry and the Pragmatic and Hermeneutic Traditions. *Theory and Psychology*, 10(4), 453–479.

Rorty, R. (1980). *Philosophy and the Mirror of Nature*. Basil Blackwell.

Ryan, J. M. (2018). *Mammalogy Techniques Lab Manual*. Johns Hopkins University Press.

Schoeller, D. & Dunaetz, N. (2018). Thinking Emergence as Interaffecting: Approaching and Contextualizing Eugene Gendlin's Process Model. *Continental Philosophy Review*, 51, 123–140.

Stuart-Dick, R. I. (1987). *Parental Investment and Rearing Schedules in the Eastern Grey Kangaroo* [Doctoral dissertation, University of New England]. Research UNE. https://hdl.handle.net/1959.11/10809.

Thornton, A., & Raihani, N.J. (2008). The Evolution of Teaching. *Animal Behaviour*, 75, 1823–1836.

Unaipon, D. (2006). *Legendary Tales of the Australian Aborigines*. The Miegunyah Press.

Wacquant, L. J. D. (1992). Toward a Social Praxeology: The Structure and Logic of Bourdieu's Sociology. In P. Bourdieu & L. J. D. Wacquant (Eds.), *An Invitation to Reflexive Sociology* (pp. 1–60). Polity Press.

Walkerden, G. (2004). How I Read the Structure of the A Process Model Text. *The Folio*, 19(1), 124–130.

Walkerden, G. (2006). Adaptive Management Planning Projects as Conflict Resolution Processes. *Ecology and Society*, 11(1), 48.

Walkerden, G. (2009). Researching and Developing Practice Traditions Using Reflective Practice Experiments. *Quality and Quantity*, 43, 249–263.

Walkerden, G. (2010). Adaptiveness and Openness in Ecosystem Management. In V.A. Brown, J.A. Harris and J.E. Russell (Eds.), *Tackling Wicked Problems: Using the Transdisciplinary Imagination* (pp. 193–203). Earthscan.

Walkerden, G. (2019). Sustaining Places: Sensibility Models as Decision Support Tools for Messy Problems. *Sustainability*, 11(6), 1–37.

Walkerden, G. (2021). Focusing, Vastness and Union: Elaborating the Focusing Practice Tradition and the Philosophy of the Implicit to Describe an Additional Kind of Space. In N. Kypriotakis & J. Moore (Eds.), *Senses of Focusing Vol. 2* (pp. 127–147). Eurasia Publications.

Walters, C. J. (2001). *Adaptive Management of Renewable Resources*. Blackburn Press.

Chapter 10

Is an intricate institution a paradox or an oxymoron? Gendlin's political optimism, the formal limitations of politics, and the relevance of activity theory

Riley Paterson

Intricate experience, generic experience, and the role of institutions

Eugene Gendlin was not a political philosopher, but his philosophy is rife with political implications. Gendlin was aware of this. His major texts and many essays gesture at politics (Gendlin, 1991, 1997, 2007, 2018; Gendlin et al., 2018), and a number of his essays directly address political questions (Gendlin, 1984b, 1986, 1987, 2006). My concern here is with a consistent theme that can be found in Gendlin's work: his claim that, socially-politically, things are getting better, and, relatedly, his optimistic view that political and economic institutions will ultimately adopt experientially intricate practices. Correspondingly, Gendlin writes of a coming society of pattern-makers and points to something like intricate institutions that will support and be supported by these intricate, pattern-making individuals.

By intricate experience or pattern-making, Gendlin means the opposite of generic or role-bound experience. Most people, Gendlin claims, experience themselves generically: they mainly have the emotions and thoughts appropriate to their social roles. "Some people cannot easily feel more than the cultural situation," Gendlin (2009) writes. He continues:

> For example, a man's brother died. You ask him what he feels and he says 'sad'. You ask for more and he says, 'I am mourning him'. You ask him what his brother's death means to him, and he answers 'Well, what are you asking me? How would you feel if your brother died?'
>
> (p. 355)

Intricate experience, by contrast, is freshly arising, embodied experience that incorporates but ultimately exceeds or transcends the generic social roles. To be intricate is to experience and understand oneself as *more* than the social categories. I may work as a therapist, for example, but I am aware that my experience is not exhausted by that role identity. Thus, a society of pattern-makers would presumably involve the development of institutions

DOI: 10.4324/9781003296706-11

that would allow people to creatively reorganize their roles to further their experiencing, *rather than* limit their uniqueness for the sake of fitting rigid rules and roles. More precisely, intricate experiencing involves a zigzag or dialectic between generic form (role, category) and concrete individual experiencing: our activity generates responses to the generic forms we encounter and in turn affects those generic forms. Institutions, by contrast, more often impose generic shapes on people rather than allowing them to reorganize the role or institution for the sake of fuller experiencing (Paterson, in press; Gendlin et al., 2018, pp. 267–271).

This paper develops political implications of Gendlin's work on the relationship between experience, roles, and institutions. I will offer two steps to help explicate these implications, the first critical and the second constructive. First, Gendlin's work could benefit from being placed in deeper dialogue with Aristotle's understanding of the limitations of law and politics. In particular, I will use Aristotle's *Nicomachean Ethics* (Aristotle et al., 2012) to demonstrate the *formal* limitations of law and politics: law, being formally generic, tends to obscure or suppress intricate experience in favor of generic roles. This aspect of politics problematizes the notion of intricate institutions, as institutions are deeply bound up with generic laws, rules, and roles. Second, Gendlin's work needs a deeper understanding of institutions, especially concerning the relationship between social structure and intricate experience. This deeper understanding can be fruitfully pursued, I claim, by comparing Gendlin's work with a form of psychology known as activity theory (AT). AT originated in the Soviet Union (Chaiklin, 2019; Leontyev & Cole, 2009) and has been notably developed by Danish psychologists (Engelsted et al., 2017; Mammen & Gozli, 2018; Mammen & Mironenko, 2015). Gendlin's work needs, in short, a richer understanding of law, and a deeper analysis of institutions and their relation to intricate individual experience. A deeper understanding of law and institutions would ultimately temper Gendlin's potentially unwarranted political optimism.

The essential issue is the complex relationship between fresh, intricate experience and established social form. This question is of great importance and concerns the fundamental relationship between law and justice, and politics and psychotherapy. This question is especially significant in that a variety of authors claim that psychology and psychotherapy often support and collaborate with the political domination endemic to corporate American capitalism (Fisher, 2010; Cushman, 1995, 2012; Sugarman, 2015; Cabanas, 2018; Cabanas & Illouz, 2021). With this in mind, my aim is to highlight the difference between individual-intricate process and political-institutional process, showing the limits of the analogy between the development of persons and political-institutional progress. The central question is thus: Is an intricate institution a paradox or an oxymoron? In *A Process Model,*

Gendlin (2018) claims that "a paradox is a new concept not yet formed" (p. 217). I am asking whether or not an intricate institution or a society of pattern-makers is a paradox, awaiting formulation, or oxymoronic, simply being incoherent or contradictory. The cautious but assertive claim of the paper is the latter.[1]

The paper concludes arguing that the limitations of this analogy and the oxymoronic character of an intricate institution mean that we must think more seriously about the *forms* of government available to us and how they enable or hinder individual-intricate experience. I will therefore take issue with Gendlin's hope that politics itself will become intricate and claim instead that we must think through something like *politics in service of intricate persons*. For if law or government in many ways resists intricacy—if an intricate institution is an oxymoron rather than a paradox—we must ask what forms of government enable intricate experience, even if the institutions themselves cannot be intricate.

The political tone of Gendlin's work: progress, optimism, and experiential intricacy

Gendlin's work shows a consistent tone of political optimism and often contains analyses of social problems and narratives of impending progress. In modern society, Gendlin regularly claims, existing social forms (roles, routines) often no longer fit or carry forward contemporary experience. In *Focusing*, for example, Gendlin (2007) points to the role of medicine in modern society, claiming "the authority aspect of the medical doctor never has really fitted the human process of personal change..." (p. 7). In the final chapter of *Focusing-Oriented Psychotherapy*, Gendlin (1996) similarly claims that the formal role of "therapist" often gets in the way of actual healing, and that often "many of our colleagues practice a kind of formal dance: They say only certain kinds of things and keep themselves competently hidden, not behind a couch but still behind a well-working routine" (pp. 301–302). In these examples, Gendlin is pointing to a gap between the rigid requirements of roles and the need for fresh and intimate contact between persons.

On the whole, Gendlin views modern social forms as rigid, reinforcing inequality and subtle medical coercion. Focusing[2] is therefore a crucial tool in such times. The opposite of being stuck in a restricted and unequal role-relation would be living freshly and directly in a way that could reorganize the roles. Thus, Focusing can help us attend to the intricacy of the lived body and its ability to generate fresh forms more appropriate to our new situations, rather than relying on preexisting social forms. The political implications of Gendlin's work hinge on this claim about Focusing and social change. I thus begin with Gendlin's optimistic narratives about the role of Focusing in social-political progress.

Gendlin's (2007) generally optimistic tone is evident in the final section of *Focusing* (published 1978), "Focusing and Society." In the chapter "New Relationships," for example, Gendlin writes about Changes groups, Focusing organizations that existed in Chicago in the 1970s and 80s. Gendlin describes, for example, the informal and egalitarian structure of Changes groups: people are free to ask anyone to listen to them, and anyone can attend meetings where formal and administrative decisions are made. Changes groups offered an alternative to the common way of relating through rote and predictable social roles. These rote ways of relating are especially prominent in professional and formal environments: "Our structured institutions," Gendlin thus writes, "today offer little opportunity for personal living and speaking. The real living of people is mostly dulled and silent, inside them, alone" (p. 174). Gendlin hopes that Focusing will be taught and learned broadly and that it will contribute to the slow change of schools, workplaces, and other institutions: "even when focusing and listening are learned by everyone (probably in schools), our workplaces and institutions will still change slowly" (p. 174). The more people are capable of pausing, sensing, and Focusing, the more people will make sensitive, politically sound decisions. He argues that Changes groups offer a model of an institution where people speak and listen carefully, and in which decisions are made in open, flexible, and intricate ways (pp. 175–179).

In the final chapter of *Focusing*, "Experience Beyond Roles," Gendlin (2007) repeats more forcefully his claim that Focusing can help people develop more intricate ways of living and relating. "In our time," Gendlin boldly begins the chapter, "an advance in the nature of the human individual is occurring" (p. 180). "Throughout history," he continues, "people expressed themselves in routine patterns of language, and understood themselves that way, too" (p. 180). The social forms, the recognizable patterns of acting and experiencing, are no longer functioning, Gendlin claims. People need new forms for living in fresh, intricate ways. He goes on, "The old patterns that are supposed to make life work—and once did—no longer serve[...].We have to make it up as we go along[...]" (pp. 183–184). Focusing is a tool for meeting this challenge, which Gendlin describes as "a new step in human development" (p. 183).

The ultimate result of this, Gendlin (2007) predicts, will be a society of pattern-makers, or a world in which people no longer simply "fit themselves into the roles and routines they [are] assigned and which [give] them an inner life of emotions" (p. 184). Thus, Gendlin optimistically, almost prophetically, writes in the final paragraph of *Focusing*: "A society of pattern-makers is coming. It cannot help but be a society in which people are also more sensitive to, and intolerant of, social brutalities and oppressions and more able to act to change them" (p. 187). Indeed, Gendlin indicates much earlier in *Focusing* that his ambitions, or at least hopes, are social-political: "The happiest change of all is that we can build the change process into society generally and not only in the doctor-patient therapy that costs so much and sometimes gives so little" (p. 10). *Focusing* thus shows that relatively early in his writing Gendlin regards Focusing as a practice that is aligned with a new development of human individuals, and that this development will ultimately become reflected in social-political structures, culminating in what he calls a society of pattern-makers.

This narrative of individual and political progress is repeated in many texts, spanning Gendlin's productive career. In *Thinking Beyond Patterns*, for example, Gendlin (1991) claims that "A great individual and social change is occurring. Today millions of people have found experiential intricacy. Business, medicine, and *society as a whole* are adopting experiential process" (p. 35, my emphasis). The preface to the paperback edition of *Experiencing and the Creation of Meaning* contains a similar narrative:

> there has been a great development in human experiencing, with therapeutic and interpersonal processes. Where people used to be silent, now they have a developed vocabulary with which to explore and express their experiential and relational intricacies. The old community in which people related mostly in roles has broken down, and new kinds of community in which we can relate from our intricacy are only just beginning to develop[...] (for example, 'focusing partnerships', 'changes groups', and many kinds of support groups).
>
> (Gendlin, 1997, p. xiv)

Similarly, in his 2006 talk "The Town and Human Attention," Gendlin (2006) claims "that we are in the middle of the beginning stages of a really gigantic development of human beings" (para. 1). Gendlin then repeats similar claims: social forms have broken down but Focusing and other practices offer an alternative whereby people can create fresh forms, express and relate more intricately. "So you can look forward to a time when things are going to get a lot better than they are right now," he thus claims. "Because if you watch management, both politically and in the business world, they want to learn this [experiential intricacy, Focusing] now" (para. 24). Even *A Process Model*, Gendlin's (2018) most rigorous and developed philosophical work contains an endnote with a nearly identical narrative:

> We are in the midst of a whole new stage of the development of the individual. Some huge proportion of people in the world are developing an inwardly sensed self that transcends cultural role-identity. The rest will soon find it too, since it is a cultural development.
>
> (p.272, n. 20)

Thus, from his early writing in *Focusing* to late in his productive career, Gendlin consistently offers narratives of both individual and political progress. Individually, people are developing psychologically and experientially. And politically, we are moving toward a time in which institutions and roles will be less constricting and more flexible, leaving room for or encouraging experiential intricacy. As he flatly says in "The Client's Client" (Gendlin, 1984a): "The listening and focusing process is of crucial *political* significance[...] A kind of human organization is coming, which would not again be the imposition of power by some over others," (p. 23). Or, as he asks in the final chapter of *Focusing*:

> How can more developed individuals make a better social structure? It is a large, unsolved problem. We know a lot about how social patterns form individuals, but if one begins with individuals... there is a gap. We don't know how individual development can ever reach the level of social structure. That is why there has been so little progress in the character of social and political units. Focusing is only a piece of the answer. It lets people find their own inner source of direction. It can be a source of new patterns, devised freshly by each individual.
>
> (Gendlin, 2007, pp. 184–185)

Gendlin therefore understood Focusing, among other developments, to ultimately imply a reorganization of fundamental governmental structures.

Gendlin's work offers tremendous resources for understanding how Focusing and psychotherapy support the emergence of intricate experience in spite of oppressive political conditions. There is much work to be done, however, on the "great and unsolved problem" that Gendlin names: How does intricate individual experiencing contribute to the development of better social structures? Why is there a gap between the development of persons and overarching social-political change? Or, asked differently, how much does the model of Focusing apply to our relationship with political-institutional process? The remainder of this paper is concerned with this issue.

An intricate institution is an oxymoron: Cultural Capture and Aristotle on the formal limitations of law and politics

In this section, I claim that the concept of an intricate institution is oxymoronic and not simply paradoxical. A society of pattern-makers is perhaps a less problematic concept, but it is precisely its institutional aspects that must be thought through. So far, we have seen that Gendlin holds two interrelated views: (1) The current state of political-institutional life leaves many feeling trapped and stifled within themselves; and (2) Focusing will be an important part of a larger process whereby society makes more room for intricate experience, culminating in a society of pattern-makers. Thus, I now wish to ask, Why are people so often captured by political-cultural life? And is this an incidental feature of our period, or a stable feature of political experience?

Drawing on Aristotle's understanding of the formal limitations of law and politics, found in Book 5 of his *Nicomachean Ethics* (Aristotle et al., 2012), I will argue that people are so often captured by social categories because there is something inherent in the nature of political life that renders people as separable units, generic forms, or machines. The crucial point is that legal-political logic, which deals with the division of labor and distribution of resources, requires that individuals be treated in generic ways, as separable patterns that can be rearranged in empty space. Politics treats people, in a word, *as machines*. It is both possible and important to teach people to Focus in these contexts, just as it is important for judges to preside over the particularities of actual situations. But I claim that *institutions themselves* will always have to engage in some form of generic or machine thinking. This fact thus justifies the pursuit of *politics in service of intricacy* rather than *institutions themselves becoming intricate*.

The question of an intricate institution is intimately related to the problem of cultural capture, or the tendency to get experientially stuck within generic social roles and categories. An intricate institution, or an institution serving intricacy, would be one that somehow mitigates or prevents the possibility of cultural capture. Gendlin (2009) offers a more detailed account of cultural capture in "What First & Third Person Processes Really Are." The central issue is our unavoidable relationship with speech and language. Human situations are moved primarily by speech: our bodies are carried forward by the use of generic symbols expressed in gesture and voice. In the section "Two Kinds of Speech," Gendlin claims that language can *both* capture and enable intricate experience. Unfortunately, however, capture is the more likely alternative "because speech *first* forms as a cultural system of sayings and doings which can capture us" (p. 354–55, my emphasis). The cultural system so often captures, Gendlin continues, because it necessarily consists of generic units: it designates generic *kinds* of situations, *kinds* of responses, and *kinds* of experiences. "Each culture consists of its *typical kinds of situations* and word-uses in them. Each *kind of situation* is a bundle of stories, scenarios, *ready* alternative actions and sayings" (p. 356, my emphasis). This does not mean we can *only* speak in generalities. Indeed, Gendlin shows how *new phrases* are particularly powerful at moving beyond generic sayings and doings, as we can "notice what the old ones *do not say*" (p.357) and thereby say more deeply what *we want to say*.

Thus, Gendlin (2009) offers a fairly straightforward explanation for the prevalence of cultural capture: "We rarely speak directly from our own whole [intricate understanding or felt sense] because our behavior context implies this elaborate system of *already-defined situations* with *already-formed sayings*" (p. 356, my emphasis). Being human means living in a situation that is at least partly generic, and cultural capture is the experience of being dominated by these generic, ready-made aspects (Paterson, in press). But why is human experience so intertwined with generic symbols and actions, sayings and doings? I turn to Aristotle's analysis of law and politics to further these questions.

In Book 5 of his *Nicomachean Ethics,* Aristotle articulates the necessarily general character of law and claims that we must take steps to correct the injustices that arise from this feature of law (Aristotle et al., 2012). It is important to note that the Greek word for law, *nomos,* is ambiguous in that it means *both* written law and unwritten law or custom. Thus, when I write "law," I ask a reader to read something like law-custom-culture: the generic categories, attitudes, and practices that make any society possible.[3] Aristotle notes that there are multiple ways of talking about justice. It is common to speak of justice as if it were exhausted by the concept of legality, i.e., that to be just is to be in accordance with law. The just, however, is a more comprehensive concept than the legal: "all law is general, but concerning some matters it is not possible to speak correctly in a general way" (Aristotle et al., 2012, p. 112). Something is therefore needed to correct this misleadingly general character of law.

Aristotle argues that *epieikeia*, translatable as equity or decency, is necessary if we are to achieve justice in spite of the generality of law:

> Hence equity is just and better than what is just in a certain sense [i.e. legally just]—not what is just unqualifiedly but the error that arises through its being stated unqualifiedly [i.e. generally]. This is in fact the nature of the equitable: a correction of law in the respect in which it is deficient because of its being general.
>
> (Aristotle et al., 2012, p. 112)

The legally just is thus a highly restricted sense of justice. Justice, in a fuller sense, requires a person who can think beyond the generic categories of law. One must be able to reckon with the *particular situation* rather than merely the generic categories that structure political-institutional life. Thus, Aristotle is frank that "all things are not in accord with law: it is impossible to set down a law in some matters, so that one must have recourse to a specific decree instead [i.e. an individualized judgment]" (p.112).

For Aristotle, this is not an incidental feature of law, but a necessary part of how political communities are organized. Earlier in Book 5, Aristotle discusses the necessity of establishing equity among society's disparate roles. How, for example, can we evaluate the relative contributions of a shoemaker and a housebuilder? We must find ways, in other words, to *equate* differing practices and roles that are all socially necessary. The dilemma can be rendered simply: the complex division of labor requires people to perform different tasks or roles. Some roles will be more enjoyable or valuable than others: it is in some ways more enjoyable to be a lifeguard than a ditchdigger, or it is potentially more valuable to be a doctor rather than a sculptor. Every society has to make decisions about what roles are valued and how members are compensated. But how can we know that the disparate roles are being compensated equitably? What is the common factor by which these different roles could be equated? As Aristotle says, "No community comes into existence out of two doctors but rather out of a doctor and a farmer and, in general, out of those who are different and not equal. But these [differing types] must be equalized" (Aristotle et al., 2012, p. 100). Aristotle points to need as the most fundamental thing uniting these various contributions. Need, however, is difficult or perhaps impossible to quantify precisely, so "money has become, by agreement, a kind of exchangeable representative of need" (p. 101). Aristotle then notes that the word for money, *nomisma*, shares a root with *nomos* or law, saying that "it exists not by nature but by law" (p. 101). Money, being derivative of law, similarly fails to establish perfect equality. The diversity of roles within political communities means that equality, strictly speaking, is impossible. It is not possible to settle in a final way the contribution of a cobbler versus an architect. Thus, something like equity is necessary. If this becomes the attitude of an individual person we could say that they are *decent*: they want to do what is just and equitable in a deeper sense, and not in the merely legal sense.[4]

Aristotle's analysis of law and justice can help us further understand Gendlin's claim that people often feel stuck inside themselves, trapped in their roles, and unable to live beyond the generic categories, culturally captured. The generic social categories, in Aristotle's analysis, are a stable feature of political life: all communities will have to confront this problem of striving for equity in spite of differing and unequal roles. It is this necessarily generic feature of social organization that leads individuals to be captured by the culture of their time and place. It is also this feature of political life that makes the idea of an intricate institution oxymoronic rather than paradoxical. If we accept that human situations are *first* systems of generic sayings and doings, then what would it mean for *the system itself* to become intricate?

Gendlin, moreover, often makes claims that resonate with Aristotle's analysis, arguing that government seems to rely heavily on generic and machine thinking.[5] In "The Responsive Order," for example, he acknowledges that governmental logic generally treats people as machines: "It can be important to know that the actual policies of one's society assume that one is a machine" (Gendlin et al., 2018, p. 274). Similarly, in "The Town and Human Attention," Gendlin (2006) claims that the American government thinks primarily in fixed concepts or units: "But in the U.S. policy-making procedure the people who think are at the bottom. By the time it gets to the top just the cut-up options remain" (para. 35).

In working with cut-up options, political life is particularly akin to *machine* or *unit model* thinking. A machine, Gendlin claims, can be defined as "a set of known patterns separated from the thing in which other factors could cross [i.e. intricately interact] with them" (Gendlin et al., 2018, p. 272). Gendlin readily admits that "science renders everything a machine," meaning that it treats everything as a separable pattern or unit that can be rearranged in empty space (p. 272). Gendlin also refers to machine thinking as the "unit model," meaning that it proceeds by dividing things "into stable units, parts, atoms, particles which are understood separately" (Gendlin & Johnson, 2004, para. 3).[6] Politics is highly intertwined with unit model thinking and generally renders everything as machines. Gendlin (2012b) confirms this point in more abstract terms in "Process Generates Structures" where he links unit model logic with generic social forms:

> The organismic [i.e. more intricate] process in us continues even though it is hidden by the empty system of location 'points' [i.e. the cultural system of roles]. The cluster of action possibilities is not really reduced, only covered over. We seem unable to think from the implicit [i.e. our intricacy] because we try to make it fit the [generic cultural] terms we have. We try to think of it as structured objects in the space of 'there-from-there' [i.e. separable units].
>
> (p. 8)

Generic social forms (roles) and machines are thus highly related concepts that both assume that people and things can be adequately rendered or captured as separable patterns in empty space.[7]

Gendlin therefore acknowledges that political life seems to be highly intertwined with unit model or machine thinking. To be locked into unit model thinking is to tacitly deny the existence of more intricate processes, to "cover over" our more complex lived experience with generic social forms. Gendlin's understanding thus aligns with my analysis of Aristotle: there is something peculiar in law, politics, and institutions, whereby general categories are both necessary and obfuscating. The generic social forms both make our communal lives possible and hinder certain kinds of individual growth. The crucial question is *can* politicians learn to think in intricate terms? And even if they did, would the *forms of political organization* ever become intricate in themselves? Or, is there something inherent in the *form* of political things that resists intricacy and collapses reality into units? Would not lawmakers still have to deal chiefly with legislation that organizes according to generic categories? I claim that institutions, like cultural systems, will always be generic in nature and that Focusing will always be something that emerges as a correction and further development within this context.

It is crucial to note that Gendlin (2009) explicitly says that cultural systems are *first* systems of sayings and doings, and only *second* does language become available for use in Focusing or more intricate processes. The structure of *A Process Model*, Gendlin's mature theory, confirms that Focusing is a *further development* of generic cultural systems, *not a replacement of. A correction* and not a substitute. *A Process Model* is developmentally or hierarchically organized, meaning that each chapter presupposes and builds on the last. The book moves from the most basic living body processes to the most complex human situations and practices. As Walkerden (2004) claims in his summary of the book, "*A Process Model* offers an explication of major stages of development as the emergence of new basic *kinds* of process (tissue process / behaviour / language / culture / ... [Focusing])" (p. 327). Thus, in the final three chapters, Gendlin tries to show how animal behavior (Chapter VI) could become human symbolic-cultural processes (Chapter VII), and how Focusing could emerge from those symbolic-cultural processes (Chapter VIII). In each case, these body processes build on what came before: we do not begin to use symbols until the animal body has developed complex and meaningful gesturing, and we do not begin Focusing until we have an existing stock of symbols that can be creatively redeployed.

Focusing, in other words, experientially and logically presupposes our existence within a stable, perhaps rigid, cultural system. Indeed, Gendlin (2018) claims that a crucial step in the development of language and culture is the formation of short *syllabic units*: "Original word-formation appears to have broken sound sequences down to syllabic units" (p. 171). The formation of these units, moreover, seems to come along with a rigidity or conservatism: "*When and exactly why did new sound-formation cease?*" Gendlin thus asks later in Chapter VII. "Language continues to change, of course, but not by taking in new sounds... Sound-formation ceased very early. Once language has formed it is amazingly conservative" (p. 185). This conservative character of language contributes to the prevalence of cultural capture.

Gendlin (2018) says, moreover, that Chapter VII of *A Process Model* is "devoted to traditional culture," which precedes the "whole new stage of the development of the individual" named in the same endnote and elaborated above (pp. 272–273, n. 20). Language thus begins as gesture and dance in the animal body, becomes unitized symbols in traditional human communities, and *only then* do symbols become available for something like Focusing. It is therefore impossible to conceptualize Focusing as anything *other than* an alternative to cultural capture. The capacity for symboling does not free us of our behavioral body, and the capacity for Focusing does not rid us of our need to engage in traditional symbolic situations in which language is primarily functional and conservative, "a cultural system of sayings and doings which can capture us" (Gendlin, 2009, p. 354–355). I will return to the relationship between Chapters VII and VIII of *A Process Model* in the next section.

Focusing therefore stands in analogous relation to cultural systems as decency/equity does to legality. In both cases, we are observing a necessarily generic system of organizing human communities (culture/law), and a practice that is able to observe and move beyond these generic categories (Focusing/decency). Indeed, Gendlin defines authenticity in part as the ability to move beyond formal rules into a more intricate space and even ties this conception to ancient views on justice. In authentic living and speaking, Gendlin (1999) writes, "Every code will be eschewed, but these characteristics are not so far from the ancient virtues of sincerity and justice" (p. 211). Despite this similarity between decency and Focusing, however, Gendlin and Aristotle seem to differ on the ultimate political meaning of these practices. As far as I know, Aristotle did not claim that political-institutional life itself would become capable of decency or perfect equity. Aristotle did not anticipate or predict anything like the coming of intricate institutions or a society of pattern-makers.

Political life will always be to some extent about the generic rules and roles that organize the division of labor and the distribution of resources. We need as many intricate persons as possible inside of our unwieldy institutions, learning to Focus, learning to be decent, learning to correct the violence done by generic categories. But an intricate institution is essentially an oxymoronic idea. Intricate experience depends on an individual person-body that can relate in new ways to the generic cultural symbols: only *persons* can Focus or be decent. Institutions are necessarily bound up with laws, rules, roles, and units; they require generic roles to be named and filled. This feels especially true of modern institutions which are deeply entrenched through physical and architectural structure. It is therefore hard to imagine institutions themselves becoming intricate. *An intricate institution would be one in which the laws (rules, roles, cultural systems) themselves could have the same responsiveness as the living body. But laws and institutions are not living bodies. Laws are symbols separated from living processes, they are separable patterns, they render us as machines.*

The rest of this paper is concerned with what to do about this predicament. If institutions themselves cannot become intricate, if an intricate institution is truly an oxymoron, then how can we relate to Gendlin's political hopes? I believe that Gendlin's work has enormous potential for continuing to think through these political questions. In the next section, I will further develop the political implications of Gendlin's thought by putting him into dialogue with the Soviet psychologist Alexei Leontyev.

A deeper analysis of institutional process: Activity theory, the double life of symbols, and the meaning of appropriation

Having demonstrated Gendlin's political optimism and having argued for the oxymoronic character of an intricate institution, I now offer positive conceptual steps. I am, on the whole, sympathetic to Gendlin's project and also hope for our societies to cultivate intricate persons. It is obvious to me that something like a society of pattern-makers should be the goal of politics. But as my analysis of Aristotle shows, something in the *generic form* of law and political life resists open, dialectical relationship with intricate processes. Focusing and politics are, in short, *formally divergent*, having fundamentally different relations to explicit formulation. We must be careful, therefore, to not assume too hastily that Focusing and psychotherapy somehow contribute to social-political progress, which is so bound up with law and formal policy change. If we wish to understand the relationship between Focusing and society, then, we must think carefully not just about personal-therapeutic process, but *political-institutional process*. I now turn to a form of psychology known as AT to more fully understand political-institutional process.

AT is a form of psychology initially developed in the Soviet Union (Luria, 1994; Leontyev & Cole, 2009; Engelsted et al., 2017), and more recently elaborated by European psychologists, most notably in Denmark (Engelsted et al., 2017; Mammen & Gozli, 2018; Mammen & Mironenko, 2015).[8] AT's origins in the Soviet Union mean that, from the outset, it was concerned with Marxist themes of the relation between individual experience and social-political structure (Luria, 1994; Leontyev & Cole, 2009).

I believe that there is significant compatibility between Gendlin's work and AT. Thinking these two projects together would almost certainly generate significant developments in both. Here I will highlight two aspects of Soviet AT: Leontyev's concept of *the double life of symbols* and his related claim that both individual and social-political progress require the *appropriation* of existing structures (Leontyev & Cole, 2009).[9] I have already pointed to something like the double life of symbols in discussing Chapters VII and VIII of *A Process Model*. Put briefly, symbols function *both* as a generic system of sayings and doings that organize communities *and* the starting point for unique personal developments. Leontyev's concept of appropriation will add further depth to this problem of how intricate experience or Focusing proceeds by repositioning or appropriating terms initially formed in a system of sayings and doings.

Activity theory and a fuller understanding of intricacy and institutions: The double life of symbols and appropriation

Leontyev's concept of the double life of symbols is most easily approached by understanding his distinction between natural and social-cultural environments. According to Leontyev, human activity is unique in that it takes place not simply in a *natural* environment, but in a *social-cultural* environment.[10] As social-cultural life becomes more complex, each generation is born and initiated into a constructed environment in which the activity of previous generations has left objective structures. Objective structures are often physical objects like buildings, roads, or tools, but Leontyev also includes meanings, symbols, and linguistic patterns. These objective structures then condition the activity of future generations, as the motives that produced them remain implicit in them. Thus, Leontyev writes in "Activity and Consciousness" that

> "in society man finds not only his external conditions to which he must adapt his activity, but also that these very social conditions carry in themselves the motives and aims of his activity, the ways and means of its realisation..."
>
> (Leontyev & Cole, 2009, p. 401)

To be human, in other words, is to *enter into* a world of already existing forms, to have our activity already shaped and influenced by tools, traditions, and institutions. This is especially true of our language, which implicitly carries previous persons and situations.

This feature of human life and language, Leontyev claims, gives meanings or symbols a double life:

> "The major difficulty here is that meanings lead a double life. They are produced by society and have their history in the development of language, in the history of the development of forms of social consciousness; they express the movement of science and its means of cognition, and also the ideological notions of society—religious, philosophical, and political."
>
> (Leontyev & Cole, 2009, p. 415)

In addition to their objective, historical existence, meanings, and symbols also have a second life, a private life in which they enter into more intimate contact with individual experience:

> "In this second life of theirs meanings are individualized and subjectivized only in the sense that their movement in the system of social

relations is not *directly contained* in them; they enter into another system
of relationships, another movement."

(Leontyev & Cole, 2009, p. 416)

Something like the double life of meanings or symbols is a consistent feature
of Gendlin's writings. Gendlin regularly points to the way that social forms
do not *merely* impose themselves on us; we are free to relate to them in new
ways and to use old words to convey fresh meanings. Indeed, Gendlin (1986)
makes precisely this point in the final sentence of "Process Ethics and the
Political Question":

> "all we can say—but it is a lot—is that this kind of process [i.e. Focus-
> ing] reveals a more intricate order which can *exceed and reorder existing
> forms*. Imposed form [i.e. objective social structure] is not the only kind
> of order."
>
> (p. 275, my emphasis)

As noted, this same point is made with greater force in "What First &
Third Person Processes Really Are" where Gendlin (2009) claims that cultural patterns can (and often do) capture individuals. At the same time,
Gendlin acknowledges that these same cultural patterns are an essential precondition for generating fresh experience. The old forms must be
engaged in particular ways. Gendlin (2009) points especially to the power
of odd phrasings to explicate and convey fresh meanings (p. 357–358).
Something like Leontyev's notion of the double life of symbols is thus present in Gendlin.

Leontyev, however, takes a crucial step that I have not seen Gendlin
explicitly take, and this is my second point: because we enter into an already
existing formal social-cultural landscape, any further development must be
an *appropriation* of an already existing structure. As Gendlin knows, there
is no stepping outside of society, no saying or doing that gets outside the
ongoing interaction with our cultural environment. We must, instead, find
a way to modify, reshape, or appropriate existing forms for fresh purposes.
Appropriation, for Leontyev, is uniquely human; animals merely *adapt*,
whereas we must *appropriate*:

> The activity of animals realises acts of adaptation to the environment,
> but never acts of mastering the advances of phylogenetic evolution.
> These advances *are given* to the animal in its natural inherited traits,
> whereas they are *posed* to man in the objective phenomena of the world
> about him [i.e. in the objective, social-cultural life of symbols].
>
> (Leontyev & Cole, 2009, p. 269)

There is thus a peculiar relation between phylogenetic and ontogenetic development for human beings. The development of the species as a whole is bound up with objective structures in our languages, tools, and institutions. We are never able to simply pick up the previous generations' traditions wholesale. We must find a way to make these structures work for our new situations, appropriate them:

> The spiritual, mental development of individual men is thus the product of a quite special process, that of appropriation, which does not exist at all in animals, just as the opposite process does not exist in them either, viz., that of objectifying their faculties as objective products of their activity.
>
> (Leontyev & Cole, 2009, p. 269)

To be a pattern-maker, to create something freshly suited to our unique situation, means to appropriate some existing structure, to bring an objectively existing symbol or meaning into ourselves, and make something new of it.

Amendments to Gendlin's political thought culled from activity theory: Two senses of development

The double life of symbols and the related problem of appropriation further problematizes the idea of an intricate institution. More specifically, Gendlin's work needs a sustained analysis of the oppressive quality of institutions and needs to more directly build concepts about the forms of government. The ultimate upshot of this section, and the whole paper, is that the analogy between intricate experience and political process breaks down when we grasp that social-political forms cannot be deployed as flexibly as they are in Focusing, psychotherapy, or philosophy. Social-political forms are not merely symbolic and linguistic formulations but are a system of sayings and doings entrenched in tools, buildings, and artifacts of many kinds (Gendlin, 2009). To see this we must further appreciate the double life of symbols and appropriation in Gendlin's work.

Many of Gendlin's writings point to the double life of symbols: he often distinguishes between the public use of words in which they function in conventional situations, and a more private, intricate use of those same words (Gendlin, 1986; Gendlin et al., 2018). The structure of *A Process Model*, moreover, demonstrates something like the double life of symbols. As noted above, *A Process Model* is a developmental text, moving from the most basic life processes to animal behavior, human symboling, and culminating in an account of Focusing (or direct reference). As Walkerden (2004) claims in his analysis of the structure of *A Process Model* (commented on by Gendlin), the book describes the emergence of various *kinds* of processes.[11] Chapters I–V describe basic life processes, comparable to the lives of plants or simple animals: "body tissue processes, e.g. drawing in oxygen and passing out carbon dioxide" (p. 322). From there, Chapters VI–VIII each elaborate a new *kind* of life process that develop out of these basic ones: "behaviour, e.g., walking and running (chapter VI), culture and symbol, e.g. speech (chapter VII), heeding 'Direct Referents' (felt senses), e.g. Focusing as we know it, (chapter VIII)" (p. 322). Walkerden explains that these life processes are layered on top of one another, each implying and incorporating prior developments: "These *kinds* of process," Walkerden thus writes, "are layered: Focusing is a form of listening-speaking, speaking is a form of behaviour, and behaviour is a form of body tissue process. Each 'higher' layer consists also of the 'more primitive' layers of organism processes" (p. 322).

A Process Model thus culminates with two chapters that demonstrate the double life of symbols, or the "two kinds of speech" discussed elsewhere by Gendlin (2009). Chapter VII, "Culture, Symbol, and Language," is primarily concerned with traditional culture (Gendlin, 2018, pp. 272–273, n. 20), or the objective life of symbols in which language mainly designates conventional roles and procedures. Chapter VIII "Thinking With the Implicit," by contrast, emphasizes how individuals are able to find a "direct referent" or felt sense of a traditional situation and to thereby develop more holistic and personally intricate concepts that (hopefully) still function in traditional situations. Thus, the final two chapters of *A Process Model* instance something like the double life of symbols. Gendlin (2018) puts this concisely in the final pages of Chapter VIII:

> "from any point in a VII [i.e. traditionally symbolic] discussion or line of thought one can move in two different ways: first, along the implications of the symbols; secondly, to direct referent formation [i.e. an intricate felt sense] (and from it to new symbolic sequences again)."
>
> (p. 240)

Our symbols split along these two possibilities: the objective implications proper to the cultural system or the more intimate life of direct reference and private meaning.

Thus, Gendlin's philosophy, and especially Focusing, instances something like the double life of symbols whereby language is both public (designating more rigid roles and procedures) and private (in which experiential intricacy can be expressed and cultural life can be remade freshly). Or, as Gendlin (1972, 2012a) says in multiple places, philosophy works by *repositioning* (i.e. appropriating) major extant terms. Indeed, allowing words this double life is an essential prerequisite to understanding *any* philosophy: "A different philosophy cannot be understood right off. A philosophy changes the meanings of its major terms" (Gendlin, 2012a, p. 4).

The relationship between Chapters VII and VIII of *A Process Model*, or the dependence of Focusing on existing social-cultural patterns, is also evident from Gendlin's (1999) essay "Authenticity After Postmodernism." There Gendlin reaffirms the claim that Focusing is a trans-cultural practice (see Gendlin, 2009, p. 358). Gendlin (1999) explains that while working in Japan he was able to engage in direct and intricate relations with others despite cultural differences: "Indeed, when I have worked there with individuals, the process is so familiar, I have forgotten that I am in Japan" (p. 211). Gendlin acknowledges that sometimes cultural detail is required

> to lead me across something I would otherwise not understand, but this is easily done. I needn't understand the whole thing, only what it means just now to this person, which is characteristically unique and more intricate than the public meanings.
>
> (p. 211)

When the intimate process of Focusing or dialogue ceases, however, a cultural opacity returns:

> "But, when my part is over and people act in groups again, then the culture becomes impenetrable to me. It is as groups that cultures are impenetrable to each other. It is the public meanings and common phrases that we cannot grasp."
>
> (p. 211)

This is a perfect demonstration of the design of *A Process Model* and the difficult relationship between public and private meanings. Direct contact with an intricate person is of course trans-cultural. But the possibility of that contact is always embedded within a set of cultural practices, a system of generic sayings and doings *that retains its basic opacity to those on the outside*. Focusing or intricate dialogue does not replace our life within the generic cultural systems, it is a *temporary emergence out of those more basic processes*. Thus, Gendlin clearly understands something like the double life of symbols and appropriation.

What Gendlin lacks, and Leontyev offers, however, is a sustained account of how collective symbols are often the basis for social-political oppression. Gendlin's tone implies that existing roles or forms are more or less available for appropriation; all that is needed is the skills and practices for developing the deeper life of these symbols (i.e. Focusing).[12] Leontyev, by contrast, follows Marx by arguing that the modern division of labor (i.e. social forms) has generated a situation whereby individuals are generally alienated from what they do, bringing a fractured and disordered quality to modern activity. "Under certain conditions," Leontyev thus writes, "the discrepancy between personal meanings and objective meanings in individual consciousness may amount to alienation or diametrical opposition" (Leontyev & Cole, 2009, p. 419). The complex division of labor, or a society based on commodity production, is especially primed to create this opposition between objective structure and individual meanings. Leontyev, further, argues that in these situations "personal meanings reflecting the motives engendered by a person's actual living relationships may fail to find objective meanings which fully express them, and they then begin to live in borrowed clothes, as it were" (Leontyev & Cole, 2009, p. 422).

This same dilemma, of a misfit between public and private meanings, is expressed in the final chapter of *A Process Model* when Gendlin (2018) asks: "Can we think clearly why direct referent formation does not *necessarily* enable livable VII-sequences in just one step?" (p. 248). A "livable VII-sequence" would be an objectively existing, structured social situation that would allow a more intimate, personal process ("direct referent formation") to carry forward in a publicly recognizable form. Why, in other words, may Focusing fail to find a way to carry us forward? Perhaps the social conditions are lacking, and what is felt experientially cannot become actual in a publicly recognizable way (Paterson, in press). Gendlin acknowledges this difficulty in a long endnote, claiming that "even with the greatest creativity an individual could be imagined to have, there is no guarantee that a way will always be found to carry forward an interaction" (p. 273, n. 20). The objective life of symbols, in other words, can be an impediment to someone's further living, no matter how deeply they can Focus or develop fresh concepts. This aspect of Gendlin's philosophy, as I have been exploring, is underdeveloped. Gendlin's work therefore needs a deeper account of how the objective life of symbols can often oppress certain groups, and how Focusing or intricate process could feed back (or fail to feed back) into these social-structural processes.

The double life of symbols and appropriation point to the question of how individuals develop themselves in relation to already existing social forms. Human growth is *always* in the context of an existing social order. The major question, then, is how social-political structures enable or hinder growth, learning, and development. It is therefore important to be precise about what forms of development are available to us and how this is related to our social-political environment.

A relevant step found in Gendlin's (2006) writings is to distinguish two related but distinct forms of development: the development of persons due to formal or technological change, and the more personal, intricate development of individuals. Technology is perhaps the most prominent objective structure in modern society: buildings, roads, machines, and their implied roles are one of the most pervasive and oppressive sources of form in our lives. Although technological development often contributes to the development of individuals, these processes are distinct. One can learn to Focus, become psychologically or philosophically sophisticated, in technologically simple situations; and one can become technologically capable without much personal psychological development. The word "progress," as well as Gendlin's optimistic narratives, often conflate technological development and the development of intricate persons. Thus, distinguishing the development of technology and the development of persons as such is a crucial first step in furthering Gendlin's political thought.

Gendlin (2006) makes this distinction in his talk "The Town and Human Attention." There Gendlin repeats his optimistic narrative: things are getting better socially-politically, governments and businesses want to learn experiential process, and the therapeutic and Focusing community have an important role to play. In the first two paragraphs, Gendlin elaborates this distinction between development brought about by technology and the psychological development of persons:

> I want to say that we are in the middle or the beginning stages of a really gigantic development of human beings.... Now in a town that you never heard of, somewhere in Northern Ghana, a kid goes to the movies on Saturday and sees television all week and knows everything that's going on; and this is a tremendous development of people. There is literacy in half the world, but even where there is no literacy, there is tremendous awareness that a mass of people have gotten much more similar and much more developed. That's my first thing to say.
>
> (para. 1)

In this opening claim, Gendlin points to the development of persons aided *more or less directly by technology* (I consider reading/writing a form of technology). Gendlin then points to another form of development, one that is more strictly psychological and interpersonal:

> Secondly, there has been a smaller development, still of millions of people, who are now psychologically sophisticated. Not just in the West or in Japan, but in many places. What I mean by that is, you sit on the bus and the woman behind you is telling her friend, 'I am not his mother!' (for instance). And you realize that there is a level of sophistication that has come, psychologically, to certainly not the majority, not to the mass of people, but nevertheless to some significant hundred million people or so who are aware of all this stuff and coming in closer to the center!
>
> (para. 2)

Thus, Gendlin acknowledges that the development of persons can happen on interactive but distinct levels: one more connected to technology and artifice, and the other more directly psychological or personal. This is the difference between being able to use a set of tools versus being able to Focus, for example. These two forms of development, moreover, correspond to the objective and subjective life of symbols, respectively.

As "The Town" goes on, Gendlin (2006) depicts modernity as a dialectic between technological development and the development of persons. The transition from agriculture to industry, for example, necessitated the mass education and development of persons. These changes, Gendlin asserts, were not *merely* in the external conditions of living, but within the persons themselves who learned to participate in industrial society:

> It required a human development for people to run machinery. They had to be taught how to read instructions, they had to be taught how to be careful with powerful machinery, they had to be taught to be there at 8:00 in the morning, because the whole factory can't work unless everybody is there... So everybody had to buy a watch, everybody had to learn numbers. There was this tremendous development of people, inside and outside.
>
> (para. 6)

This narrative no doubt contains truth: industrial society certainly necessitated mass education and certain personal developments. Gendlin goes on to argue that our moment, the early 21st century, is characterized by a burgeoning shift, one in which we no longer engage principally in industry, but interhuman attention. Gendlin is admirable in his desire to understand this dialectic between social form and individual development, and his hope to get past the split between individual and society, inside and outside. Leontyev's analysis of the double life of symbols, especially combined with Aristotle's critique of law, however, should make us careful about conflating social-technological development with the development of persons as such.

We must be careful, in other words, about how far we take the analogy between the process of Focusing and the process of social-technological development. Growth (as individual intricate development) is not the same as progress (as positive social-political development). Gendlin makes this distinction in "The Town," but it is conflated or obscured in his earlier claims about a coming society of pattern-makers and his optimistic political narratives. Gendlin, as far as I know, does not take the time to specify how a society of pattern-makers would be organized: What forms of political-economic organization, what objective structures, would need to be in place so that people would be able to appropriate them for their own meanings? If we do not ask these questions, we may content ourselves with vague, prophetic statements like: "A kind of human organization is coming, which would not again be the imposition of power by some over others," (Gendlin, 1984a, p. 107) or "A society of pattern-makers is coming"

(Gendlin, 2007, p. 187). Above all, I want to avoid the sense of inevitability that seems implied in these sentiments.

Thus, I am emphasizing the difference between *forms* of government (objective life of symbols) and the *formulations* that facilitate more intimate psychological development (Focusing, philosophy, or the private life of symbols). These concepts certainly overlap in experience. But the dialectic of Focusing is unique in that it can dispense with a formulation whenever it is appropriate: ("No, its not slippery... its more like... slimy..."). Social-political forms (laws, institutions, buildings, machines), by contrast, cannot simply be dispensed with: they have a life that extends over multiple generations, they often occupy and structure physical space, and even when they are immaterial (like words and symbols) they acquire an objective life *beyond* any one individual. *This is the fundamental limitation of the analogy between Focusing and society: individuals in Focusing (or psychotherapy or philosophy) are free to relate flexibly to formulations, discarding them when appropriate. A society, by contrast, cannot simply dispense with forms, cannot abandon traditions, but must somehow appropriate or adapt existing structures to current needs.*

It seems to me, moreover, that something about social-political forms simply resists intricacy. As my analysis of Aristotle showed, there is something in law and the form of political things that resists the intricacy of the living body present in Focusing and philosophy. Laws and institutions, the *forms* of social-political process, avoid being intricate, appear as *form without process*. It is precisely these difficulties that are obscured by Gendlin's optimistic and underdeveloped claims about a society of pattern-makers or the coming of a new form of human organization.

If social-political processes fundamentally resist intricacy, if they are more closely bound to our objectively existing cultural systems of sayings and doings, then we are left with questions about possible *forms of government* and their relationship to the development or oppression of intricate individuals. This means thinking about the fundamental political-economic alternatives: monarchy as opposed to democracy, socialism as opposed to capitalism, and agriculture as opposed to industry. These forms no doubt have a deep and dialectical relationship with intricate experience. But political thinking also seems to resist the call of intricacy. Gendlin (2006) acknowledges in "The Town" that contemporary government is relegated primarily to categorical thinking: "those people who have charge of everything, they are still thinking in the categories, so no wonder things aren't going so well" (para. 43). The question is whether or not government is only temporarily stuck in categorical thinking, or *if there is something in the nature of government itself that relegates it to categorical, unit model thinking.* Aristotle's analysis of law suggests that it is a fundamental feature of law and government that it must deal chiefly with units, with rules and roles. It is telling, moreover, that Gendlin (1996) says of a felt sense that "One cannot *legislate* [its] direction" (p. 21, my emphasis). Legislation and the intricacy of a felt sense are apparently at odds. Curiously, elsewhere Gendlin (2009) argues that a felt sense "is very precise and *governs* what we say and do next" (p. 341, n. 7, my emphasis). Gendlin, of course, is using these political terms metaphorically. But the point remains: somehow a felt sense cannot be legislated, and, at the same time, *it* is what ultimately governs our activity. This is reminiscent of Aristotle's claim that the legally just (literal legislation) is a highly limited and incomplete form of justice, as opposed to *epikeia* or a sense of decency as what metaphorically governs our activity. An intricate institution, I therefore repeat, is an oxymoron, not a paradox. Politics *in service of intricacy*, however, is a different question altogether.

It is within this context, of the tension between intricacy resisting institutions and intricate persons, that AT and the question of appropriation are most significant. For if I am correct that our current situation is one that resists the fundamental questions about the forms of government, then we must be creative in how we try to open these fundamental and controversial questions. Terms like socialism, communism, Marxism, and the like seem to be too mired in the violent history of modernity. We need to find ways to open these questions about social responsibility and the meaning of government in fresh terms that bypass or appropriate the deeply sedimented biases of our political history. This is the task this paper ultimately implies but cannot address: to think freshly and intricately about political processes that, in their nature, resist intricacy. We cannot content ourselves with teaching Focusing as broadly as possible (which is certainly an important task). The intricacy of the therapeutic model cannot extend into the depths of political process. We must consider political form as such. What words, images, and processes exist in our situation that could possibly be appropriated for opening the fundamental questions about the basic alternatives of political life?

Conclusion: A society of pattern-makers, institutions in service of intricate persons, and next steps

Here I have addressed the consistent tone of political optimism that pervades Gendlin's corpus. More specifically, I tried to assess the validity of Gendlin's concept of a society of pattern-makers and more so the corresponding intricate institutions implied in *Focusing* and promised in "The Client's Client." I argued, using Aristotle's *Nicomachean Ethics*, that the generic structure of law or cultural systems fundamentally resist intricacy, making an intricate institution an oxymoronic concept rather than a paradox. I then argued that AT can offer important resources for amending Gendlin's political thought. Leontyev's work on the double life of symbols and appropriation is particularly helpful in thinking through the political implications of Gendlin's work. The task the paper finally poses, but cannot take up in detail, is to think about basic forms of government. If institutions themselves cannot become intricate then we must think through which forms of government enable individuals to live intricate, growthful lives. The goal is not intricate institutions or politics but *politics and institutions in service of intricate persons*.

The paper implies far more questions than it can address. Therefore, it is worth considering next steps. The task is to carry Gendlin's project into the domain of politics in a thorough and proper sense. I hope to work out a set of internally consistent political concepts that take something like *A Process Model* as a starting point. Gendlin's *Process Model* is, no doubt, indispensable. But what needs to be understood in more detail is how political experiences like ours emerged from and continue within the ongoing life processes that Gendlin describes. Gendlin's whole philosophy and especially *A Process Model* offer a rich account of the human capacity for symboling, how our cultural-symbolic systems can capture us, and how we can relate to those systems without being captured. We need to understand, however, not just how individuals interact with their generic cultural-political systems, but how different forms of organization encourage either cultural capture or individual growth. Only by taking possible forms of government seriously and explicitly can we hope to bring together the (intricate) development of persons with the (non-intricate) processes of government.

Gendlin's work no doubt implies these questions and at times explicitly addresses them. But I want to ask more directly: What sorts of political-institutional arrangements would make a society of pattern-makers more likely? To my mind, universal basic income, universal health care, and guaranteed housing are examples of institutional arrangements that would lend themselves to the development of persons and the possibility of something like a society of pattern-makers. This question, however, must be understood in our current context in which it is incredibly difficult to raise these fundamental questions. The United States in particular is highly stilted in discussing the forms of government. The legacy of the Cold War quietly looms, and words like communism, socialism, and Marxism obscure more than they clarify. Raising fundamental questions about government is therefore not simply a theoretical or philosophical task, but a political one that must navigate this concrete situation.

I am thus in a strange, hopefully paradoxical, situation: I claim that Gendlin's philosophy is politically inadequate but also provides the basis for a deeper and richer understanding of our experience of politics and institutions.

Notes

1 The phrase intricate institution, as far as I know, does not appear in Gendlin's writings. He implies in several places (1984a, 2007), however, that a society of pattern-makers will involve major institutional changes. While I will argue that the idea of an intricate institution is oxymoronic, I think that the concept of a society of pattern-makers is less problematic if understood in terms of institutions that, while not intricate in themselves, serve the development of intricate individuals.

2 I consistently capitalize the word "Focusing" when referring to the specific embodied, self-therapeutic practice of checking symbols against our felt sense of situations.

3 Michael Davis (2012) suggests, our word "culture," with its mingling of explicit and implicit elements, is perhaps the closest analog for the complexity and ambiguity of *nomos*.

4 A similar argument could be derived from a dialogical reading of Plato's *Minos* (Pangle & Plato, 1987), especially when paired with Willet (2019). Or one could look to Plato's *Statesman* where he has the Eleatic Stranger claim "law could never, by having comprehended precisely what's most excellent and most just for all at the same time, command what's best. For the dissimilarities of both human beings and actions, and the never being at rest, so to speak, of any single thing among human things—these do not allow any art whatsoever to proclaim anything simply in any area concerning all things and for all time." The stranger's interlocutor agrees and the stranger continues, "But we see the law pretty much straining in this very direction, just like some human being who's stubborn and ignorant and allows no one to do anything against his own order nor to ask any questions, not even if something new contrary to the command he himself uttered should turn out to be better for someone" (Plato et al., 2012, p. 76/294b-c).

5 It is curious that despite Gendlin's deep and sustained engagement with Aristotle (especially in his *Line by line commentary on Aristotle's De Anima*), I am not aware of any direct references to Aristotle's *Politics* or *Nicomachean Ethics*.

6 It is crucial to note that unit model thinking, "which governs most of our natural sciences," erases the distinction between the living and nonliving. "In the unit model there is no basic difference between living and inanimate things because everything is assumed to be made of the same inanimate parts" (Gendlin & Johnson, 2004, para. 4). In being intertwined with unit model thinking, political logic can sometimes struggle to acknowledge that we are talking about living persons rather than interchangeable parts. It is also worth noting that militaries are generally divided into "units" with distinct roles.

7 One of the more complex and nuanced points of Gendlin's account of machine thinking or the unit model is that it necessarily implies the concept of empty space. Space, in its original and more fundamental sense, is behavior space, or our lived sense of immediate possible actions and their interrelations. Our sense of empty space is co-emergent with our capacity for symboling, which implies separable patterns that can be moved from "here" to "there" (i.e. in empty space) (See "The Derivation of Space," in Gendlin et al., 2018).

8 The concept or theory of activity is sometimes taken to be the work of a single individual, often A.N. Leontyev. Activity, however, was a guiding concept for a wide range of Soviet psychologists (Chaiklin, 2019).

9 The word appropriation is commonly used in social justice discourse to point to the exploitative adoption of oppressed cultural practices by privileged groups. Leontyev's concept of appropriation is distinct from this problem of cultural

appropriation. My hope is to keep these problems separate for the sake of this analysis, although I suspect there is much to explore in the overlap between these problems.

10   Gendlin (2018) makes a similar point in *A Process Model* when he claims that "Symboling creates a new world, as is well known and will become clearly thinkable here" (p. 123). At some point, the primary context of human activity is no longer simply the natural environment, but the context of gestural and symbolic interaction. Gendlin calls this transition the FLIP:

> "After the FLIP, the contexts are no longer the physical settings, but the interhuman gestural contexts. Their connections are not those of behavior space, not how a physical action changes the context for other actions. Rather, their connections are how a given gesturing between people changes *their* situation, the one they have with each other.... After the FLIP everything is located in the gestural external empty space, and the gestural interaction supersedes and defines what each situation is."
>
> (p. 152)

11   The book, moreover, is meant to both describe process *and exhibit process,* meaning that the concepts themselves are instances of what is being described. The concepts themselves are implicitly intricate, experientially grounded, and in the process of development. As Gendlin (2018) explains,

> "To think clearly, one needs concepts that share an internal structure, that develop together, so to speak. What each is, and what the others are, constitute a single structure so that one can grasp what each does in relation to the others."
>
> (p. 114)

A Process Model is therefore a book about process that also exhibits that process.

12   Gendlin certainly acknowledges the difficulty of the problem but, as far as I know, never quite explores it in depth. In "What First & Third Person Processes Really Are," for example, Gendlin (2009) acknowledges that *generally* culture tends to capture individuals, but it does not always (p. 354–355).

References

Aristole et al., (2012). *Aristotle's nicomachean ethics.* University of Chicago Press.

Cabanas, E. (2018). Positive psychology and the legitimation of individualism. *Theory & Psychology, 28*(1), 3–19. https://doi.org/10.1177/0959354317747988

Cabanas, E., & Illouz, E. (2021). *Manufacturing happy citizens: How the science and industry of happiness control our lives.* Polity.

Chaiklin, S. (2019). The meaning and origin of the activity concept in soviet psychology—With primary focus on A. N. Leontiev's approach. *Theory & Psychology, 29*(1), 3–26. https://doi.org/10.1177/0959354319828208

Cushman, P. (1995). *Constructing the self, constructing america: A cultural history of psychotherapy.* Da Capo Press.

Cushman, P. (2012). Defenseless in the face of the status quo: Psychology without a critical humanities. *The Humanistic Psychologist, 40*(3), 262–269. https://doi.org/10.1080/08873267.2012.696411

Davis, M. (2012). *The soul of the greeks: An inquiry.* University of Chicago Press.

Engelsted, N., Mammen, J., & Toomela, A. (2017). *Catching up with Aristotle a journey in Quest of General psychology.* Springer.

Fisher, M. (2010). *Capitalist realism: Is there no alternative?* Zero Books.

Gendlin, E.T. (1972). *Two ways of reading a philosophy—And their pitfalls.* Unpublished manuscript (22 pp.). http://previous.focusing.org/gendlin/docs/gol_2038.html

Gendlin, E.T. (1984a). The client's client: The edge of awareness. In R.L. Levant & J.M. Shlien (Eds.), *Client-centered therapy and the person-centered approach. New directions in theory, research and practice,* (pp. 76–107). Praeger. http://previous.focusing.org/gendlin/docs/gol_2149.html

Gendlin, E.T. (1984b). The political critique of "awareness." *The Focusing Folio, 3*(4), 139–157.

Gendlin, E.T. (1986). Process ethics and the political question. In A-T. Tymieniecka (Ed.), *Analecta Husserliana. Vol. XX. The moral sense in the communal significance of life,* (pp. 265–275). Reidel.

Gendlin, E.T. (1987). A philosophical critique of the concept of narcissism: The significance of the awareness movement. In D.M. Levin (Ed.), *Pathologies of the modern self. Postmodern studies on narcissism, schizophrenia, and depression,* (pp. 251–304). New York University Press.

Gendlin, E.T. (1991). Thinking beyond patterns: Body, language and situations. In B. den Ouden & M. Moen (Eds.), *The presence of feeling in thought,* (pp. 25–151). Peter Lang. http://previous.focusing.org/gendlin/docs/gol_2159.html

Gendlin, E.T. (1996). *Focusing-oriented psychotherapy: A manual of the experiential method.* Guilford.

Gendlin, E.T. (1997). *Experiencing and the creation of meaning: A philosophical and psychological approach to the subjective.* Northwestern University Press.

Gendlin, E.T. (1999). Authenticity after postmodernism. *Changes: An International Journal of Psychology and Psychotherapy, 17*(3), 203–212. http://previous.focusing.org/gendlin/docs/gol_2052.html

Gendlin, E.T. (2006). *The town and human attention.* [Transcript]. Talk presented at the Focusing Institute Summer School, Garrison Institute, New York. http://previous.focusing.org/gendlin/docs/gol_2180.html

Gendlin, E.T. (2007). *Focusing.* Bantam.

Gendlin, E.T. (2009). What first & third person processes really are. *Journal of Consciousness Studies, 16*(10–12), 332–362.

Gendlin, E.T. (2012a). *Line by line commentary on Aristotle's De Anima, vol. 1: Books I & II.* The Focusing Institute.

Gendlin, E.T. (2012b). Process generates structures: Structures alone don't generate process. *The Folio, 23*(1), 3–13.

Gendlin, E.T. (2018). *A process model.* Northwestern University Press.

Gendlin, E.T., Casey, E.S., & Schoeller, D. (2018). *Saying what we mean: Implicit precision and the responsive order: Selected works of Eugene T. Gendlin.* Northwestern University Press.

Gendlin, E.T. & Johnson, D.H. (2004). Proposal for an international group for a first person science [Internet page]. The Focusing Institute.

Leontyev, A.N., & Cole, M. (2009). *The development of mind: Selected works of Aleksei Nikolaevich Leontyev.* Marxists Internet Archive.

Luria, A.R. (1994). *The making of mind: A personal account of Soviet psychology.* Harvard University Press.

Mammen, J., & Gozli, D. (2018). Rebellion, theory, and dialogue: An interview with Jens Mammen. *Human Arenas*, *2*(2), 186–199. https://doi.org/10.1007/s42087-018-0050-6

Mammen, J., & Mironenko, I. (2015). Activity theories and the ontology of psychology: Learning from Danish and Russian experiences. *Integrative Psychological and Behavioral Science*, *49*(4), 681–713. https://doi.org/10.1007/s12124-015-9313-7

Pangle, T.L., & Plato, S. (1987). *The roots of political philosophy: Ten forgotten Socratic dialogues.* Cornell University Press.

Paterson, R. (in press). The dilemma of compliance: Roles and rules in schizophrenia, censorship, and life. *Philosophy, psychiatry & psychology.*

Plato. (2012). *Statesman.* (E. Brann, P. Kalkavage, & E. Salem, Trans.). Focus Publishing.

Sugarman, J. (2015). Neoliberalism and psychological ethics. *Journal of Theoretical and Philosophical Psychology*, *35*(2), 103–116. https://doi.org/10.1037/a0038960

Walkerden, G. (2004). How I read the structure of a process model: What is a "kind" of process? *The Folio*, *19*(1), 124–130.

Willett, K. (2019). Sacrifice and law: On Plato's minos. Paper delivered at the ninety-third annual meeting of the American Philosophical Association, Pacific Division. Paper requests: Kwillett@tulane.edu.

Chapter 11

Epilog

Showing how he means: Thinking along with Gene Gendlin

Robert Fox

I was fortunate to have discovered Eugene Gendlin in 1967 when I was an eighteen-year-old college student majoring in his newly formed Philosophical Psychology department at the University of Chicago. I had gone to the school expressly to study with him, on the recommendation of Rollo May, who had been my intellectual hero in high school.

Gene told me the first day I met him that he believed that words could say what they mean only if they *show how they mean*. From that very first day I was dazzled by the rigor and precision of his use of language in the service of *showing how* a phenomenon is to be understood rather than talking *about* properties or qualities *of* that phenomenon. In writing this epilog, I wish to show how Gene worked by showing how he worked with me through conversations. Gene's primary modality was conversation, and it is fitting that this volume carries forward a vibrant conversation. I know that the conversations we had reverberate with me to this day.

Gene's dialogical way of being showed up in his teaching—in seminars and independent studies. His relationship with me had an element of the therapeutic in it, as it did with many of the other college students who studied with him in the late 1960s. To show Gene fully requires a discussion of his intellectual history at the University, and some glimpses of how he was both therapist and teacher. I will begin with our first encounter, and then trace the unique intellectual history of Gene's way of working. I will then use four extended conversations between Gene and me which come from 1969, 1988, 1996, and the present day to illustrate the way he worked directly with me. The first three are remembered; the fourth newly imagined to be the conversation I would have liked to have with him after reading *Saying What We Mean*. I hope to show the philosopher, teacher, and the therapist in these conversations—and also the human being.

When I first met Gene, it was at his house in Hyde Park, Chicago. I was embarking on a year-long independent study with him, reading Husserl, Heidegger, and Merleau-Ponty. When I knocked on the door, a serious boy about ten years old greeted me with dignity and brought me in to meet his father. There is a poignant symmetry which evolved from that meeting.

DOI: 10.4324/9781003296706-12

Almost thirty years later, Gene arrived at my house in Newton, Massachusetts where he stayed while giving a keynote address for the New England Center for Existential Therapy's inaugural conference. When he rang my doorbell, my eleven-year-old son answered the door, greeted him with dignity, and brought him to meet his father. The subject of sons and fathers is not accidental here. I looked for and collected fathers until I was in my forties—Gene was one of the most important father-figures I have had, and perhaps the most enduring.

Join me in remembering being an eighteen-year-old in Gene's *Introduction to Philosophical Psychology* class. We would read texts very closely and carefully, but as much with an eye on where the ideas took us as to a critical appraisal of them. In his classes, he was keen on paying attention to how concepts *showed up* in the conversations between us. If someone grasped an aspect of something, Gene would say, with shining eyes, "Yes...*there* it is." By doing that he was *showing* us something that either was already there or just emerging. Everything about Gene is in those four words: Yes. There. It. Is. The "yes" was an announcement which got our attention. The "there" evoked what I later understood as the Da of Dasein—something already there that announces itself. The "it" was actually the most mysterious to me—"it" was anything worth paying attention to. The "it" *noted* itself (a profoundly reflexive procedure) as something that could not be explained or even described, but which could be attended to repeatedly, and followed. And the "is" evoked the Sein of Dasein—Sein as in something which has been revealed in the very process of attending in a particular way. Everything Gene did and said was a call to attention—the kind of attention which gave rise to his Focusing approach to psychotherapy as well as his philosophical work.

My sense of Gene's intellectual development or "history" is not an objective study but rather reflects my constantly developing and changing understanding of who he was as I got to know him within the context of the University. These understandings came from stories he told me and other students, and my trying to put them into a kind of order as I began to read the ideas to which he introduced me so as to make meaning of them. Over my three years at the University, I gradually realized that Gene was teaching me *about* phenomenology and hermeneutics by teaching me in a phenomenological and hermeneutical way. As much as I longed to emulate Gene, I failed to do so. Gene as "therapist" tried to free me to be myself rather than to be like him, and in this circular process with Gene I grew. The conversations which follow are largely discussions about hermeneutics in Freud and in Heidegger's *Being and Time,* and how hermeneutics can be understood as basic to both psychoanalysis and Focusing. Over the years certain themes continued to come back again and again—and each time somehow different and the same. He showed me *how* to think and how to be this way.

Gene was a legend at the University when I got there, even though he was barely forty years old. The philosophy department, run by Richard McKeon, was legendary as well. We cannot understand Gene without appreciating his mentor McKeon and the ethos of the University at that time. Gene received his college education and PhD in philosophy at the University from the late 1940s through the early 1960s. The University was famous for its notion of philosophical pluralism. Indeed, there are many wonderful ways of thinking about things, and we need to use all of them. The goal isn't to find the right one, or the true one—but to use all of them; and to use them in a way that does justice to each of them and creates a fine mesh when used in conjunction with each other. Gene taught pluralism in a way that later gave rise to his vital concept called *crossing*—ideas can "cross" with each other to create something far more powerful than each of them could alone. This was *not* eclecticism, because each of the ways of thinking was seen to be more or less appropriate to any given subject matter, and there was a strict discipline to the choice of which to use (and *how* to use it) at any given time. This was *not* integration, because each of these ways of thinking kept its distinct character while interacting with the others. This was *not* relativism, since each of these was understood as absolute in its own approach. This was philosophical pluralism as Gene conceived it in action.

McKeon taught pluralism in a very structured, and for Gene, pivotal way. He wrote schemas of the history of philosophy, emphasizing different types of concepts and methods of thinking, and the interplay of each with the others created remarkable thinking possibilities (Plochmann, 1990). McKeon made the study of Aristotle the cornerstone of his thinking, and Gene first and foremost required his students to read Aristotle carefully together. Aristotle had astonishing breadth—he wrote about physics, biology, zoology, cosmology, metaphysics, logic, mathematics, poetics, politics, ethics—and much more. Aristotle was not merely encyclopedic, however—and like McKeon, Gene wanted these approaches to connect with each other, but not merge with each other. He did not champion positions for theory's sake. He was interested in pragmatic use of these ideas, and the open interplay of them. This training allowed Gene to play with philosophy in a uniquely practical and "playful" manner.

Aristotle's practical intellect was attractive to Gene, and all of Gene's ideas about thinking and feeling—like "crossing"—are profoundly practical as well as beautiful. The University had long been a bastion of philosophical pragmatism—the effect of John Dewey was still pronounced at the time Gene went to college there. What interested him most in this pragmatism was using ideas to open doors to further thinking. He was not interested in trying to find the "deep" underlying meaning of things. He was interested, however, in how meaning works—how it opens and moves, and this proved to be central to his contribution.

This interest in opening and moving furthered his growing interest in continental philosophy. In the early 1960s, when Gene was finishing up his doctoral studies, most academic philosophy departments in the United States were dominated by the orientations of ordinary language, or analytic, philosophy. Most philosophy departments had just one "continental philosophy" slot, and back in those days before the emergence of Derrida, that meant "phenomenology and existential philosophy." While Gene grew up in McKeon's pluralism and the pragmatic milieu, and never lost his connection to them, he nevertheless became very interested in phenomenology and hermeneutics. The combination of his interest in this kind of thinking, along with his relationship with Carl Rogers and his rigorous grounding in philosophical pluralism, gave rise to a rich, complex, and distinctive approach to philosophy, which later informed his Focusing therapy approach as well.

I can remember his enthusiasm as he told me about what these thinkers meant to him. His admiration for Husserl was first and foremost. His interest in studying experience in its own terms was constant, and I remember early in my studying his suggesting that it would be helpful when in reading Husserl I substitute "experiencing of…" for the term "consciousness of…" Over time I grew to understand how essential that substitution was in the development of his phenomenology. I can remember the look on his face when he said, "for all my criticism of Husserl's later phenomenology, his insistence on the complexity, thickness and layering of experience…of meaning…is basic to all of my thinking."

He was deeply influenced by Merleau-Ponty's work on the phenomenology of the body, and *The Phenomenology of Perception* was a text he urged many of his students to read (Merleau-Ponty, 1962). Ponty emphasized the centrality of embodiment and how experience is always embodied *and* languaged. Ponty also introduced the term "carry-forward" (it shows up a number of times undramatically in that text) wherein every aspect of experiencing carries itself forward into further aspects. This became central for Gene, and essential for Focusing. And Ponty disrupted the philosophical dominance of the subject/object dualism and continually criticized linear causality as the methodological approach to understanding human being. Gene was dedicated to this non-dualism and in his mature thinking remained opposed to dualism and uncritical application of causal analysis in understanding. These concerns also led him toward an appreciation of hermeneutics, first in his reading of Dilthey and later Heidegger's *Being and Time.*

Reading Heidegger's *Being and Time* (1962) with Gene was the highpoint of my three years with him, and one of the things Rollo May had urged me not to miss when I got to the University. By 1967 Gene was teaching the *Being and Time* seminar every other year to college students. He told me that he came to Heidegger after all of the others, and with some reluctance. This reluctance, he told me, was largely due to Heidegger's Nazi involvement, which remains an ethical conundrum for anyone reading Heidegger and wishing to take him seriously. Furthermore, Heidegger's seemingly mystical bent (perhaps more evident in his later writing, but certainly already there in *Being and Time* with terms like "the clearing") was not attractive to Gene, with his pragmatic interest in moving things along as opposed to "getting to the bottom of things." But once he read the book, he found it essential to his thinking. He was most interested in Division I Chapters 3 and 5. Much of the language we associate with Gene comes from his development of ideas which are found in these chapters. He would say about Chapter 3:

> This is about how it works to be in a world—and where else could we be? Things show up in our working with them and coming from our involvement in them, rather than taking ourselves out of involvement with them to "analyze" them.

He loved the idea of the "involvement structure"—and as Richard Rorty has maintained, the pragmatism of these early Heideggerean ideas (Guignon, 1993).

Chapter 5 was the essential chapter for Gene, and he spent much of the seminar carefully exploring the structures of "being-in"; of what Heidegger calls the "Care structure." Much of the program of what he later would call Focusing can be understood in terms of the hermeneutics of the three structures of "state of mind," "understanding," and "discourse" which are laid out in that chapter. We used the classic Robinson and MacQuarrie 1962 translation of *Sein und Zeit*. Gene particularly disliked the translation of Heidegger's term "Befindlichkeit" as "state of mind." "*Befindlichkeit is neither a state, nor is it of the mind*," he would often say. He preferred the more literal translation of "where one finds oneself," which increasingly for him was seen as the "bodily felt sense" which later became the basis for Focusing. In the seminar, Gene would help us understand these three structures using his own distinctive language:

> Befindlichkeit describes how one finds oneself already, primarily in a mood. Understanding is our situatedness in our everyday activities which orient us in our living in the world. And Discourse is the way we express our moody understanding and carry it forward.
>
> (Casey & Schoeller, 2018)

This bringing in of the adjectival form of mood as "moody" is pure Gene. These were some of the influences that Gene talked about as central to the development of his philosophical psychology. But another influence—very

Midwest American and about as non-European as could be—loomed large. Carl Rogers' impact on Gene was hardly only clinical—it was deeply philosophical. Gene was taken with Rogers' client-centered therapy approach—it was here that he began to use clinical examples to demonstrate his philosophical ideas. He liked what he called the rigor and discipline of Rogers' operationalizing of empathy and the kind of self-awareness he called genuineness. From 1958 to 1963, Gene took a leave of absence to work with Rogers on the client-centered research project on schizophrenia at the University of Wisconsin, and during the last few years of that time, he concurrently wrote his dissertation called *Experiencing and the Creation of Meaning*, which later became his first published book. When he returned to Chicago, Rogers' impact loomed as large as any of the philosophers. Gene ultimately began to teach in both the philosophy and psychology departments of the University of Chicago and then—when the University created its "New Collegiate Division" in 1966—he developed the undergraduate studies major called Philosophical Psychology which drew me to the school in 1967.

My relationship with Gene from the very start had a quality of psychotherapy to it. He wanted to know not only what mattered to me, but how I got there. While never officially therapy, I always felt that I was both client and student to Gene. He also had an uncanny ability to make me feel like I was a colleague from the very beginning. To do justice for this "case study," I will need to show a bit of who I was at eighteen; what he learned about me and how he chose to respond to that.

The fundamental issue can be understood in this way: I was a boy who loved enchantment (both being enchanted and enchanter), and Gene was a master of disenchantment. I was drawn to philosophy for its drama, and Gene was drawn to it for its potential precision. I was enchanted with Gene and wanted to be just like him. My story is tied up with my desire to please and save my mother (herself both entranced *by* me and entrancer *of* me)—to please and save her by becoming what she needed me to be. She was deeply appreciative of the psychoanalysis she was in, and of the psychoanalyst she was in it with. At age thirteen, when she took me to meet him, I became enchanted with him and wanted to be just like him. I began to read Freud, then other analysts like Erich Fromm and finally more existentially oriented psychoanalytic writers like Rollo May and R.D. Laing. By the time I was in high school, I was enthralled by the dramatic self-in-conflict images from both psychoanalysis and existentialism. I was convinced that people were in fundamental conflict with "society" and also with themselves. I glorified these struggles, which helped me make sense of my own internal struggles which were intensified by my parents' divorce when I was fourteen. I was highly dramatic, opiniated, and I discovered over time that I was considered charismatic by many other students. My father called me a "starry-eyed boy," which may have been a term of concern but which I interpreted at the time as a term of contempt. Gene saw all of this and took it into the way he chose to be my teacher. He would occasionally also refer to me as a "starry-eyed boy," but always with tenderness and respect.

The therapeutic aspect of our relationship can be seen as an extended conversation between my devotion to the imagery of dramatic struggle (and my desire to find a set of fundamental metaphysical and psychological principles from which to ground those struggles) and Gene's commitment to pay careful attention to what shows up in any process (rather than get distracted by a need to find a grounding metaphysics or meta-psychology). I was devoted to contradiction and paradox to make sense of things, and Gene was committed to helping me *use* ideas rather than identify with them. I was taken by, and jealous of Gene's meticulousness and the complete lack of hysteria in his makeup; I fought him while at the same time tried to become like him. I used to think that we struggled constantly with my philosophical and psychological investment in conflict. What I began to see was that we were not only struggling (perhaps for Gene there was no struggling at all). We were *playing*—it was all very serious play. Only twenty years later when I began to read the work of the psychoanalyst D.W. Winnicott and the hermeneutic philosopher Han-Georg Gadamer (on "play space" and "Spiel-raum" respectively) did I begin to appreciate Gene's remarkably serious play, and how much play there is in his work.

But foremost and long before I learned about playing, there were two thinkers to whom I was particularly drawn. One was Freud, whom I began to read in early adolescence shortly after my meeting with my mother's psychoanalyst. The other was Heidegger, whom I began to read as soon as Rollo May told me to make sure I didn't miss Gene's *Being and Time* class. I was in constant conversation with both Freud and Heidegger throughout my many years of conversations with Gene. It was with Gene that I learned the art of conversation as a vehicle for critical appraisal.

In these conversations, I began to realize that I was drawn to both dialectical and hermeneutical thinking. When I began to think about Freud as a philosopher (and despite all his attestations to the contrary, his thinking was significantly philosophical), I conceptualized his developmental theory as a dialectical movement. The sequence of oral, anal, and phallic/genital seemed to demonstrate a thesis, anti-thesis, and synthesis to me— with "latency" being a consolidation of the synthesis which later became the thesis for the next sequence (e.g., of early adolescence, middle adolescence, and late adolescence/early adulthood). As such, I saw psychoanalytic developmental theory as a dialectical unfolding of an ongoing conflict between the need to be taken care of and the need to take care of oneself. I saw every "resolution" to this conflict as temporary—and over time began to take great pleasure and even solace in the fact that the tension could not be "resolved" but rather must be borne and transformed. I also conceptualized

Freud's structural theory of id/ego/superego in dialectical terms as a struggle between good and evil in oneself. I brought my delight with these aspects of Freud's thinking to Gene. As we will see in the ongoing conversations, Gene was less taken with the dialectical aspects of psychoanalysis—less taken with dialectical thinking in general, in fact. This is where I struggled with him, and he played with me.

I also recognized psychoanalysis as a hermeneutical discipline. If its *theories* are dialectical (e.g., the developmental theories, the structural theories, and the continual emphasis on drive *versus* defense), its *process* is hermeneutical. Psychoanalysis as a psychotherapy is a continual working with and through the "transference" in order to "resolve the transference neurosis." Gene brought this to my attention through his careful reading of *Being and Time* with me. Listen to how he said this to me very early on:

> You seem to like so much the way Heidegger talks about hermeneutics in the introduction to Being and Time, Bob. This is about interpretation, and you are very interested in psychoanalytic interpretation. If you want to "marry" psychoanalysis and existential thinking, this is a good place to start, I think.

Later during our independent study year, when we were reading sections of Division II on Heidegger's concept of "resoluteness," Gene gave me an important hint that I would use in the developing of my thinking about this marriage.

> Freud talks about "resolving" the transference, right? But he knows that these fundamental aches of the soul are not resolvable. It is so unfortunate that so many psychotherapists, especially in the United States, are so operational in their thinking that they see therapy as a place to solve problems rather than find new ways to be in them and to understand them. Heidegger has much to offer here. Look at this! The ache is powerful and complex—both totally unique and individual, and shared by everyone. We can understand it biologically, culturally and ontologically. Heidegger goes ontological with it, but we can take it into psychology if we want to. He tells us that "it" cannot be resolved in a present-at-hand way, nor can it be "resolved" dialectically through a "resolution" qua synthesis. This fact—that it cannot be resolved—must be held with resolution! Heidegger's resolve replaces both present-at-hand and dialectical notions of resolving. If you can work with this, Bob, you can have your existential psychoanalysis.

To this day, remembering this conversation with Gene grounds me in the resoluteness—the rigor—that I owe him. However, my increasing appreciation of Gene's use of Heidegger's hermeneutics did not replace my devotion to dialectical thinking, and particularly to the power of the language of paradox. I realized early on that I could work *with* Gene from a hermeneutic stance, but that I might have to work *against* Gene in terms to my devotion to paradox. Hidden in these last two sentences is the psychological key to our work together—my devotion to "devotion" and Gene's commitment to sober paying attention to what is. It was not really the intellectual differences that mattered to me; I wanted him to come over to my romantic way of being. I wanted my "father" to give his blessing to my identification with my mother—with her dramatic, romantic, and charismatic way of being and the way I was entranced into being with her and for her. All of my work with Gene, including posthumously, can be seen as "working in the transference." Gene would be pleasantly amused with me putting it this way—he would graciously let me have this formulation even though he would himself never put it in that way. Gene knew that I was drawn to conflict theory and interpretations, and he was happy to let me keep that. His understanding of hermeneutics was the key to all of this, and the following conversations are about hermeneutics in Freud, Heidegger, and Gene's philosophy of the implicit and his Focusing therapy project.

I will try to stay in the present tense, as I attempt to re-present these conversations in a way that keeps Gene alive. To be sure, when Gene Gendlin and I are talking together he is there for me. He is gentle, so I am not scared of him. He is relentless, and I fear what he will not allow me to avoid. Whenever Gene teaches, he uses the therapeutic skills first taken from Carl Rogers but finely hewn into his own style. How does he teach? He converses, but importantly, he avoids conversations *about* how things work and rather demonstrates *how* they do work. Conversations like this are what he calls "instances"—a happening rather than a dissection or analysis.

Importantly, everything is in play in conversations with Gene. Nothing is disembodied. Gene seems awkward in his body, but this hardly gets in the way of him being incredibly embodied. Indeed, this awkwardness is part of genuine embodiment. Experience is discussed "from" a palpable apprehensive knowing rather than a disembodied comprehension. Everything is in play, yet there is a rigorous order of steps, and he allows nothing to be skipped over. He sees that I am dreamy and somewhat disembodied, and he does not allow me to skip over myself through my romantic and theatrical uses of imagery; he does not allow me to seduce myself, so to speak. This is part of what is scary to me as well as what is so appealing. This is central to Gene's indelible contribution to my life and our field.

In recalling this unfolding conversation with Gene, there are three instances that are crucial to remember, as well as a conversation I will imagine that I would have liked to have had with him now if he were still alive. The reimaginings come from various settings and situations: 1969 in our working together on my Bachelor's Thesis on Freud and Heidegger, 1988 during one of our many times of walking and talking together when he was living part of the time in Wellesley, Massachusetts while his daughter was going to school there, and the evening in 1996 when he stayed at my house the night before he was to deliver a keynote talk at the inaugural conference of the New England Center for Existential Therapy called, not surprisingly, *Thinking from Feeling.* While these conversations are not literal (I did not record them or take immediate notes)—they live and as such change every time I revisit them. Working with Gene and remembering working with Gene is a hermeneutical event, every time.

The first conversation occurs while we are working on my thesis on Freud and Heidegger. Even as I am remembering the conversation now, I can palpably feel Gene's bodily excitement and take in the sparkle of delight in his eyes. He is excited about everything because everything is connected to everything, and anything can open anything. He loves things opening, and he is rigorous in exploring just how things open. He tells me how he likes how Heidegger wrote about the "openness" but says "...*it is not enough to write about it. It is not even enough to write lyrically and with passion about it, because that can become a mystification rather than a direct experience.*" This is pointed directly at me. He already knows that I love Heidegger's terms liked "the openness" and "the clearing" (Heidegger, 1962)—and he wants to caution me against getting swept away in the passion of my romantic response to philosophical ideas. He insists that "...we must demonstrate just how it moves, how it opens, how it gets stuck and won't seem to open." As I re-listen to his language, I am struck by his use of the word "it," the musical quality of its repetitiveness in his long sentence. This musicality has philosophical as well as esthetic meaning—and it is only available to me if I *do indeed* refrain from leaving direct experience for romantic passion.

In *Saying What We Mean* (Casey & Schoeller, 2018), Gene devotes Chapter 5 (entitled "Words Can Say How They Work") to this very task, effectively showing how things actually work. Rather than the lovely but rather mystical "the openness," he shows *how* things open. He reintroduces what he calls the ellipses (...)—originally coined in his *Experiencing and the Creation of Meaning* in 1962—which he puts at the end of a statement about an experience—demonstrating how the implicit sense of an experience or a statement about an experience carries itself forward into a constant opening. In a conversation, Gene's body acts as the ellipsis. He will say something—or more powerfully listen to something that I am saying—and will move his body in response to that. Whatever is coming up is an "it," and his very body is responding to that "it" by saying bodily: "Yes. There. It. Is." When he does this, you can feel how "it" was already there, showing up and leaving, and moving toward something, and you know that *this* is the opening which we could choose to call the "openness."

In this first conversation, I am wanting to use this difference between Gene's notion of opening and Heidegger's "the openness" to talk to Gene about psychoanalysis and its relationship to his developing approach to psychotherapy (in 1969 still called *experiential psychotherapy*, and not yet *focusing*). He tells me:

> The term carrying forward that I am borrowing from Merleau-Ponty has in ways a similar function to that of "free association" in psychoanalysis. They both are the opening of what is not yet available; they both allow for something clearly "already there but not yet available" to articulate and announce itself.

I respond, Yes, for something implicit to become more explicit, and he gently reminds me that it doesn't work that way, and "Thank God for that. You are using both words in a present-at-hand way, to think in terms of Heidegger as you like to do. We know something was implicit only later. Better to say more available than more explicit." I *feel* the rightness of this more than I can conceptually understand it, as is often the case in talking with Gene.
Gene continues:

> Free association does allow for this process, but we need to watch out for it being conceived as an expression of a reified "unconscious"—unconscious as a noun—to which these associations refer. Unconscious is not a place or a thing but rather a part of the process of articulation. We can best understand the "unconscious" as that which lies in the background. But what lies in the background is not something fully formed that is hidden; the discovery of it, the carrying forward of its implicit meaning, is part of what it is.

I say "Heidegger says that an essential aspect of a phenomenon is that it conceals itself. To do phenomenology is to respect that hiddenness and take it into account. And I think that psychoanalysis believes this, too." Gene then says "Revealing and concealing—such powerful chords. Sounds like something a god does." And then the disillusionment of the starry-eyed boy gets harder.

> I do not think of opposing forces, Bob. I do not think of something hidden because its truth is too hard to bear. Rather I think of a process of something coming to light which then is responded to and through that responsiveness, is changed. Theories and images of opposing forces can be powerful and thrilling, but the process here is more subtle.

I can see him move forward toward me and say "...it can be expressed as opposing forces but does not have to. Thinking that it must risks your confusing the excitement of the battle with the structure and function of the experiential process itself." Gene is speaking forcefully now but is aware of my vulnerability to what he knows is a challenge to my very sense of what life is about. While working with me he observes that he sees that I am learning to be more interested in the experiential process than the big "ahas" *about* that process and therefore am getting more interested in the tension of existence rather than a dramatic celebration *of* that tension.

Gene is so friendly and so fierce. He tells me,

> So you have told me that you talked to Rollo May and told him that you wanted to put psychoanalysis and existentialism together, like you think he does. Great. I suspect that he told you that I would try to help you learn philosophy so that you could do that for yourself. I think psychoanalysis is just fine. We can make it work for you. But if we do our work, you might not always recognize it in the form that was originally presented to you.

He sees my attraction to the psychoanalytic dialectic, to the clash of opposites, and to the "depth" of that. He says "The clash of opposites can take us a long way. And depth...of course we want depth. But let's not confuse the desire for depth with the avoidance of taking all the steps along the way." From the very beginning, Gene is saying "yes" to me in a way that makes me feel seen and loved, and at the same time challenged to be disciplined. Gene challenged *and* loved. This was so different than my own father's admonishments. Gene's way did not shame me and, through my desire to be more like him, encouraged me to work harder and rhapsodize a bit less.

By the mid-1980s, things have changed significantly. Gene has formally created Focusing, which has been tremendously successful, with a large international following. He is still teaching at the University, but the Focusing Institute is taking up more and more of his time. I have created the Institute for Existential-Psychoanalytic Therapy in the Boston area, where I practice psychotherapy and teach and train students in my approach, which combines psychoanalytic object relations theory (largely Fairbairn and Winnicott) and existential psychotherapy (with a major emphasis on Heidegger's ideas from *Being and Time*). I am particularly interested in exploring how Ronald Fairbairn's object relational re-working of Freud's concept of the repetition compulsion and Winnicott's notions of potential space and play space are existential as well as developmental. Gene has kept up somewhat with what I have been doing, and I want to tell him more about it.

This second recollection takes place around 1988, during a walk we took in Wellesley, Massachusetts. I have taken a number of Focusing workshops and am hoping to integrate that approach into my therapy work and teaching about theory of therapy. I want to talk to him about the therapeutic relationship in both Focusing and psychoanalysis, and I am afraid that he will not like what I want to say and that I will not like how he responds to my concerns. I realize again that I want us to be the same—even though I know we are not. He knows this about me and does not speak of it directly. But his sensitivity to this desire and fear of mine is constant, and I know it will ultimately be addressed.

I tell Gene,

Contemporary psychoanalysis understands transference and countertransference as a circular inter-subjective space. Winnicott's notion of play-space is about both external and internal relational space (Winnicott, 1971) and I understand it hermeneutically as similar to Gadamer's ideas about "spiel-raum" (room to play), (Gadamer, 1977). Gene, the psychoanalysis I am interested in is about the experience of both client and therapist and I think is about how both attend to the implicit material arising from the relational field. In this model the therapist and client together interpret this implicit material—expressed in dreams, symptoms, enactments and most importantly the strange feelings and thoughts which each develop about the therapeutic relationship itself. Neither participant's experience is privileged over the others. On the other hand, as I study Focusing it seems to me that it doesn't have the therapist involved enough in the process. The therapist seems to be actively encouraging the client's carrying-forward of their felt sense but doesn't get involved enough in it as a person. I just don't think Focusing is relational enough.

Gene gently and warmly responds to my frustration:

Bob, this is such an important thing you are saying. It can seem to some that the therapist in Focusing is merely facilitating an internal process for the client. It's so easy to make a false separation between terms like "internal" and "external"—or intra-personal vs inter-personal. Terms like "inter-subjective" have a lot of cache but can be uncarefully used. Look, right now you and I are having a significant intimate relational experience; we are having a meaningful philosophical discussion; and we are using our felt sense and carrying that forward in our conversation with each other.

I realize that he is indeed offering me an embodied transformational possibility (his eyes and bodily movements engage my eyes and energize my body). He is gently showing me that my distinction between the intrapsychic (inside oneself) and the interpersonal (with the two or more of us together) is not quite right. Gene will usually say "not quite right" rather than "wrong."

Partly out of respectfulness, but mostly because the "wrong" is almost always wrong. He continues,

> There are many ways to "interpret" responsiveness, Bob. If I wish to share my own focusing response with a client (as we focus together) there is no reason not to do so. What you are calling "intersubjective resonance" can be shown without becoming reified as a topic of analysis, which is always my concern about the practice of psychoanalysis.

I am fascinated by this...he is not talking me out of my psychoanalytic orientation nor arguing for Focusing as superior. He is showing me how the two are similar and different at the same time and suggesting a way out of a dichotomy that may be getting in my way.

We walk a bit without talking, and then Gene says: "You have been writing me a lot about your desire to marry Winnicott and Heidegger these days. You used to want to marry Freud and Heidegger—always you want to get people married." He says this in a Yiddish accent that breaks me up.

> And now you mention Winnicott's play space and Gadamer's spielraum. I think different ways of using terms like "space" and "play" can be very useful. I like how you want Winnicott and Heidegger to play together, and this playing with the way they both play with "space" can be a nice way of getting this started.

And then he brings in his concept called "crossing," which he first wrote about in *Experiencing and The Creation of Meaning* and has stayed central to his philosophy. I say,

> Crossing. Let me see if I can say what that is. Let me try this: Different words can arise from the "same" felt sense and when we "cross" those two words together they can carry forward that felt sense more powerfully and accurately than either can do alone. And it doesn't even have to be two different words—Heidegger and Winnicott can both use the word "space" and crossing their respective usage of that word (which has both similarities and differences, in my opinion) makes both of their positions richer and more interesting.

"Yes," says Gene, "but of course there is no 'that' felt sense. The felt sense is always a pre-separated multiplicity. But it doesn't know that until it begins to separate in response to the response of an image or some words." The impact of his peculiar way of speaking ("But it doesn't know that until...") makes me laugh and stays with me, almost bodily, a long while after our talk.

I am now very happy, almost drunk on Gene Gendlin-talk, and I say,

> So it seems that concepts can cross with a felt sense and carry it for-
> ward. Concepts can cross with other concepts and carry a felt sense
> forward and can carry their own conceptual power forward. Heideg-
> ger and Winnicott can cross with their respective stirring notions of
> "space" and carry much forward.

Now I stop for a moment. We have stopped walking because I am thinking
so hard. "Of course, not just their concepts—because we see that 'space' is
no longer just a concept. Ah, I think it is a poetics," I say. And this is where
Gene's eyes laugh at me again.

"Why are your eyes laughing at me, Gene?" I ask. "Because you love so
much to be carried away," he says. And then his eyes laugh a bit less and get
more serious, and I know the next part will be harder. "And the exploration
of this space, this existential space of Heidegger and this potential—play
space of Winnicott; to get this right is hard work, isn't it?" And I see again in
his gentle and teasing way he is telling me that it is not enough to get carried
away, but to be able to see and demonstrate all the steps in the exploration of
these differing conceptions, and expressions, of the term "space."

Now I can see how Focusing and psychoanalysis can help inform each other;
that Focusing can work in the relational space as well the personal space,
and that psychoanalysis can't work if it isn't rigorously experiential. Because
of Gene's phenomenological rigor, "experience" certainly means much more
than merely feeling stuff instead of explaining stuff. And his approach insists
that "interpretation" be embodied, situated, and expressive (here we have
Befindlichkeit, Understanding, and Discourse, again). While I am thinking
about this on our hike together, I am remembering that he and I talked about
this often in my college days. I had forgotten much of this. I can see that Gene
is happy to let me have my word "space" as much as I want to, but I need to
remember how and why I am using it and cannot use it to avoid the hard work
of understanding and clearly expressing what I am trying to say. Gene insists
on intellectual sobriety. He will not let me get drunk on imagery.

The third conversation occurs in 1996. We are at my house in Newton,
Massachusetts the night before he is to give a talk at the inaugural conference for the recently formed New England Center for Existential Therapy.
He is yet again talking with me about interpretation in Focusing and psychoanalysis. Sitting on my porch, smoking his cigarette, he says,

> I know you want to see how my ideas work with psychoanalysis. Let's
> continue talking about ways of using the term "unconscious." Well, for
> me the unconscious is a very useful concept when we see it experientially.
> I don't find it useful to see it as a reified place where repressed desires

and fears are somehow kept in storage. That way what is repressed is "stuff," and then we need to invent energy charges to move it around, and we then call it "psychodynamics" which is a cool word because the suffix "dynamic" is...

And I laugh and retort, "Quite dynamic." Gene continues:

Everything we are, everything we do, everything we experience, is already there for us in some way. I like how Freud sees this "unconscious" as something happening already—but it is indeed a happening rather than a place. I like that he wants us to get in touch with this unconscious, much like I want us to get in touch with implicit meaning through the felt sense. I like that he wants to call attention to the complexity of experience. But he seems to imply that what lies "in" the unconscious is put in-there and then lies there as a "dynamic thing" pushing to emerge when stimulated. If you pay attention to experience, there is always something more there which wants to announce itself— as your friend Heidegger puts it. But it emerges in dialogue with you, it emerges in the very way you choose to interpret it. It is not first there, and then interpreted. It emerges as we interpret it. This is exactly my Focusing method. Focusing is interpretation in this sense. It is interpretation in Heidegger's sense when he distinguishes experience-near hermeneutic interpretation from experience-distant explanatory interpretation.

He then goes on to remind me that Dilthey's contribution to this kind of thinking is important and wishes he had encouraged college students to read more Dilthey in the Philosophical Psychology program. I make a note to read Dilthey.

I say that I already have a sense of this. I tell him that I am working on conceptualizing the unconscious in terms of Heidegger's modes of "being-in" and am seeing it as the location of being "thrown" into a Befindlichkeit. Gene responds:

Yes. Thrownness is thrownness into something, and it is available for reflection only as part of a complex process. My concept of the felt sense comes partly from Heidegger's use of that term. It is Befindlichkeit; it is to where, as Heidegger puts it, one is delivered over. But the felt sense only exists as responded to by the images and words it generates. Unconscious desires and fears matter only in the concrete situations which call them forth and which interpret their meaning.

And then Gene reminds me that there is no experience in itself. Every experience is a felt sense carrying itself forward and then somehow recognizing itself.

Gene's eyes are not laughing now but still passionate. He is not only playing with his favorite ideas; he is *using* those ideas to create something that I can use. This is philosophy as therapy. The more he calls my attention to a discipline which is implied by Freud and Heidegger, but much more articulated and demonstrated by himself, the more I am able to understand what I do and who I am, and what I need to try to do differently.

These conversations—reconstructed and reimagined—going back as long as fifty-five years ago—evoke how Gene taught in his therapeutic way with those he mentored, trained, and guided. Let me emphasize two things that stand out to me here about his distinctive way of working. One is that we are very much in relationship with each other, and we refer to that relationship. Gene, however, doesn't make transference interpretations. He doesn't point out internal conflicts. But he observes patterns in my way of being, and he teases me about them because he knows they keep me from a more direct experience of what is real. In very short sentences, or by merely pausing and using his body and his eyes, he carries forward a feeling or an image—or makes room for the carrying forth of that feeling or image. Secondly, he does not interpret in a way that implies "what this *really* means is this." However, I suggest that everything Gene does is interpretive in the hermeneutic sense; the conversation opens new meaning for me by referring to the sensing of a way for us to be together in it. Gene interprets by recognizing it, letting it be the metaphor it is, and allowing for a new form of understanding.

I attend the After Post-Modernism conference at the University of Chicago in 1997, which was extraordinary in its scope, and leads to the collection of essays edited by David Levin called *Language Beyond Postmodernism: Saying and Thinking in Gendlin's Philosophy.* Many members of the New England Center for Existential Therapy attend with me and also appreciate how important his way of thinking is. After this time our projects increasingly diverge, and our long conversations shift to shorter friendly exchanges.

While there was no Gendlin conference entitled "Beyond Psychoanalysis," one could argue that there didn't need to be as his philosophical and psychological work was not oriented in that direction. Nevertheless, my conversation with psychoanalysis deepened. Now I imagine another conversation with Gene as I reread his classic papers, his later development of thought, and works published posthumously. As I write this epilog to these extraordinary applications of Gene's work by contemporary philosophers and psychotherapists, I find that I am in an ongoing conversation with Gene still. Indeed, I imagine it would unfold in a particularly palpable and poignant way. Here is how it might be:

Sitting with Gene, I tell him how I struggle with the differences in our work. I say: "I have been wanting to talk to you about something for a long time. Please be patient as I try to explain it to you." "Of course," he replies.

You know, Gene, that I like the irony in Freud's thinking about fate. His belief that we are fated to recreate the misery from which we came—to somehow remain loyal to our parents' shadows in the very process of trying to free ourselves of them—seems uncontestable. There seems to be a core existential paradox about freedom and loyalty, which feels related to the paradox of our wanting so much to know the truth about ourselves and our fear of knowing that truth. To me therapy is the process which helps clients live in that struggle rather than resolve it.

Gene says: "Yes, I know that about you. That has always been important to you. What more do you want to say about this now?"
     I say,

As I read and re-read your classic paper "Befindlichkeit: Heidegger and the Philosophy of Psychology" (Casey & Schoeller, 2018), I realize how much of what I teach comes from your understanding of Heidegger's section of Division I Chapter 5 of Being and Time on the structures of "Being-In." There is so much Gene Gendlin in my teaching of Being and Time. But I also am concerned about what I think you devalue in this important chapter of Heidegger's, and I want to talk to you about my concern about this devaluation.
     You write so persuasively about the importance of three of the four existential structures that Heidegger lays out in Division I Chapter 5. Your discussions of Befindlichkeit, Understanding, and Discourse are wonderful, and I can see how much of Focusing comes from this.

Gene says, "Yes, we have talked about this many times before." I think he is still wondering about just what it is I think he has devalued.

Well, Gene—what about the fourth existential structure: Fallenness? You give it no attention at all in your chapter. This is the existentialist in Heidegger, I think: we "fall" away from taking responsibility for our thrown situatedness by allowing others in our culture to define what that is supposed to be. Only in coming back from our fallenness, by responding to a call which occurs when there is a break in our normal functioning, can we become free to own what he calls our authentic self.

Gene is closing his eyes and nodding his head, demonstrating that he is listening very carefully. He is following me all the way.

And here we get to where I think this links up with psychoanalysis. Heidegger has two ways of understanding fallenness. One is what I would call "structural": all human beings fall into the world of everydayness, and paradoxically, only in falling out of that world into an anxious non-grounded place he calls unheimlichkeit (not-at-homeness) can we come back to ourselves. He also has a more dramatic way of approaching this concept: "falling" can be understood in a more motivated sense whereby we flee the anxiety of taking responsibility for our thrownness, because this makes us feel so alone and ungrounded. This second approach—more psychological than ontological—has much in common with the thinking of Kierkegaard and Nietzsche and has a strong affinity to psychoanalysis.

Gene nods and says

Yes, this part of Heidegger is very popular, and I can see its affinity to psychoanalysis. If I remember correctly, Being and Time was written around the same time as Freud's seminal papers on anxiety, and we could say they both arise out of a similar historical moment.

(Freud, 1926)

I say:

Yes, indeed. This notion of fallenness is central to my understanding of therapy, and one of the reasons I remain drawn to psychoanalysis. The implication here is that human beings need to be supported to face the anxiety of unheimlichkeit. For Heidegger this is about the nothingness and ungroundedness that all of us essentially are—especially given the kind of meaninglessness implied by finitude and contingency. For Freud, this is about the anxiety over the return of repressed feelings and memories. Both Heidegger and Freud join in conceptualizing that we as human beings are divided against ourselves, wanting both to be in the truth and afraid of it.

I pause and find myself almost afraid to look at him. I so very much want Gene to join me here as well.

I continue:

Gene, when I was working on my thesis on Freud and Heidegger, I read a then recently published book by Paul Riceour called *Freud and Philosophy*, (Riceour, 1970). He makes this incredibly useful distinction between what he calls the hermeneutics of everydayness and the hermeneutics of suspicion. In this light, Heidegger's structural understanding of fallenness is a hermeneutics of everydayness; falling and return from falling are just the way human beings are. For therapy, dreams, symptoms, enactments, cultural experiences and interpersonal relationships are all opportunities to come back to oneself from the abandoning of oneself through allowing the others to define us. I am struck how

Heidegger uses the phrase "Dasein's abandonment to itself" repeatedly in Division II. The goal here is to pay attention to the call to return to ourselves again and again.

Heidegger's motivated understanding of fallenness Riceour calls the hermeneutics of suspicion. This is a delightfully evocative phrase. Here it is not merely noting that we fall away, but also that the falling away is motivated by anxiety. We can see anxiety as functioning to recognize a break in the context of our everyday living and thinking. And we can go further and see it as pointing to the recognition of the unbearable burden of being human and the impossible choices that go along with that burden. A hermeneutics of suspicion carries forward Nietzsche's belief that humans are afraid of the truth and afraid of their freedom and have good reason to be.

(Dreyfus, 1991)

Of course, Gene already knows Riceour's book and says: "I think I see where you are going with this, and I am really appreciating the hard work you have done with this marriage of Freud and Heidegger." I say:

Yes—the hermeneutics of suspicion is ironic—we need to be suspicious that our very avoidance of something points to the very thing we are avoiding. Psychoanalysis embraces this irony and offers a way to hold the tension of desire and fear.

And now I turn my face to Gene's and say:

You seem to reject the hermeneutics of suspicion outright. You reject it in Heidegger, demonstrated by your lack of interest in the existential structure of fallenness and your relative disinterest in the sections of Division II of Being and Time which deal with guilt, anxiety, resoluteness and the call. You reject it in Freud and psychoanalysis. It seems to hold no place in your Focusing method. In so doing I feel you are rejecting some of the most basic aspects of being human. This is truly my main concern about your philosophical psychology.

And of course, it is my concern about him as my intellectual and surrogate father.

And I tremble here. If I am right, I will face my disappointment in Gene head on. If I am wrong, I will be a terrible disappointment to myself. How will Gene respond to this?

Gene is now neither intense nor playful, but quietly serious again. He tells me:

A model which bases itself on fundamental struggle can be very attractive, but it must take into consideration its impact. We find struggle everywhere we look for it, if we look for it. Remember, there is no truth outside of our relationship to it; we find only what we are prepared to see. If a struggle comes up when you pay attention to something, follow that. But don't start out by assuming it or looking for it. I don't want to accept a hermeneutics of suspicion based on its rhetorical power, its power to persuade. But I am open to the notion of struggle and conflict when it emerges compellingly as a response to my paying attention.

He then references something he taught when I was a college student.

Remember when I told the class that Rogers was not merely a nice guy who made everything nice? When there was a struggle, he noted it. But he didn't assume it and interpret it everywhere he went.

Gene looks at me with affection.

We both love hermeneutics. My work can criticize current hermeneutic theories, but I have no problem saying that my work is hermeneutic. I also like a lot of dialectical thinking, and you know I use Socratic methods in my teaching. It's the rule bound dialectical historical process that is a problem for me.

My "philosophy of the implicit" has gone through a lot of changes since the After-Post Modernism Conference. But even before that, in 1997 I wrote a chapter for "Man and World" on philosophy of science which speaks to my appreciation of hermeneutics in philosophy and psychotherapy. Now I call it "The Responsive Order: A New Empiricism."

(Casey & Schoeller, 2018)

Somehow, I had not read this paper and it opens up like a gift as Gene begins to read Chapter 14 from *Saying What We Mean*.

Reading from the book he quotes himself: "Hegel gave his dialectic a permanent formulation. There can be no formulation of how formulations change in explication. Currently what is used of dialectic is only the constant possibility of contradiction and paradox" (p. 267). He looks up at me and smiling says: "*Of course, I am suspicious of the rhetorical power of contradiction and paradox. These devices have great explanatory power, but they cannot be used as the basis of the experiential process.*"

He continues reading:

In dialectic the role of the implicit is not always recognized. In the hermeneutic process one cannot miss it.

He looks directly at me while reading.

With our new terms we can say: when experiences function implicitly, they cross with every new event. Statements bring an implicit mesh which grows even if the statement remains the same.

(pp. 268–269)

And then he emphasizes one more crucial line:

Hermeneutics is a way of thinking which does not need unchangeable parts or individuated units. The parts neither stay the same nor become different. But this is not a contradiction: it is the relation we have been calling "carrying forward." It cannot long seem strange—it is the most ubiquitous kind of transition we find in thinking. We only lacked the terms to talk about it, and to think deliberately with it (p. 269).

I am mesmerized, as I always am when he speaks like this. I can't feel it as much when I merely read it. "It cannot long seem strange"—My God, how he touches me, even now.

He is finishing up now and reads:

Hermeneutics places the logical order *within* the wider implicitly crossed order...Hermeneutics provides a process of thinking which moves back and forth between the explicit and the implicit, without reducing them to each other. We can employ logically structured statements that remain fixed, and also think with implicit meanings.

(p. 271)

He looks up from the book and then says

You see, Bob, we do not need a hermeneutics of suspicion to articulate the tension that you so prize. That tension comes through crossing and carrying forward, and when it is there, it can be used in our thinking and feeling. The hermeneutics of suspicion in psychoanalysis and early Heidegger is a romantic hermeneutics that attracts notice, but it is not careful phenomenology. It skips over so many steps. Bob, you can enjoy it as much as you want—especially in a literary way. But you do not need it. All you need is the responsive order.

I say: You are telling me that the hermeneutic process is not one of explicating the implicit, but rather—to quote you—"(it)moves back and forth between the explicit and the implicit without reducing them to each other." I pause. "That gets easily misunderstood, doesn't it, Gene?"

Gene replies:

Yes, it does. I don't agree with Gadamer when he says that hermeneutics is primarily a way of being, and only secondarily a method (Gadamer, 1977). I like how he, following Heidegger, shows that Dasein is hermeneutical, but that is a more literary understanding of the term.

Hermeneutics, like phenomenology, and very much like good therapy, is indeed about method as well. And it is a method we can do poorly or well. The conflicts you celebrate, between the forces of knowing and unknowing, light and shadow, authenticity and inauthenticity—are worth exploring. I'm glad you do so. But the tension that interests me is the one between paying attention to implicit meaning and the responsive order, and not doing so. Any theory of motivation that explains that tension interests me, but only in so far as it carries itself further into a responsivity rather than drags itself down to either a metaphysical position or a deconstructive dead end that stops movement.

I respond:

I like the romance of contradiction and the drama of paradoxical formulation. And I really like when this is connected to hermeneutics as well. Eliot has a famous line from the Four Quartets: "We will not cease from exploration and the end of all our exploring Will be to arrive where we started and know the place for the first time" (Eliot, 1971). This is my favorite way into feeling the hermeneutic process. I find the lines stunningly paradoxical. I like what initially seems to be an overt contradiction slowly turning into something else.

Gene says: "I can play with a circular set of steps which can be carefully followed."
  I push back: "The feeling, the poetics of this paradox are rendered magical."
  Now he is smiling again with his eyes. He knows he is about to end a conversation where I have been taken seriously and been cared for, where nothing I have said is "wrong." He knows that he has planted seeds of a more carefully nuanced way of thinking that can help me modulate my romance with magic. He knows about the beauty, the entrancement, and the dangers of magic. He says:

Yes, paradox can certainly be rendered magical. We can work with this magic. I think it also can be rendered as a magical precision. Eliot sees, like only a poet philosopher can, that the same can be different and the different can be the same. When we think differently, when we allow language to move us to different understandings, there can be the magic of a return which feels like a transcendence.

I smile because Gene does not ordinarily use words like transcendence. It is a gift to me.
  This matters to me as a teacher and a therapist. Teaching and therapy can be entrancing—truths can be rendered as enthrallments. Heidegger certainly did this, at least at the beginning of his life and work, perhaps before some of the dangerous consequences of that way of teaching frightened him

away from it. Gene certainly does not. For him, teaching and therapy are unadorned and disciplined steps—the beauty is in the precision and not the oracularity of the pronouncements.

"I guess we are different," I say awkwardly and somehow saddened. My jealousy of his skill is now felt as grief, and I miss him so much. But I can see him smile after I say that "We certainly are," he says with a grin. "And we can work with that."

And I, as long as I live, will work with that.

References

Casey, E. S., & Schoeller, D. M. (Eds). (2018). *Saying what we mean: Implicit precision and the responsive order.* Northwestern University Press.

Dreyfus, H. L. (1991). *Being-in-the-world: A commentary on Heidegger's being and time, division I.* MIT Press.

Eliot, T. S. (1971). *The four quartets.* Houghton Mifflin.

Freud, S. (1926). *Inhibitions, symptoms and anxiety.* W. W. Norton.

Gadamer, H.-G. (1977). *Philosophical hermeneutics.* University of California Press.

Guignon, C. B. (ed). (1993). *The Cambridge companion to Heidegger.* Cambridge University Press.

Heidegger, M. (1962). *Being and time.* Harper and Row.

Merleau-Ponty, M. (1962). *Phenomenology of perception.* Routledge and Kegan Paul.

Plochmann, G. K. (1990). *Richard McKeon: A study.* University of Chicago Press.

Riceour, P. (1970). *Freud and philosophy: An essay on interpretation.* Yale University Press.

Winnicott, D. W. (1971). *Playing and reality.* Penguin books.

Index

Printed in the USA
CPSIA information can be obtained
at www.ICGtesting.com
LVHW020034051023
760125LV00006B/712

9 781032 280042